THE MASTER PLANT EXPERIENCE

THE SCIENCE, SAFETY, AND SACRED CEREMONY OF PSYCHEDELICS

MAYA SHETREAT, MD

Difference Press

Washington, DC, USA

Published 2023

DISCLAIMER

Cover design: Jennifer Stimson

Editing: Natasa Smirnov

Author's photo courtesy of Michelle Johnson

CONTENTS

To Gaia. May we celebrate the miracle of Me and We every single day.

INTRODUCTION

Have you ever imagined how a baby feels as it travels through the birth canal to be born? After a comfortable, protected existence, it must feel terrifying, jarring, even painful to be expelled into the chaos of the unknown.

Then the baby emerges into a world so much more vivid and interesting and beautiful than the muffled darkness of the womb. We call this process birth, and we're told that it happens only once, at the very start of our lives.

But this process doesn't happen just once. Many times in your life, you may be expelled from your seemingly comfortable existence, usually through pain or loss – of a loved one through death or separation, of a job or career, of a key part of your identity, of your health, by experiencing severe illness in yourself or someone you love. And through that pain, you transform.

As with birth, there is no going back to the old you. It is a kind of death of your prior self. But in dying and being reborn, you emerge into a world in which everything becomes clearer, more acute, and filled with possibilities that your old self could never have fathomed.

Rarely would anyone willingly commence such a journey

through the birth canal, even if their prior existence wasn't particularly pleasant. But you don't always get to choose the moment of your coming to consciousness. More often, it chooses you.

As you go through the transformation, know that you are reawakening to your life's purpose. Know with all of your heart that you are being held and guided through this process (even when it doesn't feel that way). And most importantly, know that you will be okay. You are emerging.

I've certainly been there myself.

In the year before flying to the Amazon, I'd been saying to my then-husband: I feel like I'm dying. He reassured me that I was just tired – I had three young children, a dog, a busy medical practice, and an urban farm, and I was traveling and speaking around the country. Outwardly, I was a powerhouse. But as someone who had given birth to three children over the course of grueling medical training, I knew what tired felt like. This new feeling wasn't physical, though I had no vocabulary to accurately describe it.

Was it emotional? Spiritual? Whatever it was, I knew that something was very wrong.

I was already well-known as an integrative adult and pediatric neurologist, herbalist, and urban farmer who worked with children and adults from all over the world to reverse chronic and refractory illness. I was an expert. And though I knew that focusing on my physical body wasn't the solution, I had no idea where to start or even whom to ask for help. Though admittedly out-of-the-box, I was trained as a doctor and scientist. What I knew was that the answer was something far more intangible. It was my energy body. It was my spirit. It was my soul. And it was a deep knowing I couldn't ignore – or rather, by ignoring it, I'd pay an impossibly high cost.

At the time, I felt all alone in this knowing. But eventually I learned I wasn't. And since then, I've helped thousands of people recognize they're not alone in this discovery.

But many people still deny this knowing even once it's revealed to them – at their own peril. In that denial, they feel isolated and alone even when surrounded by friends because they are not seen for who they are. For some, these unexpressed parts can get loud and manifest as very real mental, emotional, or physical symptoms: explosive rage, depression, anxiety, addiction, insomnia, chronic pain, and conditions including autoimmunity and neurological disorders, even cancer. We label people who are suffering with what we call "diseases" and offer them pharmaceuticals as though their problems are purely physical or mental. Then we wonder why so many of these people don't respond to what conventional, integrative, and even mental health professionals offer. The root cause may be something else entirely.

To be fair, conventional and even integrative doctors get no education in what it means to be sick of heart or spirit, though it is as epidemic in medical practitioners as in everyone else. And this understanding is missing not just in healthcare. Since the European witch hunts, our society has systematically stigmatized intuition, sensitivity, spirituality, and the sacred. Even those who feel connected to the intuition or the sacred assiduously avoid referencing them for fear of being laughed at, discredited, or dismissed as being "woo-woo."

Science – in all its linear, rational certainty – has become the only acceptable lens through which we can understand ourselves. If we can't see or measure it, it doesn't exist. Yet our lack of language to describe our invisible terrain makes it no less real. And without this vocabulary, we feel incomplete, limited in our ability to know ourselves, and we hunger for the invisible more than ever. No diagnosis, medication or therapy can address that sense of isolation from ourselves.

What was epidemic before 2020 – depression, anxiety, addiction, and suicide – became exponentially worse during the pandemic. When the numbers of overdoses shot up, doctors at first asked if COVID-19 made death to overdose physiologically more likely. The answer (obviously!) was no. It was profound loneliness and separation from community. One of my colleagues discovered that his mother's rapid downward spiral into deep dementia during her nursing home lockdown miraculously reversed when restrictions were lifted. In truth, we may never know if the true body count of the pandemic was as related to extreme isolation from family and community – including forcing hospitalized patients to be without family to care, caress, or advocate for them – as it was to physical symptoms. We have limited ways to assess deaths of despair in their many forms.

The "unprecedented times" we've been living in since have been a period of spiritual initiation. In every great myth and story, the hero faces one or more moments of initiation – an often-harrowing experience that catapults them out of their normal, everyday life – that leads to a powerful spiritual awakening. They reach a new level of sensitivity and awareness that inevitably reveals a more authentic identity and gifts that they can ultimately share so their community can heal and evolve.

Such initiations can be individual and usually are instigated by a personal loss: of a relationship, job, home, or health. They can also be collective.

The pandemic, for example, jolted us from our normal daily existence. Finding our way back to normalcy – or what we imagined was normalcy – has been considerably harder. Quarantine eliminated many of the ways we self-soothe in the midst of discomfort. With nowhere to run and nowhere to hide, most of us came face to face with our demons. In the process, we have felt displaced from our communities and our sense of identity.

Indeed, ancient mystics would not have seen that as a bad thing. They believed that being thrust out of normalcy held gifts.

They believed we should be periodically forced to evaluate whether the norm is really what we need or even want. So often, we stay in situations that are not best for us and don't bring out the best in us because they feel safe and certain.

Yet 2020 reminded us that certainty doesn't exist. Experts don't always agree. Science is never settled. Medicine is an art. Governments don't always have our best interest at heart. Even if these concepts are not new to some of us, we're each forced to relearn these lessons again and again.

We believe ourselves to be more advanced than ever before. We've collected data and analyzed, researched, peer reviewed, and published protocols. But we haven't mastered compassion. We haven't learned humility. We don't know how to be in right relationship – with ourselves, with each other, with the land, or with the invisible.

And to indigenous elders, certainty is not even a goal. There is no certainty. Being in a state of humility and not knowing is an achievement, allowing mystery to find us. To be in an ongoing conversation with mystery is in and of itself sacred.

Indeed, true science means letting go of being an expert, unlearning what you think you know, and being unattached to any outcome in order to allow for the unexpected. Science is an ongoing dance with uncertainty and a celebration of our ever-present relationship with mystery. It is no accident that many great scientists – Pythagoras, Maimonides, Tesla, Einstein – were mystics in their way. Science is but one language we use to describe the invisible world.

Master Plants are an indigenous way of referring to powerful, neuroactive flora, fauna, and fungi who instigate transformation within us and who are considered wise (and sometimes demanding) teachers and guides to humans. By connecting us to realms beyond this one, they remind us that we are never alone. Through reverence, humility, wonder, awe, gratitude and kinship, we can truly show up in a good way in our visible and invisible relationships, so that we never need to feel isolated or lonely again. And though Master Plants are by no means limited to psychedelics, this book will mostly explore the science, safety, and sacred ceremony of psychedelics.

Welcome to the Master Plant Experience.

AUTHOR'S NOTE

The term "indigenous" does not refer to one monolithic group that adheres to one cohesive viewpoint, but to diverse people and nations around the world – past and very much present – who possess a diverse array of unique viewpoints and cosmologies. Here, indigenous refers to those who still fundamentally operate from ancient traditions and a worldview of kinship, connection to place, and interconnectedness of all beings, rather than one from a modern, reductionist worldview.

1

WHAT'S WITH ALL THIS TALK OF PSYCHEDELICS THESE DAYS?

W hat if you could take one dose of a medicine and it could help you to heal from conditions like major depression, anxiety, PTSD, OCD, addiction, chronic pain disorders like migraines, eating disorders, dementia, and even sexual trauma? And when I say heal, I mean the effects last.

Amazing, right?

I'm talking here about the fascinating and cutting-edge research coming out weekly on medicinal mushrooms and psychedelics.

You've probably seen the headlines somewhere, because they've been *everywhere.*

The science of psychedelics is in the process of changing the entire landscape not just of mental health, but medicine. It's exciting. And honestly, it's about time.

For years, I've seen profound transformations in so many people who have worked with psychedelic medicines – especially those suffering from the health effects of adult or childhood trauma. Even people who felt stuck – in physical or mental health issues or simply like they couldn't move beyond a compromised, unhappy, or less-than-fulfilled place – were able to step into a healthier, more vital, and joyful life.

You may be thinking, Why the heck are doctors so excited to be serving up illegal drugs to the world's populace?

It's true – many of us have been told that psychedelics are drugs, that they're harmful, and that they should be illegal, and most people accepted that.

But now, research is showing us that these indigenous medicines that come from the earth can offer much more than even some widely-used mainstream treatments. And in the process, scientists are developing a lexicon to describe the connection between our physical, mental, emotional, and spiritual selves – and beyond.

Widespread stories of benefit – including personal experiences by scientists and doctors themselves – have led to an explosion of psychedelic studies.

Extensive research has been underway over the past many years in the most prestigious academic institutions from around the world – Johns Hopkins, Harvard, Stanford, NYU, the Imperial College of London – with research papers published in many of the most respected medical journals. In these clinical trials, those suffering from untreatable depression, severe anxiety associated with terminal cancer, crippling PTSD, and alcohol and drug addictions are reporting mystical experiences that are profoundly life-changing. And for many of these study participants, the benefits even from one dose of mushrooms, for example, can be long-lasting.

In a 2006 trial studying the potential of psilocybin, more than 70 percent of the participants rated the experience as one of the five most important in their lives. Nearly a third rated it the single most important experience. In studies conducted by NYU and Johns Hopkins, published concurrently in November 2016, about 80 percent of cancer patients showed clinically significant reductions in anxiety and depression lasting some eight months after an initial dose. The paper concludes that "discovering how these mystical and altered-consciousness states arise in the brain could have major therapeutic possibilities" and "it would be scientifically shortsighted not to pursue them."

As with any natural or pharmaceutical medicine, it's absolutely essential to be educated and intentional in the way we engage with these medicines. And as we'll see, Master Plants are much, much more than a mere pharmaceutical or natural supplement, and as such, education, guidance, and support around how to engage with them has become that much more important.

This book is a journey into considering psychedelics differently than most of us have perhaps ever considered them before.

Given that most pharmaceuticals are taken daily, what's profound about the current studies on psychedelics is that in some cases, just *one dose* of these medicines can *reverse* conditions that are very challenging to treat. And the effects are long-term.

One dose of psilocybin-containing mushrooms can transform treatment-resistant depression, anorexia, and PTSD.

With *one dose* of iboga alone, people have been able to refrain from using heroin, methamphetamine, and other substances that are very difficult to stop otherwise.

With two doses of psilocybin, over 80 percent of people stopped smoking – and almost 70 percent stayed away even after a year. And those same two doses helped heavy drinkers of alcohol cut their drinking by more than half over an eight-month period.

People are discovering that they can engage with these medicines in micro or even smaller quantum doses over time – with no psychedelic or journeying effect – and still successfully address brain health, mental health, mood, pain syndromes, and more.

Are these for everyone? Probably not.

But can these medicines change the lives of those people who *are* good candidates?

Absolutely yes.

TRAUMA LIVES WITHIN US

Let's back up for a moment and consider where we are at this moment in time, and why.

Millions of people around the world are struggling with chronic physical and mental health conditions and have tried different pharmaceuticals, diet changes, nutritional and herbal supplements, and other treatments and therapeutic techniques to address them. These approaches work for a good number of people. Many get better or at least get by, at least for a period of time. But in my practice, a percentage of people still didn't get better, and I usually saw them at or immediately after the moment when everything fell apart. Something deeper clearly was afoot.

And the question I kept asking myself was this: Why does a similar condition – let's say strep throat, or Epstein-Barr virus (which causes mononucleosis), or a seemingly benign car accident, or even divorce – cause one person to get knocked off the horse for weeks or even months or years, while for another person, it barely causes a blip in terms of function for more than a week or two?

When I was in medical school, I was taught the answer to everything that happened to us was likely genetic – diabetes, migraines, mental illness, cancer, all the way down to our level of resilience or shitty coping skills. Who hasn't heard – or said – "it runs in my family"? Yet while it's true that all these physical and mental health conditions can have familial and even genetic components, research has shown that genetics likely play a far smaller role than we initially were told. And since genetics are mostly set in stone, I wanted to explore where opportunities existed to change those health and other stories passed down to us. I knew there had to be more to the story, and there was.

As we'll explore together in these pages, the real answers are both simple and very complex. But we now know that trauma is a key factor in setting those different responses. And by that I mean not just current, ongoing, or acute events but even terrible moments or periods of life that could have happened decades ago or sometimes even generations ago. These events imprint upon us down to a cellular and mitochondrial level, and even affect how our DNA is read. Sometimes trauma can result from an event that didn't even look very dramatic to someone on the outside. And sometimes there was no "event" that someone could point to – it was simply a painfully dysfunctional garden in which they grew every single day of their early childhood.

For a long time, trauma wasn't a concept even discussed in the mainstream. Then – finally! – mainstream psychology and medicine began to acknowledge that trauma plays an often disempowering or even toxic role in our adult behaviors, responses, and relationship patterns, in ways ranging from overeating to addictions to depression to what we commonly call personality disorders.

Very recently, research has begun to show that adverse childhood events (ACEs) impact even our physical bodies, and can lead to not just mental illness but also some of the most difficult-to-treat physical ailments we suffer from today – autoimmune diseases, metabolic syndromes like diabetes and obesity, ADHD and dementia, and even chronic pain and cancer.

We know much about what happens in the brain and body as a result of individual trauma from studying a variety of childhood events. ACEs include experiences of divorce; addiction; incarceration; physical, mental, or sexual abuse; and loss of a family member, many of which are not uncommon life experiences.

Some people have higher ACE scores (meaning a greater number of difficult childhood experiences) than others, and may suffer more effects as a result. And of course, high or low ACE scores do not always correlate to a particular adult outcome, because every single person's particular experience of difficult events is uniquely painful to them. Full stop.

How do the physical, mental, and other changes have a long-standing impact in our bodies and minds, even causing disease later in life? When these experiences occur, our nervous system structure changes. On an MRI, higher ACE scores correlate with less gray matter in key areas of the brain, including in the prefrontal cortex, which supports decision-making and self-regulation, and the amygdala, which processes fear. If a child's developing brain undergoes chronic stress as a result of ACEs, the hippocampus, which processes emotion and memory and manages stress, shrinks.

ACEs can affect our resting heart and respiratory rates, eye contact, posture, coping mechanisms, and our emotional responses to situations. And though the events may have taken place in childhood, the effects can last for life, partly because the resulting behaviors tend to become invisible to us. They simply become part of our unconscious behavior.

All of this offers context for why many of us walk around ready to rumble (or crumple!) at the slightest instigation. The imprints of trauma disrupt our decision-making, self-regulation, fear-processing, memory, and stress management. And when we're triggered, we fall more readily into a dysregulated fear response.

The fear response is designed so that we can't see subtlety. After all, what good is nuance when we're running from a lion? The problem is that many of us feel like we're constantly running from lions, even when we're not. Every nightly news story or newspaper headline is crafted to activate that response. Social media algorithms, too, are designed to act as triggers to the sympathetic nervous system so that we get "fired up" and stay longer on the site. And anyone who reads the comments section of any controversial post on Facebook can vouch for how even triggered strangers can trigger us, causing a chain reaction of activated trauma.

Trauma mind shows us only directly what's in front of us, our one and only path to survival, and nothing else. The result of a society in chronic survival mode is that half of the population seems to entirely disagree with the other half on any number of issues. We have seen in real time around the world how easily we can become weaponized against each other when we are triggered. Not surprisingly, black-and-white thinking can be a symptom of trauma response. Yet such thinking further isolates us and heightens our sense of danger – even, as we'll see, on a cellular level.

Most of all, trauma is fracturing and stigmatizing. The experiences – and how we internalize them – lead us to feel all alone, victimized, and like we are damaged, broken, and less valuable. Traumatic experiences psychically (and sometimes literally) separate us from what we may perceive to be "respectable" or "normal" society, leading to a sense of victimhood that can cause us to perceive our pain and suffering as unique, different, and something that no one else can really understand. That is the nature of the experience.

While our particular set of experiences is unique to us, pain and suffering are not unique. As a physician, I discovered early on that no matter how wonderful things may look from the outside, people can struggle with crippling issues of all kinds for a variety of reasons.

Years ago, my daughter took a gap year before college and found herself feeling isolated and alone in a relatively small, homogeneous group of people that she felt had more in common with each other than with her. Everyone else seemed to be making friends and having a great time except for her. When she shared her sense of exclusion and loneliness with the guides, they said: You're not alone. It may not look that way, but a lot of other kids here feel lonely, isolated, and like they don't have any friends.

That night, they gathered everyone into a circle for an exercise. They gave everyone a handful of pennies, placed a bowl in the middle of the room, and turned out the lights so no one could see anything. Then they asked questions: Do you feel lonely? Do you feel anxious? Do you feel depressed? Do you feel like you have no friends? If the answer was yes, they were instructed to throw a penny into the bowl.

After each question, the room filled with the sounds of pennies upon pennies landing in the bowl. Inside, everyone felt like they had no friends. Everyone felt lonely, anxious, and depressed. Some just pretended better than others.

When she told me the story afterward, I asked her if she felt better knowing that she wasn't alone. "No," she said. "Because I'm *really* suffering; they just think they are."

We all think our pennies are worth more.

From there, we live life in an "us versus them" stance, which becomes our instinctual response.

This automatic response, however, need not remain automatic. Trauma isn't what happens to us, but what happens within us.

Here's what I mean.

Like us, our cells exist primarily in one of two major states – growth or protection. Either the cell experiences pleasant stimuli, which instigates the cell to open arms wide to accept connection and communication like nutrients and information, or it turns away from overly stressful stimuli, which causes the cell to close off to nutrients, communication, and even releasing waste. In the latter situation, the cell isolates and no longer operates as part of a community. And in extreme periods of protection, the cell becomes stuck in "danger mode" and diverts its function permanently to protection instead of growth.

The cell danger response (CDR) describes how trauma lives within our bodies on a cellular level as a biological response to physical, mental, or emotional insults. Usually, our cells can activate or deactivate CDR fairly quickly in response to a challenge. But sometimes, the cell continues to live in high alert at all times and siphons resources away from optimal function, operating from the position that it remains in danger indefinitely. This CDR is the underlying physiological mechanism of almost all chronic physical and even mental illnesses. And as we reenact mental or emotional trauma until we heal it, so too will our cells reenact this response physiologically, and vice versa, again and again, until something shifts.

OUR MICROBES RUN THE TRAUMA SHOW

Trauma – whether ancestral; mental or physical abuse; a car accident; or countless other sources of physical, mental, or emotional pain –imprints not just on our cells but also, as we'll see, on our very DNA, and even the microbes that reside within us. This trauma imprinting disrupts the composition of our microbiome – the organisms that live in and on our bodies, primarily in our digestive tracts. These three to five pounds of billions of bacteria, viruses, yeast, and fungi are a complex universe within us that supports not just our digestion but also our immunity, sleep, memory, and mood.

These microbes are influenced by what happens to us in our lives, and we, in turn, are exquisitely sensitive to what's happening in our microbiome. A period of trauma can alter the makeup of microbes that predominate in our gut, causing dysbiosis or microbial imbalances. And that alteration translates to persistent adverse physical and mental health effects from the stress of that trauma. Our inner microbial community literally holds our traumatic events as their own and invisibly amplifies and propagates and prolongs them in our bodies.

This means that something that happens to us when we're seven years old can imprint on our microbiome, and that shift then facilitates long-term negative impact – just from that single stressor! – for the rest of our lives or until that part of the microbiome is shifted back in balance again.

It turns out that our microbes are fundamental drivers of how we deal with the world around us and how we perceive the world. When trauma imprints on the microbiome, that imprint rewrites how we experience our daily life – literally down to our stress levels, anxiety, depression, brain fog, impaired memory or immunity or autoimmunity, chronic pain, and more – in the context of that trauma.

And it doesn't even have to be trauma with capital T.

We can be affected this way by our parents not comforting us when we're crying or calling us "crybaby." Or by a caretaker coming late every day to pick us up after school. Or by an abusive first-grade teacher who publicly embarrasses us all year in front of our class when we make mistakes.

An important note is that another child in the family or kid in the classroom may not have experienced similar challenges in the same way as we did. For them, insults that flattened us may have rolled right off their backs. Similarly, not everyone demonstrates the same physiological changes as a result of the very same events.

Contrary to what we've been taught, "trauma" is not the event itself. It's how we experience the event or period of our lives and how effectively the changes take up residence with us – whether it ultimately embeds into the makeup of our cells, microbes, brains, and beyond. It all depends on how acutely and intensely each of us experiences the particular set of stressors in the context of our particular inner nature, and the level of resilience and resource we derive from other parts of our lives.

All of this may sound a little far-fetched. After all, how can a mass of microbes – that aren't even human – be so affected by our grief, sadness, and anger? And how do they in turn affect our behavior and our health?

At the most basic level, traumatic experiences dramatically shift our microbial balance away from the beneficial gut organisms that we do need and toward the opportunistic organisms we don't, all in a very short period of time. And then they really cause problems, because these excessive "opportunistic" organisms begin to create excess inflammation throughout the body. They increase intestinal permeability causing leaky gut and elevated inflammatory cytokines that travel far beyond our intestines – creating a chronically hyper-sensitive, hyperactivated hypothalamic-adrenal-pituitary (HPA) axis, which leads to chronically increased surges of stress hormones like cortisol and adrenaline. Now we are living in an ongoing fight-or-flight response.

When the HPA axis is so sensitive and thus more susceptible to activation, small things that would be seemingly easy to deal with create a much more amplified stress response. Everything feels like a 10 out of 10.

Starting to get the picture?

The constant surges of cortisol, adrenaline, and other stress hormones that activate our fight-or-flight response trigger the sympathetic nervous system and immune system in ways that amp our inflammatory pathways.

Welcome to chronic inflammation, which becomes the founda-tion for chronic disease. This constellation of events sets the stage for developing autoimmune diseases, chronic pain syndromes, and neurodegenerative conditions like Alzheimer's, Parkinson's, and dementia. They can also act as a fundamental instigator of metabolic disease. So now our risk for developing diabetes, heart disease, and obesity dramatically increases because of this fundamental state of elevated inflammation.

In a nutshell, trauma keeps us on high alert, amplified by daily stressors, leading to chronic inflammation, which can cause chronic physical, neurological, and even mental illness down the road.

What does this all mean for us, practically speaking?

Let's say we experience a common daily stressor – for example, crappy traffic. We're driving to work, somebody cuts us off, and we get pissed. Totally normal. Our heart rate goes up. Our stress hormones surge. Our flight-or-fight response kicks in.

Sometime in the next twenty to thirty minutes, that stress response should return to baseline.

But if we have a trauma-altered body and gut, that single stressor will perpetuate the flight-or-fight response for hours. Instead of being a minimal, temporary stressor, the day becomes filled with anxiety and inflammation. To add insult to injury, we are now set up for chronic illness. Everything else starts to fall apart because of that embedded stressor within the system.

Of course, the more profoundly the stress persists, the more we try increasingly dramatic approaches to calm the response. Some people enter "freeze" mode and simply go numb or check out. Others develop addictive behaviors or seek substances in desperate attempts to extract themselves or even just cope with the stress response.

Whoa.

When we hold the imprint of trauma in our bodies and minds, even simple uncertainty of any kind can act as one of many physiological and emotional triggers. The resulting insatiable need for control can look like perfectionism, people pleasing, hypervigilance, always expecting the worst (catastrophizing), and other adaptive behaviors.

But take a minute. Breathe. Because it's important to know that this response need not be inevitable or permanent.

MY SEARCH FOR ANSWERS IN THE UNSEEN WORLD

Until we find a way out of these trauma loops, our automatic responses can lead us to repeat familiar childhood dynamics in our adult relationships, even if they were extremely unpleasant. And as a result, we can feel that we're unsafe, that we cannot trust ourselves or those around us, and that we have to disconnect from ourselves and our needs to be accepted or loved. We can walk around dissociated, not noticing physiological cues like hunger, thirst, the need for rest, or even pain, or we can live in a state of chronic brain fog, where we struggle with focus, clear thinking, or memory. We may avoid intimacy, even with our spouses or those close to us. We may be hypervigilant, our dysregulated nervous system always looking for danger and ready for lights to flash and sirens to blare, or we may catastrophize, expecting the worst of everybody and preparing for the worst possible scenario at all times. We can ruminate, overthink, perseverate, and worry, worry, worry.

These are not innate responses, but likely result from experiences we had with our families of origin very early in our lives, which in turn can reflect familial and sometimes even ancestral trauma. As long as we are unaware of ways that we automatically live into patterns that may have been in some way modeled for (or inflicted upon) us, we may perpetuate them by repeating them with different sets of actors when we're adults.

As I mentioned, when I began my own journey into understanding Master Plants, I was already known as an integrative adult and pediatric neurologist, herbalist, and urban farmer who worked with children and adults worldwide to reverse chronic and refractory illness. I was an expert, but even with all of my training, I couldn't account for the different outcomes I saw in my patients with similar conditions who followed similar treatment regimens. I knew it wasn't just "genetics." Something deeper was at play for my patients struggling with treatment-resistant syndromes.

With my detective hat on, I searched for answers, this time in the unseen world. I took the endeavor as seriously as my prior medical training. I traveled to the Amazon rainforest, the Andes mountains, and the Valley of Longevity to explore different perspectives on how nature heals. In the years that followed, I trained with indigenous elders. I learned about ancient astrology and numerology, read original writings of ancient mystics, and dove deep into my own personal, familial, and ancestral trauma. And I began to grow my own Master Plants, tend to them, learn from them, and listen to them.

In the process, I began to walk the bridge between the ancient, indigenous technologies that modern science has only begun to fathom and my prior training and practice of medicine. I began to make sense of what had previously felt inaccessible. I developed vocabulary for what I had always sensed around me but struggled to describe, which I came to call the invisible terrain within and around us.

Many of us have denied the impacts of our trauma – at our great peril. We may abandon our own needs and desires for the sake of others, put our effort into trying to make things okay for other people at our own expense, struggle to say no, and do anything to avoid conflict. We may develop addictions to substances or even activities in order to escape feeling uncomfortable or avoid unbearable inner pain we have no words to describe and minimal tools to address. And as we've seen, these unexpressed, unseen parts can become loud and manifest as very real mental, emotional, or physical symptoms: explosive rage, depression, anxiety, addiction, insomnia, chronic pain, and conditions including autoimmunity, neurological disorders, and even cancer.

The famous Swiss psychiatrist and psychoanalyst Carl Jung said: "Until you make the unconscious conscious, it will direct your life and you will call it fate." Today, we are discovering how profoundly accurate his words were on every level.

And so we suffer. We can feel persistently isolated and alone even when surrounded by friends, because we are not seen for who we are. We can feel chronically fatigued or lack energy partly because we invest so much in pretending we're fine.

Loneliness itself has the same health risks as smoking almost a pack of cigarettes daily or abusing alcohol. And loneliness doesn't mean we are literally alone, but simply that we feel alone.

Many people who suffer from these conditions are labeled with what we call "diseases" and are offered pharmaceuticals, as though their problems are purely physical or mental. And while the symptoms are very real indeed, often they don't fully or even minimally respond to these conventional, integrative, and psychological treatments.

The root cause may be something else entirely.

WHAT DOES HEALING LOOK LIKE?

We are capable of change, and we can recalibrate our responses. The first step is to learn to listen to ourselves and trust the intelligence of our transmissions, beginning at the level of our nervous systems, hearts, bodies, souls, and beyond. From this place of trust, we can begin to find meaning in our life experiences, and see them as a call to mystery, community, and opportunity. Ultimately, this process allows us to encounter, embody, and continually evolve into our truest selves.

It sounds esoteric or unattainable, I know. But we're going on this journey together.

When we realize how deeply we really are connected – to the world within us, the world around us, and even the world outside of ordinary space and time – we begin to shift out of the "us versus them" perspective. We can access a new kind of knowing that most of us have never been taught. And we can develop a sense of resonance and alignment rather than fruitlessly pursuing fulfillment through false acceptance. The more authentic we become, the more we recognize and even magnetize our soul family, so we never need to feel that sense of loneliness – existential or otherwise – again.

With this, our cells shift out of danger mode, and our chronic physical and mental health conditions can improve and even reverse. Mitochondrial scientist Dr. Robert Naviaux calls this active recovery and healing capacity of our cells from danger mode "salugenesis." This term is closely related to sociologist Anton Antonovsky's concept of "salutogenesis," which describes how we can employ our hard-won coping skills to enhance our daily lives on a larger scale.

What this means is life is not "all downhill from here." No matter what challenges we've encountered, we can feel well, joyful, and more alive, even (especially!) after hardship. And we can better navigate future difficult times as well.

Moving toward healing and connection – on every level – is our natural state. Sometimes our bodies, minds, and spirits just need a reminder that we're capable of it, and a guide to help us begin the journey back to a state of well-being.

Most of us have been offered few options to address our past experiences and patterns other than recommendations for talk therapy, psychiatric medication, meditation, or keeping a stiff upper lip. Some of these approaches may work for some people, but the vast majority of people are looking for more effective – and faster – relief.

Psychedelic medicines – and Master Plants in particular – have captured the imagination of medical and mental health professionals, largely because they're blowing up much of what we've believed about not just our physical and mental health, but also our emotional, spiritual and even communal and ecological health.

In this book, I invite you to consider Master Plants as a profound way to open new portals to healing and connection. However, this is not a push-of-a-button, one-size-fits-all solution. Master Plants require a particular approach that includes the proper support before, during, and after. They ask us to think beyond reductionism – the paradigm of breaking ourselves and the world around us into tiny, separate pieces and particles – and to instead embrace interconnectedness in the broadest sense of the word.

2

ME AND WE

We know that a certain amount of suffering and challenges are an inevitable and inherent part of the human experience. Much as we may want to eliminate that, the nature of our current reality is that we all encounter difficulties over the course of our lives. The ten-million-dollar question is how do we become resilient in the face of those periods of inevitable hardship? How do we bounce back?

In Chapter 1, we discussed that a common underlying reason we suffer is because we live under the perception that we are separate, isolated, and unable to be seen for who we are. And those same perceptions of separateness are mirrored in our physiology – in how our hearts beat, how we breathe and oxygenate, our stress response, our posture, literally down to the function of our cells.

Yet everything mainstream we are told to do to "heal" perpetuates our sense of separateness – even from ourselves. We've come to see our bodies and their many parts as disconnected and divorced from us, to the point that we literally see fit to declare war on them. We wage war on our bodies, on fat, on germs, and on cancer, not to mention on the natural world – declaring war on weeds, bugs, and, of course, "drugs." Yet as astrophysicist Hubert Reeves said, "We're in a war with nature. If we win, we're lost."

What if we've been taking entirely the wrong approach to healing?

Famed humanistic psychologist Abraham Maslow's widely taught hierarchy of needs puts forth a model of society in which our physiological needs and safety are fundamental to our need for connection and self-actualization, which he portrays as a proverbial cherry on top of higher priority "essentials." One outcome of this model is the portrayal that survival becomes more primary than connection, which feeds our perpetual "war on" mentality.

It turns out, however, that Maslow's theory was largely influenced by (some say generously borrowed from) a summer in 1938, that he spent with one of North America's largest indigenous nations, the Blackfoot people. There, he was deeply fascinated and moved by a community very different from his own, where self-actualization was the norm, which he defined as "the desire to become more and more what one is, to become everything that one is capable of becoming." This approach included wide cooperation, generosity, minimal inequality, restorative justice, met needs, and a sense of satisfaction.

Yet Maslow placed self-actualization as the pinnacle for the individual to achieve. In contrast, the Blackfoot way of life assumes we're each born self-actualized, as inherently sacred beings who deserve to be treated with dignity from our very first breath. Each person's responsibility is to earn this status through continuous practice – with self-actualization serving not the benefit of the individual or as part of any hierarchy but always in service to the community. In turn, the community's responsibility is cultural perpetuity – to make decisions informed by the experience of the seven generations before and to consider the consequences for the seven generations to come.

In this paradigm, self-actualization only has meaning in the context of community, lineage, and spirit – all of which ensure access to food, water, shelter, safety, and connection, as well as satisfaction and self-actualization for us and for generations to come.

No hierarchy necessary. Cooperation, kinship, sharing, service. Everybody takes care of everybody. That makes sense, right?

Given that Maslow was a product of the modern scientific paradigm of the times, the version of the Blackfoot worldview represented in his hierarchy of needs is no great surprise.

We're still very much living in those times.

Modern science breaks complex systems into their parts and studies each in isolation. This approach was innovated in the 1600s largely by influential philosopher, mathematician, and scientist René Descartes, who believed that the human body was essentially a machine made up of various parts, such as organs, muscles, and bones. His concept of "mechanical philosophy" argued that the natural world and all living beings therein could be understood as complex machines made up of pieces that function together to produce the phenomena of life. He separated mind from body and science from religion, and in the process, transformed science into a sort of religion.

Over the ensuing centuries, Western science has taken a zealous approach of reductionism, operating under the belief that just as breaking a car down into the smallest parts possible should allow us to fully understand how the car works, so too should that work in living systems like our bodies or forest ecosystems. Scientists therefore explore the behavior of disembodied cells in isolation and extrapolate from their behavior in Petri dishes what the cells might do in complex systems. Environmental influences are taken into account insofar as they're considered confounding, or interfering with the true function of the cell. Even blood tests, bacterial cultures, and biopsies remove part of a living organism, analyze it in isolation, break it down more and more, and then make assumptions about what that could mean in a living organism, according to our expectations. Undoubtedly that can sometimes be tremendously helpful. But what might we be missing?

The trouble is that we are not a collection of independent cells that work neatly side-by-side but a robust, messy universe, filled with redundancies, in ongoing complex intelligent exchange. And this exchange is not just between parts of ourselves but also with the universe around us. We must face that much of science until now has been looking through a distorted lens and reporting a profoundly simplified – and at best, partially true – version of us.

Also, the modern scientific method operates with the understanding that we can be objective observers; however by the principles of complex systems, the observer and the observed are unavoidably and irrevocably in relationship. We are inherently part of the experiment, always influencing the outcomes of science.

All of this to say: While the reductionist approach may have some merit, holding it up as the only way of knowing for centuries and to the exclusion of all other approaches has become dangerous.

I AM BECAUSE WE ARE

The robust and rapidly growing science of connection explores how living beings – from cells to humans to entire ecosystems – interact with each other and the world around them. From the microbes living in our guts to the connection between our bodies, minds, and spirits, to the relationships that we have with our loved ones, we are connected to others in a multitude of ways.

Leading up to and during the pandemic, we clearly saw this. We need each other. We wither without companionship. Just as the invisible relationships within us allow our bodies to survive physically, our relationships with people, place, and even the invisible allow us to find meaning and joy during challenging periods. Connection nourishes our hearts and souls.

All living beings rely on each other in a myriad of ways. Plants rely on soil, sun and mycelium for nutrients; insects and plants jointly survive through pollination; and animals eat insects and plants. In this web of life, all living beings must be connected to survive and thrive. Everyone needs everyone else.

We may think of community as the people we see at the grocery store, the online friends we've made who post the funniest memes, or the neighbors on our block. All of those would be correct. But let's take it just a little further.

A community is also a group of interdependent organisms growing together in a specified habitat. What if, when we thought of our community, we included every cell, microbe, and drop of water within us? And everything around us? Sun, seed, soil, wind, water, and beyond?

What if we considered the terrain within and around us as our kin?

We know that swarms of bees and schools of fish can accomplish what one bee or fish cannot. We now know that forests work as communities at the level of the canopy by sharing sunlight, through mycelial networks underground by sending support in the form of nutrients and phytochemicals, and in ways far more complex. We are even learning that fungi communicate with one another in a way that looks uncannily like human speech.

In Zulu, the term *ubuntu* means "I am because we are." In other words, a person is a person through their interactions.

Human beings are social. We interpret stimuli based on possible social relevance. We spend tremendous time assessing our own and each other's social relationships. The social brain hypothesis theorizes that our large brains evolved in response to the demands of our complex social systems.

If only we'd realized how complex our social systems really are.

All the way down to our mitochondria, the energy makers of our cells, we love to be connected and work together. Mitochondria do much more than produce energy; they act as sentinels in the cell, continually sampling the environment to determine safety based on infection, toxins, and other stressors and deciding whether the cell should live or die, a process called apoptosis.

If we were to picture mitochondria, we'd probably imagine that all mitochondria look exactly alike, along the lines of whatever illustrations we memorized from our high school biology textbooks. It turns out that's wrong. Mitochondria are very individual in their structure, depending on their environment. When they are in what they perceive to be a "safe" environment, they are structured like branched spaghetti, exchanging information and nutrients and functioning at a very high level. When they perceive themselves to be in danger, they roll up like meatballs and don't share information or nutrients – and thus aren't able to function nearly as well – all in the name of protection.

Even our mitochondria become alone and isolated when they don't experience their community (us!) as safe and supportive.

We already know from Chapter 1 that we are utterly dependent on our relationship with the billions of microbes that live in and on our bodies. But where do they come from?

When we come into contact with others – people, animals, plants, soil, water – we share microbes. It may sound a little scary, but this isn't necessarily a bad thing. Our immune systems are social and thrive on meeting and greeting diverse organisms and compounds. Think of it as just another way we talk to one another.

As a result, we leave every encounter with another living being changed, with countless new organisms that speak to our immune and nervous systems and even to our mitochondria. Our *mitobiome* describes the communication between microbes and mitochondria, seemingly disparate but cooperative beings that reside in the universe of us that we now know evolved from common bacterial ancestry. The ongoing mitobiome conversation literally alters the mitochondrial messages sent to the nucleus – influencing the transcription of hormones, cytokines, and neurotransmitters we make – based on their exchange.

We are not the same minute to minute, hour to hour, day to day, week to week, in part because – depending on who we see and where we go – our microbiome is not the same, and that's *good*.

Our shared microbiome is constantly shifting and growing, depending on how we feel, how we care for ourselves, and how we connect with family members, friends, pets, and wild animals, as well as the plants we eat and tend, the soil beneath our feet, and the forests that surround us. These microbes support our digestion, immune systems, hormones, bones, and aging and help prevent us from developing diseases. More than that, they communicate directly with our mitochondria to instigate cellular changes responsible for cravings, feelings, productivity, a sense of well-being, and even athletic prowess.

We are a series of infinite ongoing conversations made manifest, and our bodies beautifully reflect this.

Our networks of microbes "talk" to our mitochondria, which "talk" to the cells' nuclei, who then send out neurotransmitters, hormones, and cytokines to "talk" with other cells throughout the body. Our fascial network is now known to be a communication system of connective tissue that surrounds every organ and body structure, and talks by way of molecules, electrical signals and even photons. And researchers have recently discovered that the extracellular "space" surrounding our cells is not empty but comprises a communication network called interstitium, which connects every cell in the body. Some researchers are now calling the interstitium an organ in its own right due to its critical functions in regulating fluid balance, immune responses, and signaling.

We are even connected – cell by cell, organ by organ – through our heart's powerful electromagnetic field that entrains the brain and other organs in the body to all synchronize as one community. Based on modern understanding, the brain controls the body and serves as the home to our consciousness. But extensive laboratory research comparing EEG and EKG tracings shows that it is in fact our hearts that perceive and anticipate our environment before our brains. Our heart rate variability – the variation of pauses between our heartbeats – predicts our emotional state with impressive accuracy. In this way, our hearts act as organs of perception and communication by emitting a measurable electromagnetic "biofield" that can be detected up to ten feet away.

We are increasingly realizing we're less one human organism and more like a rainforest, a swarm, or a universe inside a universe inside a universe. We didn't realize how robust these many systems were because until recently, we were too busy taking everything apart.

We're seeing in real time that despite everything we've been told, we're not independent and self-reliant. We are interconnected. We all have to care for and be cared for by each other. We must create a society that encourages us to show up for each other and check on each other. And we must make decisions not from the top down, but side by side, in ways that benefit individuals and all living beings.

We can cultivate these relationships that nourish us. That begins with our relationship with ourselves. Think of our bodies as a series of nested relationships – microbiome, mitochondria, epigenetics, cells, fascia, heart, brain, and other organ systems.

WE ARE MADE OF RELATIONSHIPS

Let's talk about our terrain. Our terrain is physical, emotional, mental, spiritual, and ecological.

Terrain is within us; let's call that the bio-terrain. It's our heart, lungs, brain, gut, kidneys, bone, and blood. It's our microbiome, the three to five pounds of invisible-to-the-naked eye bacteria, viruses, fungi, and parasites (that's right!) that live in and on our bodies and keep us regulated and healthy. It also includes our DNA, our epigenetics, our emotions, our spirit, and our soul.

Terrain is all around us, too; our eco-terrain is sun, soil, seeds, wind, water, the food we eat, the people we surround ourselves with, the microbes around us, the art, the music, the toxins, the way we spend our time, even the news we consume.

Invisible conversations between all of these entities and elements influence us in measurable ways. For example, research shows that we are healthier when we spend regular time immersed in nature. "Bathing" in the forest regularly improves focus, executive function, and memory; reduces anxiety; promotes better sleep and feelings of happiness; lowers stress hormones like cortisol; boosts our immune systems; and reduces our risk of cancer.

Spending regular time in sunlight (while avoiding sunburn) or getting our hands in the soil are two deeply evidence-based interventions that can help us become healthier and prevent illness. One 2016 study from the Karolinska Institute looked at thirty thousand women over a twenty-year period and found that those who assiduously avoided the sun doubled their risk of dying for any reason. In fact, the risk was considered equal to that of smoking cigarettes. A different study looked at healthy women who spent regular time in the forest and noted that their bodies increased production of natural killer cells and anticancer proteins. These benefits come simply by prioritizing interactions between ourselves and the forest and sun.

We also rely on plant and animal communities around us in ways that are not immediately obvious. For example, research shows that when trees die, humans that live near those trees die at higher rates. This observation does not clearly reflect anything that we've yet been able to directly assess (like cleaner air), but rather complex relationships that are beyond our ability to currently measure.

And as we'll soon see, forests themselves are living, intelligent organisms that depend upon all the many different organisms and entities within and around them for well-being, including miles of mycelium living in the soil beneath them.

When our inner and outer terrains align, we – and all living beings around us – experience greater health, well-being and balance.

Terrain is everything – from our body's ability to protect itself and stay in balance; our mind's sense of well-being; and our sense of purpose and joy to the food we eat; the land we stand on; and the quality of our connections to the visible and invisible world within and around us.

When facing health hurdles or other unanticipated life challenges, one course of action is always certain: attuning to and tending our terrain. When we are in physical, emotional, spiritual, and ecological balance, we become resilient and less likely to be derailed by any given stressors – personal or collective – from confronting novel organisms to political unrest.

This entanglement is good news. We need not think of ourselves as being entirely responsible for everything. We are intimately embedded in and thus supported by a massive life force. Our inner and outer garden is being tended to and nourished by vast numbers of beings. The task of our individual and collective well-being isn't a job for each of us alone. It rests in the quality of our infinite visible and invisible relationships.

What this all means is that each of us is not just me but WE.

Everyone is in beautiful conversation with everyone else, and together, this becomes a diverse, complex concert that makes our bodies, minds, and spirits sing.

These conversations even transcend time and space. We think of our ancestors as distant from us, but even the lives of our ancestors are not long gone. They manifest through us every day. This is not a metaphor.

The past experiences of our ancestors are woven into our epigenetics and determine how our DNA expresses itself in tangible and practical ways. For example, significant events in our great-great-grandparents' lives, such as famine, war, or farm chemical exposure, can affect how our genes express in the present moment. While DNA remains relatively stable over generations, the way it is read does not. Our epigenetics (meaning "on top of" genetics) are the labels that influence where and when proteins begin reading certain parts of DNA and where they stop, based on exposures to food, toxins, exercise, traumatic experiences, time in nature, and more. Think of them as yellow sticky notes all over our DNA that tell translating proteins to START HERE NOW. Or STOP. These labels help explain why we go gray, bald, or enter menopause at particular ages or even why familial conditions manifest in us or not.

What's fascinating is that though our epigenetics are inherited, they are reversible. This is why it is said that when we heal ourselves, we heal generations both backward and forward. On the one hand, mystics have always maintained that time and space are nonlinear. On the other hand, the science of epigenetics demonstrates this phenomenon in ways even the field of genetics previously never would have imagined.

Our survival – and, more than that, our ability to thrive – begins and ends with this giant web of unseen connections that transcends time and space.

Part of what makes us unique is the invisible world within us. Some aspects can be assessed. Others cannot, at least not with tools we currently have, and some are esoteric and thus simply not measurable. We are each individual, with our own genes, our own microbial community, and our own inner terrain. We are each the result of a vast coevolution, a moment-to-moment outcome of countless ongoing microbial contacts and encounters with diverse beings. Nothing about this process is static. Each day, we are made and remade of complex symbiotic relationships and infinite encounters. We exist because of our relationships – beginning with microbes, food, dirt, plants, animals, water, air, and people. And these systems are self-organized; there is no hierarchy there.

Engaging with our terrain means cultivating intimacy and trust as we lean into all of these nested relationships and the natural cycles of Mother Earth. As with any defining relationship, these invisible connections hold us and also challenge us. The trust we inhabit by embracing our role as both Me and We permits us to stay more resilient, curious, and even playful in the face of mystery, which includes all that we don't or can't know. From this place, we can awaken to sense a numinous layer of communication, with opportunities and solutions that present in subtle and unexpected ways – in signs, symbols, synchronicities, and epiphanies. This attunement to our terrain invites us to remember the universal language that has no words, allowing us to rejoin a bigger conversation.

MASTER PLANTS HELP US HEAL ON A COMMUNITY LEVEL

In Western medicine, any conversation about the body refers only to the physical structure we inhabit. Yet as miraculous as our bodies are, they are not only physical – but also psychological, emotional, and spiritual. Centuries living in the Cartesian paradigm has made us forget that psyche means soul, or spirit. And as we're seeing, our bodies are relational. They are part of a family, a community, a village – which means that if a problem arises within us, the community can be present to help. In fact, most cultures consider community intervention mandatory because the problems of one affect all.

As anyone who has dealt with a sick family member knows, no person in the family will function in quite the same way when their loved one is suffering because everyone's well-being is inseparable from the well-being of the one. And though we've strayed from this fundamental knowing in our "rugged individualist" culture, we're paying a heartbreaking price in a plethora of ways. The truth of this interconnection remains inescapable for our families, communities, and society at large.

Our society is only ever as strong as the support we offer our weakest members.

Master Plants help us directly engage with the traumatized or compromised within and around us – be it our cells, psyches, souls, people, other living beings, and beyond. They offer us opportunities and guidance to find our way out of derangement and into a more profound experience of physical, mental, emotional, spiritual, ecological, and relational balance.

The so-called "psychedelic renaissance" being touted in widespread headlines is really a renaissance of relationship. Because while these sacred plants work within us as individuals, they are considered also to recalibrate us on a community level – and not just the human community or even the greater-than-human community, but the ancestral community, the spirit community, and beyond. In an indigenous paradigm, none of us are mere "individuals" but rather custodians in service to – and simultaneously part of – something much more. As such, these plants offer healing that includes and also goes far beyond each of us, which is why they can be so effective.

As we'll see over the course of the coming chapters, Master Plants demonstrate why we must shift our paradigm from "Us versus Them" to "Me and We." Even the language of modern science has begun to show us ways that these plants boost our connectivity, empathy, gratitude, wonder and awe, and sense of meaning.

Indigenous people around the world have long engaged with psychedelic Master Plants as a way to contact with divinity that exist everywhere. By imparting knowledge of the therapeutic virtues of plants and fungi, as well as the sacredness of nature, all life, and beyond, has earned particular plants the status of Teacher or Master. By offering a window into the depth of our connection – with ourselves, each other, the natural world, and the invisible – they show us how we can begin to cultivate greater compassion and self-compassion, trust, gratitude, and curiosity, so that we can heal and grow individually, relationally, and communally.

3

MASTER PLANTS ARE
RETURNING IN FORCE

When I wrote my first book, *The Dirt Cure*, people asked me, "What's the difference between a germ and a microbe?" "We've always been told germs are bad, but it turns out microbes are actually good?" The answer: they're the same. *Germ* is simply a pejorative term for *microbe*. The definition rests in the nature of the relationship. The quality of our entanglement makes all the difference.

I now get asked: "What's the difference between a drug and a psychedelic?" The answer is similar. At a certain point, drugs became a pejorative term for psychedelic Master Plants. And again, the nuance resides in the relationship, in how we and the plants interact with one another. As with any relationship with a powerful Master, we must ask: are we coming with a sense of respect?

Wait. Respect for a plant? What does coming to a plant with respect even mean?

Consider whether we have cultivated reverence in our collective approach to the array of sacred plants long familiar to our culture – coca, cannabis, tobacco, and others. Most people would readily admit our engagement has demonstrated the very opposite of respect.

When I was in Ecuador years ago, I learned that communities who interfaced with Northerners referred to them as "junkies." They based their view not just on an overall proclivity for substance abuse, though that observation informed their opinion. The term emerged from what they saw as a constant and endless commoditizing and consuming of everything, even the most revered plants, with little to no respect for the sacred relationship or cultural scaffolding inherent to their benefit.

In their eyes, Northerners – seekers, scientists, pharmaceutical companies, and the rest – only come greedily for themselves, with no consideration of the well-being of anyone else: the plants, the land, the people who transmit the wisdom of those plants, or even the ancestors and the spirit world associated with the plants.

All *me*, no *we*.

WELCOME TO INDIGENOUS SCIENCE

Until now, many mainstream scientists and academics have not regarded indigenous science as true science, which is mostly a case of "it's hard to see what you aren't looking for" (or refuse to see). Yet while the principles underlying indigenous science have endured, our reductionist scientific paradigm is now being challenged to its very core by cutting-edge approaches like systems biology and quantum physics. These new perspectives allow us to explore the nonlinear entanglement of living processes, embracing complexity in ways that linear models can't entertain. And as we'll see, emerging models align far more with longstanding indigenous science. In fact, familiar methods and measures of modern science support these principles of interconnection.

As discussed, in their indigenous communities of origin, psychedelics are referred to not as drugs but as Master or Teacher Plants. They may also be referred to as Grandmother or Grandfather, Mother or Father. These Master Plants are considered to be very old and powerful kin; they convey an ancient wisdom and lineage that can help us heal as individuals and evolve as a community. In contrast to the way we perceive medicine in modern culture, these plants are not meant to be "taken" or "used"; they are regarded as revered members of the community – honored elders, teachers, and allies – and as such, are approached extreme reverence and humility, carefully, with offerings in hand. Any benefits derived are considered to be sacred gifts from the plants.

Skeptical? That's no surprise. Those from the Global North have long operated under the assumption that certain societies, particularly those of indigenous peoples, are primitive, backward, or "undeveloped." This view is partly based on the fact that they are preliterate or extra-literate, and thus unschooled in the repertory of European literature, history, and research that comprise an "acceptable" education. By this logic, indigenous communities therefore do not practice any science, technology, or advanced forms of knowledge commensurate with the standards of "modern" society.

This topic is worth unpacking in any conversation about the future of psychedelic medicine because indigenous knowledge is the past, present, and must remain a fundamental part of the future of the widespread engagement with Master Plants.

For example, this prevailing "primitive" paradigm conveniently ignores that many of our advanced scientific and other "discoveries," including those of psychedelics, primarily come from long-standing indigenous knowledge. At least 75 percent of pharmaceutical companies' plant-based remedies have come from indigenous societies. Fewer than 2 percent of all plants have been fully explored, with the vast majority of those plants living in tropical forests inhabited by indigenous communities.

Take ayahuasca, for example. Many people may not realize that the ayahuasca vine alone has no significant hallucinogenic activity. In order to become the psychedelic brew called "ayahuasca" that's been prepared for millennia, two plants must be brewed together for hours. One of the plants – which in the Amazon is often the chacruna plant (*Psychotria viridis*) – must contain the hallucinogenic substance dimethyltryptamine (DMT). However, that plant alone also has no hallucinogenic effect when consumed orally, because it is broken down by an enzyme in our stomachs called monoamine oxidase. Enter the ayahuasca vine (*Banisteriopsis caapi*) – which contains compounds that render that enzyme inactive, allowing for the DMT to survive digestion and absorption – allowing the combination to penetrate systemic circulation and the brain's inner sanctum.

Of roughly 100,000 or more plant varieties in the Amazonian jungle alone, many unrelated indigenous communities somehow discovered not just the ayahuasca vine but also the necessity of combining the vine with just the right second plant, and the hours-long process required to prepare them together to have a psychedelic effect. Oh, and all of this happened without what most of us would consider the necessary scientific knowledge or technology to identify enzymes, alkaloids, and other compounds involved.

What's more, when they're asked how they obtained this intricate, detailed, and very specific knowledge, they say the Master Plants *showed* them.

And yes, they mean this *literally*.

They refer to Master Plants – or really, the Spirit or Mother of the Master Plants such as ayahuasca – as a doctor, a teacher, or a force with intelligence and the capacity to create an alliance with humans *if* the humans come in a good and respectful way. For those who dedicate themselves to the relationship, Master Plants can transmit knowledge and power - not for personal gain but for the good of all.

Most people's automatic response when they hear all of this is that it's clearly some hallucinogenic fantasy. Learning botany and pharmacology...from a plant? Anthropologists have written extensively about this claim, which is widely held by indigenous communities in the Amazon and around the world. With few exceptions, anthropologists say it simply cannot be taken seriously.

Moreover, most scientists to this day refuse to recognize that indigenous people could have developed ways to use nature's molecules and compounds by any means other than chance experimentation. And they maintain this stance in the face of extensive evidence that the complexity of remedies used, sometimes for millennia, is as advanced as anything developed by modern science.

Another example is curare, the synthetic medication used universally by anesthesiologists to paralyze patients during surgery. Originally developed by indigenous people to paralyze tree monkeys they hunted that would otherwise remain hanging high up in trees after being shot with arrows, curare ensured that they fell to the ground. To create the treated arrows, however, the people had to identify and gather several different plants, boil them together for hours to create a paste (all while avoiding breathing the poisonous fumes), and then determine that the preparation was only effective when administered under the skin rather than ingesting it.

Are we to really assume this all happened by dumb luck?

No matter. We – by way of anthropologists, botanists, the pharmaceutical industry, and many others – have been only too happy to utilize and commoditize all of this advanced knowledge, or intellectual property (as we would call it), even as they disregarded and disrespected wisdom holders, plants, and spirits who have shared them. To add insult to injury, anthropologists pejoratively labeled the ones who often transmitted the information – now universally called "shamans" – as psychiatrically or medically unstable.

This same attitude also has permeated the way we view indigenous myth. These days, myths are mostly set aside for storytime. However, once upon a time, myth was fundamental to everyone's understanding of the world – and not just metaphorically.

Every culture has its own dominant mythology – a story that explains how the world is and provides guidance for living. Most of us, for example, have been indoctrinated with a very particular mythology of our dominion over nature and other beings, the commoditization of living beings and eternal elements – animals, plants, trees, land, minerals, water, people – and our entitlement to build that into a model of unlimited growth and unbridled benefit for ourselves.

There are, however, other mythologies – ones that were once

widely held not just as colorful stories but also as transmissions of eternal knowledge – that are far older. What's more, all of this information and much more has been memorized and recited as a sophisticated memory coding technique as opposed to being written and maintained in volumes of books.

In indigenous cultures around the world, once a plant or animal or spirit transmits knowledge to humans, the information then would be embedded and orally conveyed by way of myth.

Myths, accompanied by song, dance, and art, are cataloged knowledge passed from the ancients to now, generation by generation, initiated to initiate. For Australian Aboriginal people, for example, these *dreamings* and *songlines* are guides through the land and historical events, as well as sources of advice on how to live and survive. Some record events going back over 10,000 years.

Indeed, indigenous communities have always conveyed rich and detailed knowledge via stories, symbols, models, and metaphors assisted by art, music, and spiritual practice, all of which guide people in respectfully caring for each other and their human and greater-than-human kin. The stories communicate historical events that transformed the earth over time, and the necessary guiding principles and values for living in harmony within their community and with the world around them, also known as "right relationship."

Myths metaphorically demonstrate fundamental principles like interdependence; respect for plants, animals, and places; and how each generation must behave to maintain a reciprocal relationship with the natural world. But they are not just stories. They have long been used as instruments to encode generations of knowledge, in some cases from ten thousand years or more. The Navajo people, for example, shared the names of seven hundred species of insects with researchers, all from memory – with names, sounds, behaviors, and habitats all remembered through oral transmission of myth accompanied by cues embedded in song and dry sand paintings. For Australian Aboriginals, rituals that describe hunting magic are not just ways to engage with supernatural beings and invite good fortune – the associated songs catalog details of animal behavior, the visible constellations of stars that show the most effective time of year to hunt, and landmarks to find the animals, while the dances imitate the activity and characteristics of the animals, ways to avoid being detected by them, and patterns they might use to disperse.

In indigenous cultures, myths are a matter of survival. And a myth rarely represents only one form of knowledge but includes overlapping categories like history, literature, botany, geology, hunting, safety, ethics, law, or spirituality. An initiated elder might know over a thousand stories that act as maps for landscape features, plants, animals, elements, and other necessary resources, all remembered with no volumes of written words on which to rely.

As with a game of telephone, too many people sharing the information can distort the integrity of the transmission. This means that when we hear indigenous myths that sound like children's stories, it's probably because they are. At the most basic level, those myths are the simplest and most colorful versions of information that they will memorize, meant to introduce children to the much more complicated layers that they'd eventually learn in the process of lifelong initiation into the knowledge of their community.

It's of the utmost importance that this repository of information be woven together with ethics and maintained only by the initiated, because indigenous elders have long understood that any information – no matter how profound or powerful – can become a weapon when wielded without wisdom.

The same is true for Master Plants.

THE RIGHT INTENTIONS AND THE RIGHT CEREMONY

Indigenous communities express a great deal of concern around the use of Master Plants as a means of "sorcery." While such talk makes many of us uneasy, sorcery, at its core, means to use their exceptional power with evil intent, for example, to attack, cause disease, or even destroy enemies. In many indigenous paradigms of disease, physical and mental illness can be traced to psychic attacks and negative intentions (whether conscious or not). And Master Plants in the right hands, with the right intentions, and with the right cere-mony, can allow the healer to see into the suffering person and help them purge the spiritual sickness.

The importance of ritual and ceremony in the use of Master Plants thus centers on this very issue and is considered a funda-mental reason to uphold sacred and ceremonial "rules of engage-ment." The rules vary by community and Master Plant, but the concern that humans could easily devolve into using their profound power with malefic intent is universal.

As such, while considered sacred by indigenous communities, no one maintains that Master Plants only offer healing benefits. Master Plants are, however, indisputably powerful, and let's face it, humans who engage with great power don't always demonstrate their finest behavior. Again, this is where initiated elders play a critical role, holding others accountable by passing down ritual laws, historical events, ethics, and responsibilities encoded into myth, song, dance, and ceremony to select initiates.

Until very recently, it could easily be argued that overall, the Global North's first interactions with psychedelics in the 1950s demonstrated a less-than-responsible, less-than-ethical approach that could be called the opposite of sacred.

For example, it's thought that humans have likely consumed psychedelic psilocybes, or magic mushrooms, for millennia. It's also thought that the context for ingestion was likely sacred and cere-monial, which was certainly true for the Mazatec people of Mexico. That changed on June 29, 1955, when a vice-president of J.P. Morgan named R. Gordon Wasson traveled to Mexico with a photographer to the home of the Mazatec *curandera* (medicine woman) Maria Sabina, and they became, in Wasson's words, "the first white men in recorded history to eat the divine mushrooms."

Wasson found that many cultures across the world worshipped mushrooms and had constructed religious ceremonies around their consumption. He was especially interested in the Aztecs after learning of early Spanish missionary accounts of the Aztec mush-room ceremony of eating the teonanacatl, or "God's flesh."

It wasn't until 1955, in the Oaxacan village of Huautla de Jiménez, that Wasson achieved his goal. He asked a town hall official for help learning the secrets of the divine mushroom and was taken to a mountainside where the mushrooms abundantly grew and then to the home where Maria Sabina lived.

Maria Sabina was well-respected in the village as a curandera. She'd been consuming psilocybe mushrooms regularly since she was seven years old and had performed the mushroom ceremony for over thirty years before Wasson arrived.

The all-night ceremonies she conducted were always intended to commune with God to heal the sick. The spirits would tell Maria Sabina the nature of the sickness and the way it could be healed. Vomiting by the participants was considered an essential part of the ceremony to purge the sickness. Each participant in the ritual would ingest mushrooms as Maria Sabina chanted invocations to coax forth the divine.

Maria Sabina was reluctant to introduce Wasson to the ceremony because Wasson and his colleague weren't in need of healing. Wasson and his friends were the first foreigners to come to town in search of the "Saint Children," but in contrast to the tradition, they didn't suffer from any illness. Their reason was simply to find God.

Over time, Wasson witnessed nine ceremonies by Maria Sabina. On one trip, he brought French mycologist Roger Heim, who identified the species of mushrooms and sent samples to Albert Hofmann, the Swiss chemist who twenty years earlier had synthesized LSD. Hofmann isolated the chemical structure of psilocybin, created a synthetic version, and began sending doses to research institutions across the world.

The subsequent *Life Magazine* article written by Wasson in 1957, "Seeking the Magic Mushroom," opened a Pandora's box that led to the emergence of the American psychedelic counterculture, the defilement of the mushroom ritual, and, ultimately, the banning of psilocybin across much of the world. The article also eventually impacted Maria Sabina and her community profoundly as Westerners came to her by the hundreds.

Wasson gained the public eye, at least for a time, as well as a research career, going on to publish several volumes in the field of mycology and ethnobotany.

Wasson's story also attracted the interest of the CIA for its covert program Project MK ULTRA.

Not surprisingly, psychedelics brought about some darker components of US history. Over the 1950s and 1960s, the military and CIA conducted their own experiments through MK Ultra with LSD and psilocybin as part of their broader research on mind control and behavior modification. This research was conducted at universities like Harvard as well as other academic institutions in partnership with the government or military.

The program involved administering LSD and other psychoactive drugs without consent or warning to both willing and unwilling subjects, including CIA employees, military personnel, and members of the general public. The goal of the program was to investigate their potential use as weapons, as well as to study the effects of these substances on the human mind.

Sorcery is considered a superstitious term, far removed from the modern world, but what was this, if not using the power of Master Plants and psychedelics to bring ill effects or destruction on enemies?

To this day, the full extent of the CIA's experimentation with psychedelics remains unknown. The programs were controversial and eventually said to be terminated.

Yet whether or not he was aware, Wasson became an agent of sorts for the program after the CIA secretly funded Wasson's trips to Mexico under a shell organization.

After reading Wasson's article "Seeking the Magic Mushroom," psychologist and Harvard professor Dr. Timothy Leary traveled to Cuernavaca, Mexico. Rather than partake in the sacred mushroom ritual, he purchased mushrooms from a local curandera and ingested them by the pool of his villa – removing the mushrooms from the ceremonial setting.

From that experience, Leary stated that he'd "learned more

about my brain and its possibilities and more about psychology in the five hours after taking these mushrooms than in the preceding fifteen years of studying and doing research in psychology." Leary returned to Harvard and started the Harvard Psilocybin Project with his colleague Dr. Richard Alpert (later known as Ram Dass).

Leary and Alpert proceeded to develop pioneering concepts in psychedelic therapy, testing whether ingesting psilocybin could reduce recidivism in prison inmates or catalyze religious experiences in divinity students. Though the published results enthusiastically endorsed psilocybin's mystical and therapeutic potential, they ultimately were judged to lack credibility due to their excessively positive spin – for example, omitting descriptions of the intense anxiety experienced by many of the participants.

Leary and Alpert were doing more than simply testing psychedelics in controlled experimental settings. They were using LSD every weekend and encouraging their students and colleagues to do the same. The academic community became divided over this widespread, indiscriminate use of LSD, all driven by the belief that every researcher should be mandated to have a mind-opening experience. Ultimately, Leary and Alpert were fired. Soon after, Leary began his public campaign to "turn on, tune in, and drop out." Alpert traveled to India, studied with a guru, and returned as Ram Dass.

The overemphasis on the positive aspects of psychedelic experiences and downplaying of the negative became more of a problem when psychedelics reached the streets in the early 1960s. As psychedelic researcher and director of MAPS Rick Doblin wrote: "Some of the backlash that swept the psychedelics out of research labs and out of the hands of physicians and therapists can be traced in part to the thousands of cases of people who took psychedelics in non-research settings, were unprepared for the frightening aspects of their psychedelic experiences, and ended up in hospital emergency rooms."

For these reasons and more, from the mid-1960s onward, LSD research came to a halt, and in 1966, the United States outlawed potential LSD treatments for PTSD and alcoholism. The medication became a Schedule I narcotic, meaning it had "a high potential for misuse" and "no currently recognized medicinal use."

While public health played a role, this policy also had political motivations, particularly in light of promising research. And one of Nixon's top advisors John Ehrlichman admitted in an 1994 interview more than two decades later that the drug war was in part a ploy to undermine Nixon's political opposition:

"You want to know what this was really all about? The Nixon campaign in 1968, and the Nixon White House after that, had two enemies: the antiwar left and black people. You understand what I'm saying? We knew we couldn't make it illegal to be either against the war or black, but by getting the public to associate the hippies with marijuana and blacks with heroin, and then criminalizing both heavily, we could disrupt those communities. We could arrest their leaders, raid their homes, break up their meetings, and vilify them night after night on the evening news. Did we know we were lying about the drugs? Of course, we did."

For better or worse, the initiative worked. After President Richard Nixon declared a "war on drugs" in 1971, the number of people incarcerated in American jails and prisons escalated from 300,000 to 2.3 million. Half of those in federal prisons are incarcerated for a drug offense, and two-thirds of those in prison for drug offenses are people of color. Disproportionate arrest, conviction, and sentencing rates for drug offenses have had devastated communities of color in the United States.

Meanwhile, streams of hippies, scientists, seekers, and celebrities flooded Maria Sabina's village of Huautla de Jiménez.

For her part, Maria Sabina frequently expressed regrets over introducing Wasson to the mushrooms and always emphasized what she saw as the mushroom's true purpose. Still, she rarely turned seekers away. Yet all the publicity and tourism were disastrous for the Mazatec community, who blamed Maria Sabina for bringing misfortune to her community and defiling the mushroom ritual. Her house was burned down, and *federales* raided her home many times, accusing her of selling drugs to foreigners. The tourists took over her town and surrounding towns, had bad trips, and behaved in disruptive ways, including running naked through the streets.

In the 1970s, Mexican authorities banned the use of the mushrooms. The influx of tourists receded, but in Maria Sabina's eyes, the damage had been done.

"From the moment the foreigners arrived to search for God, the Saint Children lost their purity," she said. "They lost their force; the foreigners spoiled them. From now on, they won't be any good. There's no remedy for it."

Wasson himself expressed remorse for his role in popularizing the recreational use of the mushrooms.

Maria Sabina died penniless at the age of ninety-one in 1985. Because she is held up as a sort of sacred figure of the psychedelic movement, her face graces mugs and T-shirts sold to the tourists passing through her hometown, and the site of her former home is now a public museum.

Yet she was held in no small part responsible for ruining her people's traditional way of life. She stuck to her ancient craft as a curandera but ultimately regretted that she'd let the secrets of her people's tradition escape into the wider world, even for spiritual purposes.

She said: "Before Wasson, nobody took the mushrooms only to find God. They were always taken for the sick to get well."

THE RETURN TO HEALING THE SICK

Fast-forward to the 2000s, interest in better approaches to addiction as well as major depression began to revitalize the psychedelic clinical research field. In 2008, Dr. Matt Johnson paired high-dose psilocybin administration with a more standard cognitive behavioral therapy for smoking cessation: to help the person quit, identify their reasons for quitting and their motivations for engaging in that pattern of behavior, and untangle that web of addiction. They interspersed within that a high dose of psilocybin to accelerate the process. The initial pilot study was in highly motivated individuals that had been smoking for decades on average, and the results were exciting. The majority were able to quit smoking immediately after two high doses of psilocybin, along with supportive counseling. And the majority of those people maintained biologically-verified smoking abstinence through a six-month and then twelve-month follow-up. Even years later, many were still abstaining.

These results were far better than for any other approach anywhere else in the world. In a typical group of people trying to quit smoking, around 30 percent are usually successful in quitting longer term. But by six months or a year later, they relapse. In contrast, this study had an 80 percent success rate at a six-month follow-up of participants who were not smoking. Sixty-seven percent were not smoking at the twelve-month follow-up. These results were unmatched by any other approach attempted for nicotine addiction.

Similarly unprecedented results are emerging from clinical trials to resolve addiction to other substances as well as major depression, PTSD, and eating disorders, with studies on many more conditions in progress.

In 2014, *Scientific American* called for an end to the ban on psychedelic research.

Reforming laws around the use of psychedelics is a significant development for at least two reasons. First, psychedelics may offer a level of therapeutic benefit that could literally save lives for people suffering from the impacts of trauma and much more. Second, legalizing psilocybin may prompt a radical rethinking of the prohibition of other Schedule I drugs, which might serve as a catalyst for ending the largely racially motivated "war on drugs."

To date, several American cities and even some states have moved to decriminalize psychedelics, either due to ballot initiatives or decisions made by municipal councils. The use and possession of psilocybin-containing mushrooms were made legal in Denver for the first time in May 2019. Since then, Legalize Nature, a decentralized group, has directed grassroots campaigns in more than one hundred American cities to decriminalize psilocybin and other entheogenic plants and increase access to them.

And the initiatives are picking up speed. Psilocybin and other naturally occurring psychedelics will henceforth be treated as the "lowest law enforcement priority" in cities including Oakland; San Francisco; Santa Cruz; Ann Arbor; Washington, DC; Somerville; and Cambridge, among others. All eyes are on Oregon, the first state where Schedule 1 substances in small quantities are legal.

More than forty years after research into their therapeutic effects was all but outlawed, psilocybe mushrooms and other Master Plants are now being studied for use in a manner much closer to what María Sabina considered to be their true purpose: to heal the sick.

4

THE SCIENCE OF PSYCHEDELICS

Now that we're hearing of so many seemingly miraculous recoveries people are experiencing from some of the most difficult-to-treat conditions out there, not to mention spiritual awakenings, the billion-dollar question remains: how are psychedelics achieving the profound and lasting shifts within us – physically, mentally, emotionally, and spiritually?

When I asked this question of one of the top Johns Hopkins psychedelic researchers, he said: "We don't know. There are things we think we know, but we're probably far from really understanding it all."

Psychedelics continue to keep scientists on their toes.

As we know, most pharmaceuticals do not actually address the underlying root causes of illness; they just treat the symptoms and require ongoing administration – sometimes lifelong. In the right context, psychedelics, on the other hand, seem to take people beyond symptom reduction alone into a place where true healing can happen.

As psychedelics like LSD, psilocybin, and others are being decriminalized and growing closer to FDA approval as psychiatric treatments, the medical and science establishments have recognized a need to understand mysticism beyond simple curiosity.

But how?

Do they work at the levels of our bodies and brains alone? Do they work – as indigenous peoples who have been guided by these plants for hundreds or thousands of years believe – on a soul and consciousness level? How would we even describe that in the lexicon of modern science?

The answers are likely far more complex and nonlinear than we can imagine and will instigate new sets of questions that have yet to be considered. The key is that this process calls for a both/and perspective. And it's requiring more complex approaches to the usual scientific and medical paradigms to even begin to understand how psychedelics work.

Meanwhile, let's buckle our seatbelts and get ready to nerd out for a little while as we dive into some of the fascinating science of psychedelics. At least I think so – and I hope you'll agree.

WHAT ARE PSYCHEDELICS AND HOW DO THEY WORK?

Psychedelics are substances that reliably induce states of altered perception, thought, and feeling that most people do not easily experience otherwise, except in dreams or at times of religious exaltation. The word *entheogen* is another descriptor, derived from the Greek roots *entheos*, combining "God [*theos*] within," and *genesthe*, "to generate." In other words, these entity generate contact with the divine within us.

Given their ineffability, it should come as no surprise that there's still disagreement on what chemically defines a psychedelic. Some of that controversy centers on whether LSD, ketamine, and MDMA are even technically psychedelics. Here, our focus will remain primarily on Master Plants rather than synthetic psychedelics (which is simply a choice rather than a value judgment). And as we explore some of what we know so far about underlying ways that certain Master Plants interact with us, know that there can be any number of exceptions to any rule.

Also keep in mind that as already discussed, most modern research focuses on chopping plants up and distilling them to their compounds; thus, some of these conversations will be about particular receptors or plant compounds. Moreover, we will be exploring the underlying mechanisms shared in common by many psychedelic Master Plants, but know that they are each tremendously complex in ways that may not be fathomable, let alone measurable, by the current research paradigm – but what we do know is certainly fascinating.

Let's start with tryptamines. These two linked ring-shaped molecular structures are considered to be the operating currency of classical psychedelics. They are also the currency of signaling between cells in plants, fungi, and animals.

That's right, plants, animals, fungi, *and* humans all share common chemical signaling.

You may have heard of at least one of them: 5-hydroxytryptamine (5-HT), also known as serotonin.

Classic psychedelics disrupt neural activity by diffusing through the brain and activating a particular serotonin receptor known as the 5-HT2A receptor. While recent research indicates this serotonin receptor is not entirely responsible for the psychedelic experience (as if!), the 5-HT2A receptor is thought to be central for the simple reason that blocking it abolishes the hallucinatory state.

Different psychedelic compounds activate these and other receptors in their own unique combinations of ways. For instance, psilocybin seems to act principally via the 5-HT2A receptor system. As we'll soon see, DMT, a principal component of the ayahuasca brew made of – yep, tryptamines – acts on the 5-HT2A system and SIGMAR1 involved in neuronal signaling. Mescaline, a principal compound of peyote and San Pedro cactus, is a type of phenethylamine that acts on 5-HT2A-C receptors and also activates dopamine receptors. Meanwhile, *Salvia divinorum* is a total exception to the rule, with salvinorin A having no known 5-HT2A activation but instead stimulating a kappa-opioid receptor.

The affinity – or level of attraction – of different psychedelics for the 5-HT2A receptor varies and correlates with their potency. LSD, for example, binds more strongly to our serotonin receptors than serotonin itself – two hundred times more strongly! And fun fact, experiments conducted with tiny doses of LSD in the 1950s led to the development of SSRIs, the popular and controversial antidepressant class widely used today. But while SSRIs are generally intended to diminish the intensity of experience so that reality becomes less overwhelming, psychedelics do the opposite. They amplify the intensity of perception and emotions.

After all, we all know that an experience with Prozac is nothing like one with psilocybin or ayahuasca.

This amplification of perception is true not just for LSD but also for Master Plants. In people who took a relatively high dose of psilocybin, for example, PET imaging shows that its psychoactive metabolite psilocin occupied over 70 percent of the brain's 5-HT2A receptors. The more receptors were occupied, the greater the intensity of the psychedelic experience.

Why doesn't serotonin (or SSRIs) instigate psychedelic effects when it shares a common receptor with psychedelics? Good question.

The answer: Location, location, location.

Most neurotransmitters bind to receptors that sit on the cell's outer membrane. Serotonin molecules, which bind to the 5-HT2A receptors on the cell's surface, are no exception. Same with SSRI molecules. Then, the "activated" receptor sends necessary messages to the rest of the cell on behalf of the activating molecule.

It turns out, however, that an entire stealth population of 5-HT2A receptors recently were discovered on the *inside of the cell.* The weirdest part is that serotonin can't easily access its own "internal" serotonin receptors, which would make no sense...except psychedelic molecules can. Psychedelic compounds can easily slip across the cell membrane, activating those particular receptors on the inside of the cell.

When these internal 5-HT2A receptors are stimulated, something unique happens. Entire populations of neurons suddenly become more excitable, and this blanket activation allows for what's known as neuroplasticity. Widespread new connections are forged. Greater community develops within and between neural networks.

We'll explore shortly why this plasticity matters so much practically, but here's the preview from a neuroscience standpoint: neurological and psychiatric conditions often show up microscopically in our brains as fewer neuronal connections. Think of the abandoned streets and closed shops of New York City during quarantine. In general, neurons do not thrive when lonely; our neurons like to chat, shop, and engage in a density of connections - less like mass quarantine and more like a huge gathering in Central Park on the first beautiful day of spring. Psychedelics helps create an environment in the brain that brings together strangers (and long-lost friends) to connect, vibe, and come back to hang out again and again.

The key is that this plasticity only results when *internal* 5-HT2A receptors are activated.

These 5-HT2A receptors are found throughout the brain, most abundantly in areas of the cerebral cortex responsible for cognition and self-awareness. They're also highly expressed in the visual cortex – which may contribute to psychedelic visions – and on the ends of axons that cortical neurons send elsewhere in the brain, such as the thalamus, where sensory information is processed, which may partly explain shifts in perception.

Why would the humble serotonin receptor become so central to psychedelic stimulation?

I'm glad you asked. Some researchers believe that it's because we produce our own endogenous (made by our body and brain) psychedelic compounds that directly stimulate the very same 5-HT2A receptors specifically – namely, DMT (aka N, N-dimethyltryptamine).

DMT is well-known to be an essential component of ayahuasca brew, usually derived from the chacruna plant, and also found in mimosa, Syrian rue, and other potentially psychedelic plants. And though it can be synthetically manufactured in a lab, DMT is also produced naturally by our own neurons, likely promoting higher-order brain functions like improved learning, memory, and information processing.

What we have learned is that DMT is more than a "mere psychedelic molecule" – for one thing, it is abundant not just in plants but also in mammals, including in our blood, brain, and cerebrospinal fluid – and is thus called an endogenous hallucinogen (meaning it is made by us, for us).

In short, nature is drenched in DMT. Why?

DMT molecules not only stimulate serotonin receptors, but also are the only known activator of another very powerful and unusual receptor called the SIGMAR1. **Stick with me here, because SIGMAR1 resides throughout our bodies and is pivotal in developing, preventing and *even possibly reversing* the epidemic diseases of our modern times.** I'm talking about neurodegenerative diseases, traumatic brain injury, cancer, diabetes, chronic pain, and more.

A couple of fascinating facts. First, the human SIGMAR1 gene is unique among all our genes in that, unlike any other, it shares only 30.3 percent similarity with any other mammalian protein, but it shares 66.7 percent of its identity with an enzyme found in fungi. Hmm, that's weird. Second, this enzyme is involved in the biosynthesis of a component of fungal cell membranes first identified in the fungus *Claviceps purpurea*, which produces ergot alkaloids.

A human gene that has more in common with fungi than other mammals would by itself be remarkable. And that this *human* gene codes for an enzyme that builds *fungal* cell membranes? Also, pretty strange. But in the wildest twist, *Claviceps purpurea* is the very fungus that happens to produce ergot alkaloids, *including the precursor of synthetic LSD*. Um, what?

Could all of this be a coincidence? Maybe, maybe not. But the confluence of these and other fascinating facts led researchers to explore whether SIGMAR1 could also be involved in producing psychedelic effects in contrast to the prevailing view that 5-HT receptors alone mediate the psychedelic effects of tryptamines.

Researchers are looking more closely now at how DMT – in cahoots with SIGMAR1 – could address and transform physical, mental, and emotional trauma.

In Chapter 1, we talked about the ways that traumatic experiences persist by literally living in our bodies – changing our nervous systems, our fascia, our cells, our microbiomes, our mitochondria, all the way down to our epigenetics (the way our genes are read).

Remember how our most difficult-to-treat conditions result from our cells getting stuck in danger mode? And how our mitochondria stay chronically in meatball configuration, accepting fewer nutrients and retaining more toxins and waste?

When this phenomenon persists, it's called *cellular memory*.

The SIGMAR1 wears many hats, regulating stress, energy, communication, and plasticity. In other words, they have the perfect set of tools to both transform the memories embedded in our cells that impede our function and shift the cell's operating system from danger mode to growth and connection.

Here's what we know so far about how that could happen:

DMT activates the SIGMAR1, which then enhances the function of cells throughout our bodies – including in the brain, retina, liver, lungs, heart, and immune system. As it happens, the highest densities of SIGMAR1 are found in brain areas like the amygdala and hippocampus, which are responsible for, you guessed it, traumatic memory formation, retrieval, and updating. This is one powerful clue that suggests DMT-induced SIGMAR1 activation plays a role in the reshaping of traumatic memories.

Another clue is that SIGMAR1 can regulate certain gene expression by way of our epigenetics (remember those yellow sticky notes all over our DNA sequences from Chapter 2?). As a result, when DMT activates the multi-talented SIGMAR1 receptors, they can recalibrate aberrant gene expression and epigenetic signatures that resulted from trauma or PTSD. They offer us a whole new set of sticky notes, allowing our DNA to be read through a lens of growth and connection instead of fear and protection.

And voilà! Our cells shift from danger to growth mode. And our mitochondria transform from meatballs into beautifully connected, branching spaghetti configurations.

The influence of activated SIGMAR1 on both cellular memory and epigenetic processes makes a strong case for DMT having the superpower to modulate cellular memory. Translated, this means that DMT could help us to heal mentally, emotionally, and even physically from ailments that manifest as a result of traumatic experiences.

Yet the next step gets even better– when DMT binds and activates SIGMAR1, our cells become more resilient. They can survive stress that normally would disrupt function or even lead to cell death. Our cells even can better fine-tune innate and adaptive immune responses.

Talk about superpowers.

So although DMT is best known as a compound that can induce powerful psychedelic experiences under particular circumstances, the DMT plus SIGMAR1 combo acts as an indirect antioxidant, altering how our DNA is read, becoming a superhero agent of neuroprotection, neuroplasticity, neuro-regeneration, and immune modulation.

SIGMAR1 is also known as a molecular "chaperone" that stabilizes the formation of "client" proteins under stress conditions. This role is particularly relevant because when chaperone proteins become dysfunctional, we develop diseases from Alzheimer's, Parkinson's, ALS, cancer, cardiomyopathy, retinal dysfunction, perinatal and traumatic brain injury, frontal motor neuron degeneration, major depression, HIV, dementia, and psychostimulant addiction.

Just to name a few.

Knowing that makes all of this emerging psychedelic science

very hopeful, and explains why DMT, along with the activated SIGMAR1 receptors, may effectively address a host of common (and currently very difficult-to-treat) conditions, including cardiovascular disease, drug abuse, schizophrenia, clinical depression, and cancer as well as mood disorders, strokes and concussions, neurodegenerative disorders, and chronic pain.

REBOOTING YOUR VERSION OF REALITY

So how does the dive we've done into neurophysiology translate practically to what we actually experience during and after psychedelic experiences? To understand that, we must widen our lens and travel from our microscopic cellular connections to larger structural connections in our brains.

Meet the default mode network (DMN).

The DMN is an interacting set of brain regions that becomes active when a person is focused internally rather than on the outside world. Operational beginning in late childhood, this network of areas of the brain lights up with activity when we consider who we are (identity), imagine ourselves in the context of future events (mental time travel), try to get into the minds of other people (perspective shifting), or when we have no cognitive tasks to perform, and our minds wander. In other words, it's active when the brain is in its "default mode" – hence the name – daydreaming or reflecting in our calmer moments, and ruminating and perseverating in our more anxious moments.

The DMN links the cerebral cortex, responsible for higher functioning, to deeper and more ancient parts of our brain like the limbic system – which plays a pivotal role in our fight-or-flight response, long-buried memories, emotions, and primal behaviors like feeding and sex – always alternating the focus on our inner world with attentional networks that draw our attention outward.

Think of the DMN as choreographing a dance between expressing and repressing.

Called the "Me" network, the DMN acts as the conductor of the orchestra, by coordinating the competing systems of our brains and ensuring the active parts play nicely together, while simultaneously keeping other parts in check. When active, the system acts mostly in an inhibitory way, repressing the limbic system. The DMN acts as our filter, determining what comes in from the outside world as well as what we experience from our inside world.

Most active during focus, attention, and functioning in the outside world, it's great for survival and success. But when the DMN goes offline, our emotions, memories, and long-buried childhood traumas that have been otherwise suppressed may float to the surface – which could obviously be distracting when we're trying to perform at a high level in our daily lives.

The DMN is also responsible for a phenomenon called predictive coding, which we do every day even though we don't realize it.

Imagine walking into a room for the first time. Most people would say that they notice, observe and assess all or at least most of the details. It turns out that's not usually the case. Our brains are actually designed to select just a few key details from the present moment and then fill in all of the remaining details from relevant past experiences.

In a nutshell, that's predictive coding.

Essentially, the DMN allows our brains to predict what is most likely to happen based on the least information available. Again, this skill allows us to survive. Think about it: if we were to walk into a room with a tiger waiting to pounce, there's no way we'd have time to assess every little detail – big sharp teeth, striped fur, giant claws, long ropes of drool, fierce eyes – before we'd want to run like hell. Of course, we want to – and must – employ the wisdom of our past experiences to avoid danger.

But what about the flip side? We constantly project old memories and prior narratives onto new situations. So even if we once encountered a ferocious tiger (or the equivalent) when we walked into a room, most rooms we walk into probably won't have fierce tigers waiting to pounce. Maybe in that room sits our partner, who needs to discuss a problem they're having in our relationship. Or maybe the room is full of potential friends! Whatever the case, if we walk into the room and the ferocious tiger memory is triggered by any details, we will fill in the remaining details that could lead us to react as though the fierce tiger is there when she isn't. Heart rate shoots up, breathing becomes shallow, adrenaline courses through our veins. We're officially freaking out.

Not so easy to make potential friends or navigate a difficult moment with a partner when our body and brain want us to run like hell from the tiger.

In other words, our experience of reality is not literal or universal, but simply an illusion woven by a unique combination of what we perceive through our senses and the models constructed from our memories. Turns out, our normal waking reality is just a product of our imagination that gets confirmed again and again.

Pretty mind-blowing.

As with everything, we want to find the perfect balance in our DMN activity. Problems can occur from too much activity as well as too little. For example, low DMN activity can facilitate highly creative states but also early psychosis. On the other hand, too much activity plays a role in developing depression, obsessions, OCD, eating disorders, and addiction.

So, how can psychedelics help us reprogram our DMN?

Taking the DMN and its predictive coding offline temporarily allows for just enough chaos to disrupt our perceptions of familiar reality. As a result, we can return to our lives with new eyes to see the world and conceive of new possibilities beyond what we could previously access.

TRAVELING BACK IN TIME

How do psychedelics benefit us so profoundly and in such a lasting way? As discussed above, the answer, while complex, at least in part lies in neuroplasticity.

In my medical training, I was taught that the loss of neuroplasticity was a hallmark of adulthood. The prevailing thinking was that we hit our twenties with all the neural networks we were ever going to have. Our brains could only go downhill from there.

Luckily, that was wrong.

As it happens, our brains can change and grow during periods of adult neuroplasticity. Adult neuroplasticity allows for distinct neural networks to become less distinct, and new connections to spring up between different regions of the brain that would normally not communicate. As a result, our brains become more integrated, flexible, interconnected, and mentally diverse. Practically, we become better able to think in outside-the-box, novel ways, with better problem solving and greater openness. Until relatively recently, no one thought that such shifts were easily attainable. Though we now know many ways to access neuroplasticity, psychedelics reliably offer all that and much more.

Here's why.

Imagine being able to travel back in time and somehow heal the traumatic childhood experiences that shaped us – whether we consciously remembered them or they were buried and long forgotten. No science fiction needed. Well, studies are showing psychedelics may enable us to do just that, or the equivalent.

Childhood trauma is the topic du jour these days, from therapists to influencers, and a for good reason. What makes childhood trauma so central to our adult experiences? Part of the reason our childhood experiences impact us so profoundly and even stay with us for life is that they occur during a unique time of life during which our brains are exceptionally malleable. Unlike adults, plasticity is *naturally* superpowered early in life during what are called critical plasticity periods (CPPs). No psychedelics necessary.

It makes sense, evolutionarily speaking. Consider how quickly our brains need to adapt to master walking, talking, and potty training all in a relatively short period. During early development, our brains have to grow and develop by leaps and bounds more than any other time in our lives. CPPs describe periods during which young children's brains are primed to rapidly create new connections and dramatically reshape their brains in ways they are less inclined to do later in life.

The flip side of these supercharged periods of brain development, however, is that we are much more profoundly susceptible to any adversity that we encounter during these sensitive "windows." In other words, we are as supercharged to learn as we are super vulnerable to events that we experience as traumatic. That's why difficult experiences that occur early in our development (like the adverse childhood events, or ACEs, discussed in Chapter 1) can negatively impact our lifelong physical and mental functioning.

This is both good and bad news. As an adult, experiencing difficult events outside of these window periods may not have as significant and lasting an impact as if you were two years old – yay! On the other hand, recovering fully from our childhood trauma once we become adults may prove far trickier and more elusive. Boo.

I can feel all the parents and grandparents out there panicking as they read this. Try to stay calm. The "emotional brain" develops as a result of a number of different overlapping sensitive periods. In other words, many factors over several sensitive periods play into what we look back on as our childhood (including "childhood trauma.")

Simply put, CPPs serve as both blessing and curse because they enable our brains to be disproportionately affected in ways both good or bad by circumstances that happen to occur during these (many) developmental windows.

Where do psychedelics fit into critical plasticity periods?

We already know that under the right conditions, psychedelics may have the power to temporarily reopen these windows of development, allowing us to become sensitive to events imprinting on us – that is, we get another chance for an *intentional* experience to have lasting impact for the duration of our lives.

We are still learning what facilitates opening and closing of CPPs – some of which we learned following studies that show unprecedented complete adulthood recovery from near-sightedness long after the age it can typically resolve. One therapeutic mechanism of psychedelics could be that they allow the brain to reenter a CPP "open state." By retrieving traumatic memories under conditions that feel safe and therapeutic, they can be modified.

Keep in mind that successful outcomes also depend on the specific type and intensity of psychological support framing the experience. In this CPP framework, the therapeutic mechanism of psychedelics are thought to put the brain in an "open state," while simultaneously retrieving traumatic memories or fear responses for modification – but now in a container of safety. If the experience doesn't feel safe, the potential to be retraumatized exists. This risk cannot be emphasized strongly enough.

Studies have repeatedly shown that the specific type and intensity of psychological support that frames the experience is strongly correlated to clinical and efficacy outcomes. In other words, the transformations of psychedelics are not inherent only to the compounds in the Master Plants but are also dependent on the context – before, during, and after – in which they're taken (much more on that in Chapters 7 and 8).

It's also important to note that not all neuroplasticity has positive implications. Cocaine, for example, induces plasticity, which likely plays a role in its potent abuse potential. Opioids and amphetamines do the same. Many other powerfully addictive substances have that same potential for neuroplasticity, which can take us in directions that truly wreak havoc on our bodies, brains, and lives.

As a result, some scientists have worried about the designer psychedelic molecules that companies are rushing to develop and get approved. *Ayahuasca without the vomiting! Psilocybin without the hallucinations!* While these promises sound great – everything we want and nothing we don't – could reopening CPPs by extracting molecules, as we did with the coca plant and the opium poppy, become our downfall with Master Plants yet again?

THE EDGE BETWEEN STABILITY AND WILD CREATIVITY

Until recently, modern science simply hasn't had adequate tools to understand how psychedelics could possibly change our consciousness. Really, the trouble stems from its reductionist paradigm, which regards the sum of the parts as equivalent to the whole. But when it comes to consciousness, the whole is so much greater than the sum of its parts. What's heartening about some of the most exciting psychedelics research is when it takes a broader perspective that marries ancient paradigms with modern methods, allowing us to explore consciousness within and outside of the brain in more expansive ways.

Whether we believe the "mind" to be localized within the brain, as modern science posits, or to exist within every cell in our bodies and all around us, as maintained by indigenous science, consciousness could be considered akin to music. Whereas one small part of us, let's say a neuron, is like a solo violin – intricate and capable of making beautiful music on its own – systems within our brains or bodies have the complexity, richness, and power of a section of an orchestra, in which several instruments each making their own individual music decide to do so simultaneously. Our consciousness is the music created by this entire, massive orchestra.

An emergent system is a concept that describes self-organized, nonhierarchical, complex systems that work in nonlinear ways. They exhibit properties and behaviors that are not directly attributable to the individual components or independent parts that make up the system. In other words, the whole is more than the sum of its parts. Emergent systems can be found everywhere, from an orchestra to flocks of birds to our microbiomes to the functioning of the human brain.

Our brains are in fact a prime example of an emergent system – composed of many individual agents that interact in complex ways. The complex interactions of every cell in the brain give rise to emergent properties and behaviors that are not present in any individual component. Just as a flock of birds might appear to move as a single entity, each bird makes independent decisions based on its own observations of its surroundings and the behavior of other birds in the flock. And as we've now seen, our brains, and indeed every cell and microbe in our bodies, are doing the very same thing.

If we thought of each of our neurons as playing instruments and our brains as making music, what would those musical notes look like visually if they were mapped across the human brain? And when we change our state of consciousness – particularly with the help of psychedelics – how does the music of our brains change?

Consciousness researcher Selen Atasoy and her research team have asked these very questions. She was fascinated by how complex patterns repeat in nature – a snowflake, a flower, an orange. Inspired by cymatics – the art and science of making sound visible by way of sand or water on a metal plate that vibrates with the frequencies of music being played – she explored whether these principles might allow her to visualize repeating patterns created by frequencies emitted by the brain. As a neuroscientist, she wondered if this could help her better understand complex patterns indicating difficult-to-capture phenomena like consciousness.

So she developed an approach to visualizing brain activity as though it were music by measuring different frequencies in the brain, and then mapping those different harmonic patterns directly onto the human brain. Not surprisingly, each of our brains has its own unique set of harmonics, which are like the sound waves of a musical instrument. And each harmonic wave is the building block of complex patterns created by what's happening at the level of our consciousness.

This approach, called connectome-harmonics, compiles all of the brain activity derived by functional MRI as though it were complex music, and then uses a mathematical formula to break it down into its musical notes and analyze the many emergent parts within the system.

The results were fascinating.

Their seminal study recorded the brain activity of twelve people under both the influence of LSD and under the influence of a placebo – and before, during, and afterward, music was played for them. What they found with LSD (and later with other psychedelics, including psilocybin and DMT) was that these psychedelics changed the music of the brain, or harmonics, in similar and significant ways. Namely, psychedelics suppressed the activity of low-frequency brain states and amplified a very broad range of high frequencies.

What does this mean? More high-frequency activity allowed for a more positive mood. Less low-frequency activity allowed for ego dissolution and mystical experiences that for many, define the psychedelic experience, and are thought to be key to their therapeutic benefit. The people also had greater access to emotional states. Music amplified those higher energy states even further, indicating that psychedelics made the brain more sensitive to the effects of music.

The researchers described the brain as shifting its frequency, like tuning a radio to a new station. Certain brain frequencies died off – or were suppressed – while others that weren't very active before became very active under the effect of psychedelics. The equivalent would be an instrument playing more musical notes simultaneously.

Psychedelics enriched the repertoire of the brain "connectome," the unique ways different parts of our brains connect.

Enriched repertoire is akin to the brain engaging in jazz improvisation – using many more musical notes than are officially written in a spontaneous *and* nonrandom fashion. Our brains on psychedelics can combine many more harmonic waves spontaneously yet in a structured way, the equivalent of playing more notes simultaneously than it normally could.

Most exciting was that psychedelics took the brain temporarily to a new steady state that created a delicate balance between two extreme tendencies – order and chaos.

Usually we don't like chaos, nor do we consider extreme states to be useful – and typically they may not be. But maybe sometimes they are.

Criticality is a term used in neuroscience to describe the balance between quiescent order and chaotic disorder. Think of order as a group of soldiers who dress the same way, look the same direction and move at the same time with the same angle and speed. Now, think of a group of toddlers let loose onto a playground, with everybody letting off steam and doing what they want with little voluntary interaction or cooperation. That's chaos.

Now, imagine a group of people dancing, where each individual moves uniquely, in their own way, but those movements are in harmony with the others. So, even though each individual is doing their own thing, there is a sense of meaningful interaction and coordination between individuals. This approach is far more elastic and adaptable than that of the soldiers, and also far more ordered and even predictable than that of the toddlers.

This is the place where criticality resides. This point of balance between order and chaos allows for more complexity and potential for more imagination, possibility, and aliveness.

In the psychedelics study, at that delicate point of criticality, the brain could access increased complexity in ways that allowed for certain advantages, including a greater capacity to code information and rapidly process information.

These findings pertain directly to the perceived sense of chaos that can define some or even most psychedelic experiences. Most people dislike feeling out of control or navigating disrupted or unfamiliar reality. And that is absolutely understandable; chaos can feel uncomfortable and scary, even if it's likely to last for a finite period. As a result, many people – even those experienced with psychedelic medicines – tend to feel reticent about engaging in psychedelic experiences.

Yet both science and spiritual traditions maintain that we need a certain amount of unpredictability in our lives. Criticality is that sweet spot between certainty and the unknown. Without some structure, we can accomplish nothing. But without some chaos, we miss inspiration and opportunities that allow us to change our lives in a single moment. It's there, in that liminal in-between, where we can access possibility and see how it could come to fruition – at the critical edge between what we know and what is unknowable, between science and mystery.

It turns out criticality may be the essential formula necessary for complex and advanced brain function – a level of stability (order) required for coherent functioning and a degree of disorder is needed for functional flexibility, adaptability and perhaps even leaps of evolution. These skills come into play when we are trying to solve really difficult problems and can't see a way out. Here, our brains can thrive from exposure to the unexpected. Operating from criticality allows us to be inspired and think outside of the box by interrupting what we think we know and in a sense, starting from scratch.

Under the right circumstances, psychedelics allow us to venture to the edge between stability and wild creativity, which can act as a portal to profound moments of awareness as well as inspiration, inventions, healing, and evolution.

5

MASTER PLANTS I HAVE KNOWN
AND LOVED

T he human relationship with Master Plants has been kept fairly secret throughout history.

This is not by accident.

Consider that the very first evidence of psychedelic Master Plants comes from cave drawings, or petroglyphs.

Most of us were taught in school that cave-dwelling people recorded the mundane activities of cave life in pictures before they developed language. The strange drawings reflected their primitive skills and tools. Not surprisingly, this perspective may not be quite accurate.

Cave drawings are rarely found at the entrance of caves, where plenty of natural light would have been available to see and draw. Rather, they're located very deep inside caves, in an environment of pure darkness, isolation, sensory deprivation, and even lowered oxygen levels – the perfect recipe for altered states of consciousness. Indeed, the presence of drawings is thought to indicate that the caves themselves were particularly sacred.

The pictures often resemble shamanic visions of creatures that are half-human, half-animal, not to mention depictions thought in certain cases to be Master Plants like psychedelic mushrooms or cacti. What's fascinating is that the drawings from caves around the world going back 40,000 years are similar to one another, and include spirals and other geometric patterns commonly described by those experiencing altered states and psychedelic journeys. As we'll discuss, some caves contained DNA evidence of Master Plants.

Cave art turns out to offer solid evidence that ancient humans from the Upper Paleolithic era journeyed with Master Plants in sacred caves tens of thousands of years ago...not exactly what we were taught back in the fifth grade.

The longstanding secrecy around Master Plants may in part reflect that both the effects and transmissions of the Master Plants were taboo and therefore remained concealed, even more so as monotheism grew and eventually spread.

The minimal written evidence likely also indicated exclusivity rather than shame or fear. Strange as it may sound in these days of Google searches and huge libraries, oral tradition was considered more private and reliably maintained. Once a book is written, no one is required to memorize and hold that knowledge in their minds and hearts any longer. The information can also more easily be stolen, destroyed, or abused. Ultimately, Master Plants very likely served as sacraments for the initiated only and kept private otherwise, as many rituals and sacraments have been over time.

If anything, the dismissal of interspecies communication that's developed over time – humans offering gratitude or asking for help from particular plants (or plant spirits) and plants enlisting human help for their own agendas – was far preferable to the alternative of too much interest. For example, indigenous people in the New World were oppressed by Spanish explorers and missionaries, and were forced to mask the rituals and sacraments by including pictures of saints on altars and prayers in Spanish. This hybrid approach persists in many communities to this day. Many people died at the hand of Inquisitors who labeled the religious rituals "demonic," even as some engaged in the ceremonies themselves and, in a few cases, made written records of it.

Even in light of any taboo or attempts at suppression, Master Plants remained pivotal to indigenous religious traditions.

As we'll see, evidence of indigenous engagement with Master Plants goes back hundreds and sometimes tens of thousands of years. However, as discussed in Chapter 3, many details of scientific as well as sacred information have been neatly embedded into mythology and associated ritual objects as well as dance, song, and art, which served as a valid and tremendously effective mode of primarily oral transmission that only offers hints of the depth and details of the relationship.

Scholars therefore have had to read between the lines in their exploration of the unspoken or the role Master Plants may have seemingly invisibly played in even the Western history we've been taught.

Some may be wondering, what about the Bible?

Glad you asked.

Theology and other scholars looking deeply at biblical history – the burning bush, manna, the receiving of the Ten Commandments, even Temple rituals – have theorized that the spirits of Master Plants may have been at play.

Could the burning bush Moses inhaled that brought him to his initial prophecy have contained vaporized elements of the psychedelic compound DMT, which, as we discussed, is found in many plants as well as in our brains?

Could hallucinogenic components have been in the manna, the edible substance God gave the Israelites during their travels in the desert to transform the trauma of slavery into a state of liberation?

As it happens, two plants in the Sinai desert contain the same psychoactive combination of molecules as the plants from which the Amazonian brew ayahuasca is prepared. One of the psychoactive plants, harmal, found in the Sinai and elsewhere in the Middle East, has long been regarded as having magical and curative powers by people in the region. Could the thunder, lightning, and blaring sounds described in the Book of Exodus as emanating from Mount Sinai have come from the visions of a people in an altered state of awareness? It's not uncommon during potent ayahuasca experiences to see light accompanied by profound religious and spiritual feelings.

None of this negates the impact, importance, or even potential truth of these as religious transmissions directly from the Divine. Indeed, the light seen in visions is perceived by many to be God. These theories invite plants into the conversation as divine mediators of sorts.

Some believe the Master Plant cannabis was present in holy incense and anointing oils in the Temple.

Even the Oracle at Delphi, who lived in late Mycenean times, was described as sitting in a cave on a tripod above a chasm as "vapors" poured forth. She inhaled the vapors and prophesied.

Much later, the founder of the Hasidic movement, the Baal Shem Tov, who was an off-beat figure, spent time in the mountains, learning about herbs and plant medicines – which some speculate had psychoactive properties – and acted as both medicinal and spiritual healer, similar to what would now be called a shaman.

The term shaman originally comes from the indigenous people of Siberia, meaning "one who knows" or "one who sees." Today, the word has become synonymous with a traditional healer who works with the spirit world with or without Master Plants to assist in treating aspects of the human condition. Countless other names describe those with similar roles across cultures, including medicos, vegetalistas, curanderos, pachakuti, yachak, and others from South America; Nganga, Sangoma, or Boburo from various parts of Africa; Qilaut or Amauti from the Inuits in the Arctic; and Dukun, Mudang, and Bonpo in East Asian cultures.

In modern times, a new version of this role has become popular: the neo-shaman, usually a Westerner in a self-appointed role. Yet in traditional communities, those who inhabit the role have encountered extreme life challenges and suffering and are considered chosen, often training from a young age. Their lives may be colorful, but are rarely easy.

As we will see, the lore and even personalities of these plants are as colorful, potent, and appropriately mind-bending as the journeys they offer.

MEDICINE OR MALICE

In conventional medicine, we tend to think of pharmaceuticals as being positive and beneficial. Any unwanted outcome is called a side effect and considered separate from the medication because it's not what we wanted or intended for the medication to do.

In contrast, as discussed in Chapter 3, many indigenous paradigms hold that even the most sacred of Master Plants have the capacity to access both sacredness and "sorcery." In the Amazon, this dual nature of Master Plants is referred to as medicine or malice. The plant may want us to see or know about both for any number of reasons.

Thus, each plant has power – a spirit or soul capable of healing or doing harm. But it's the person who decides how they will engage.

The nature of the outcome relies entirely on each person's relationship with the plant. This means that every aspect of how we approach the plant matters tremendously – from intention, training, and discipline to preparation beforehand and integration afterward.

Consider what we just explored in Chapter 4 about the dual nature of neuroplasticity. On the one hand, opening windows of plasticity allows us to learn, remember, and become smarter long after those processes have usually concretized. On the other hand, cocaine, opiates, and tobacco can all open those windows with the primary effect of strengthening addiction in the person's body and brain.

People often ask me to use a scientific approach to identify which psychedelic is the "right one" for them. While many factors could play into choosing one over another, Master Plants, like people, are not commodities or even compounds like mescaline or DMT, but companions, guides, teachers, and ancient masters.

Just as many have discovered in this age of dating apps, finding the right loving, respectful relationship with a great partner isn't as simple as shopping down a list of potential suitors and swiping right. Lean into that same sense of mutual chemistry, attraction, and, yes, longing – as well as practical matters of suitability and getting along with one another.

An important point: Attraction does not necessarily mean ingestion is the next step. It may be a calling to grow the plant, wear them as jewelry or even apparel depicting them, meditate on them, or read or learn about them. These are the beginnings of a true relationship with Master Plants.

Medicos or *vegetalistas* tend to have a particular Master Plant with whom they've established a particular intimacy. Through a series of visitations in dreams or visions, the Master Plant teaches them about the world, nature, healing, and alchemy. Some only use one plant that serves as their sacred portal into the mystical realms of nature. Some may maintain relationships with as many as a dozen. As there are many more than a dozen possible power plants, even in localized regions, different medicos can have different teachers, methods, and traditions.

Do not approach Master Plants with an expectation of getting answers. Instead, embark upon an exploration into the teachings of these many ancient, mysterious teachers with reverence and curiosity. Consider each of these Master Plants to be potential allies and elders – or not – and notice what feelings arise while reading the words. Notice moments of joint chemistry.

Speaking of chemistry, Master Plants are much more than what makes them "psychedelic" or single "active compounds." We'll likely be hearing more and more about the compound ibogaine instead of the plant iboga, mescaline instead of peyote, psilocybin rather than the psilocybe mushrooms themselves, and on and on. While designer pharmaceutical molecules become the norm rather than Master Plants – and they may offer certain uniformity and pharmaceutical – we must consider where the medicine lies.

The "active ingredient" in psychedelics is most commonly an

alkaloid. Alkaloids, considered a form of "plant poisons," often represent what are thought to be the most potent contents responsible for their most desired effects such as alteration of consciousness. Pharmaceutical companies and researchers often focus entirely on extracting that one most powerful alkaloid, creating a synthetic twin, patenting the new compound, and reproducing it as a pharmaceutical.

Yet the vast majority of herbalists and vegetalistas agree that plants will be most powerful when used in their entirety for healing. A purified, amplified dose of one component is a pharmaceutical compound, or what would popularly be called a drug. The alkaloid alone may or may not necessarily be bad, but one element is not the same as the Master Plant. The whole is always greater than the sum of the parts.

For example, a recent study analyzed several species of psilocybe mushrooms and discovered not just the expected alkaloid psilocybin but also the presence of an array of neuroactive compounds typically found in ayahuasca – harmine, harmane, and others. In ayahuasca brew, these compounds interfere with our ability to break down psilocybin, making the mushrooms' effects last longer and stronger in our bodies. Another study showed that noribogaine – but not ibogaine, usually touted as the "active compound" in iboga – promotes structural neural plasticity.

In another example, nearly every study done on extracted versions of the Master Plant cannabis – say, on CBD or THC – has shown that they're less effective in treating the desired conditions as compared to working with the whole plant. This particular cannabis phenomenon has been termed the "entourage effect," which is a sexy way of saying what indigenous people and modern herbalists have continued to maintain: plants are more than just a compound; they are a universe, as complex and even intelligent as we are, far more ancient than humans. Imagine someone thinking they knew who we were because they looked at cells from our livers or a sample of our blood. And this approach is the one we take with powerful Master Plants that have persisted for millions or even billions of years – and will likely outlast us, particularly if we continue with our current practices.

Consider this chapter an introduction to the lore, history, personality, and, yes, some of the science that makes these Master Plants who they are.

PSILOCYBE MUSHROOMS

If you've ever heard the term *sacred cow* – referring to an idea, person, or institution that's held above reproach – have you ever wondered why this saying emerged, and why cows in India have long been considered sacred?

In the ancient Vedic scriptures compiled around 1,500 BCE, the cow is associated with motherhood, Mother Earth, and Aditi, the mother of all the gods. Over time, she became a sacred being who was forbidden to be eaten or harmed in any way.

Scholars have pointed out that those very same Vedic writings refer to a sacred preparation called soma, which instigated visions and profound spiritual experiences. The identity of soma remains unknown, but writings and ancient art hint that it may have been or contained a mushroom. And that mushroom probably would have been Psilocybe cubensis, which has long been indigenous to India.

So where's the connection to the sacred cow?

Mushrooms – the psilocybe genus in particular – are known to grow in cow patties. It's thought that cows were not just the source of milk and symbol of motherhood and the abundance of the Earth, but also the source of these entities used for ceremonies that connected people to divine spiritual experiences and thus to the sacred.

Mushrooms grow and have been celebrated on every continent except perhaps Antarctica. The oldest evidence of probable use was in the Tassili n'Ajjer cave in the Sahara Desert, in which stylized and abstract mushroom drawings feature a rounded cap and thin stem. Aspects of the 9000-year-old Tassili cave drawings suggest a shamanic practice. For example, many of the human figures are shown with exaggerated or distorted features, such as elongated limbs or oversized heads, which may indicate altered states of consciousness or visionary experiences. Some figures are also shown with animal features or wearing animal masks, and the depiction of spirit animals or totemic creatures. And the mushrooms are depicted alongside the human figures, suggesting that they played an essential role in the spiritual lives of the people who created these drawings.

The Mixtec Codex is a 14th-century Mesoamerican manuscript that depicts a ritualistic ceremony in which psilocybin mushrooms were used as a sacrament. The Mixtec people, who lived in what is now Mexico, believed that mushrooms had sacred and transformative properties that could connect them to the spiritual realm. The Mayan Codices are a collection of pre-Columbian 11th-century texts that contain references to a variety of psychoactive plants and fungi, including psilocybin mushrooms. The Mayan people, who inhabited parts of Mexico, Guatemala, and Honduras, used mushrooms in religious and healing ceremonies to induce altered states of consciousness and communicate with the divine.

In Nahuatl, the language of the Aztecs, the name for psilocybe mushrooms is teonanácatl, which has been translated to "flesh of the gods." There are over 200 known species of psilocybin-containing mushrooms. These mushrooms are part of the genus Psilocybe, which is found throughout the world in a variety of habitats, including forests, grasslands, and tropical regions. They are popularly called "magic mushrooms" or simply "psilocybin" and are perhaps the most widely known Master Plant (a term that includes fungi!) with the greatest influence on the collective cultural imagination.

As discussed in Chapter 3, modern non-indigenous awareness of psilocybes came through Maria Sabina, the first person to share ritual secrets of the mushrooms outside her own Mazatec community. Born in 1894 in Oaxaca, she first consumed the Children, as she called them, when she was seven years old after discovering them growing. During that early experience, the mushrooms told her they would help her if she needed it.

A year later, her uncle got incurably sick, so Maria returned to eat the mushrooms and asked for their assistance. They guided her to the herbs needed to address the evil spirits causing her uncle's suffering. Within days of her administering these herbs, her uncle's condition reversed. From then on, she knew that the mushrooms – or children, as she referred to them – would become pivotal to her life purpose. Though her life was far from easy, Maria Sabina – meaning "wise one" – helped thousands of people heal over her lifetime.

Maria would talk about the sacred mushrooms: "There is a world beyond ours, a world that is far away, nearby, and invisible. And there is where God lives, where the dead live, the spirits and the saints, a world where everything has already happened, and everything is known. That world talks. It has a language of its own. I report what it says. The sacred mushroom takes me by the hand and brings me to the world where everything is known. It is they, the sacred mushrooms, that speak in a way I can understand. I ask them and they answer me. When I return from the trip that I have taken with them, I tell what they have told me and what they have shown me."

For the Mazatec people, mushrooms are considered a gift from the thunder god, partly because when it thunders and rains, the mushrooms sprout – and when they are born it is a gift. They can only be gathered in ritual. It is thought that if we ask from the heart, with love and lots of sincerity, they will give us what we want.

Curanderos do not necessarily automatically work with mushrooms; they must be selected. Few are called to the work in general, and even fewer work with sacred mushrooms.

Mushrooms also are not the first stop for someone suffering. They may already have gone to Western doctors or other curanderos, for example, a person who works with herbs or reads the smoke of smoldering copal. If and only if they found no answers, they would go to someone who specializes in mushrooms.

Traditionally, only children were allowed to gather the mushrooms because they were the only ones with their innocence still intact. They would go on the full moon with the curandero to the mountain where they grew, pray to ask for permission to cut them, sing to them as they picked them, and gently wrap them to bring them back unharmed. They would return to town on less-traveled paths to avoid problematic encounters that might affect the mushrooms' abilities to heal – a dead animal and a funeral procession, for example. If the mushrooms were considered contaminated, they wouldn't do their healing in the same way or teach the same lessons.

No one was allowed to handle or even look at the mushrooms until it was time for the ceremony. They wrapped them in large tamale leaves until they were served to avoid spiritual contamination.

Today, mushrooms are still served in pairs or even numbers to represent female and male energies. They are only consumed on certain days of the week for certain purposes. Prayer is a vital element in the mushroom ceremonies. Particular songs and rituals are associated with specific intentions, for example, healing or talking to the ancestors.

Another essential component of ceremony requires listening to plants. This doesn't mean the mushrooms must be ingested; indeed, ingesting mushrooms is not required to hear their directives.

Those preparing for the ceremony are advised to abstain from alcohol, red meat, cigarettes, and sexual relations. In addition, participants are told not to go to a cemetery, wake, or funeral because the mushrooms are very sensitive and pick up on that energy.

After the ceremony, participants are instructed not to go out into the street or public areas because their sensitivities will increase. Participants could absorb ill intent or be affected by surrounding events in unintended ways.

Anything outside of the very particular parameters is considered to negate the lessons of the mushrooms.

Everything following the experience should continue to support preserving the sacredness of the ceremony. There are secrets the mushrooms have revealed that it is our responsibility to have to protect. They should not be discussed. The experience is considered private, and integration must also be kept private.

From the perspective of the Mazatec people, members of their own community are at minimal risk of abuse or misuse of mushrooms, for example taking them too often or without preparation. On the other hand, foreigners abuse and misuse mushrooms by taking them for fun and not respecting the sacred.

Mushrooms create a sense of enchantment and revelatory quality to the world around them – a sense of aliveness, beauty, and meaning in everything: a leaf, a tree, a bug, a ray of sunlight. In addition, people can experience unexpected philosophical insights or awakenings of the divine.

Visual perceptions can widen, allowing for greater sensitivity, including colorful kaleidoscopic visions even with closed eyes, intensification of colors, distortion of the shapes of objects or surfaces that undulate or move, and an increased appreciation of music and sounds. Synesthetic experiences can occur, in which stimuli corresponding to a certain sensory field are perceived and processed by another sense; for example, sounds that are perceived as visions. The sense of touch can also be altered, with an increased tactile sensitivity, sensations of cold, heat, tingling or energy running through the body. Some species can induce muscle paralysis. People can experience these altered sensoria as very intense in ways positive, terrifying, or both.

Mystical experiences can include numinousness, profoundly positive states, a sense of unity, altered time and space, a sense of unity and interconnection with all things. Yet frightening experiences, known as "bad trips" (discussed in Chapter 7), can include sensations of agonizing fear, paranoia, a sense of dying or going crazy, feelings of depression or anger, high anxiety, agitation, confusion, and disorientation. Psychotic experiences are rare but can herald the first symptoms of psychosis in those thought to be predisposed. In most cases, however, the experiences induced by mushrooms induce enjoyable and less enjoyable components that can be more challenging. In addition, participants may experience ego dissolution, with sensations described as "oceanic," which can be perceived as a transcendent experience but sometimes results in anxiety.

Experiences in which personal biographical memories or understandings relating to significant others can also arise.

Many studies have been done in the past decade exploring the benefit of psilocybin in adults with depression, anxiety, OCD, PTSD, eating disorders, severe fear of death in those with terminal cancer, and addiction.

A 2022 study showed it is highly and significantly effective over placebo in 93 participants for alcohol overuse. The active dose was a standardized 25 mg dose of pure psilocybin (equivalent to about 2.5 grams of dried mushrooms) compared with placebo – a dose of diphenhydramine given to about half the participants. Psilocybin was combined with psychotherapy with a trained and experienced facilitator. Overall, people in the psilocybin group reduced their heavy drinking days by more than half compared to those treated with diphenhydramine. The treatment was determined to be safe and effective for alcohol use disorder.

The billion-dollar question is, can making psilocybe mushrooms available and accessible transform the depression and anxiety that affect so many people?

After all, studies show that those who ingest them experience enhanced empathy, reduced incidence of petty crimes, and lower rates of domestic abuse of women.

The answer is: it depends.

Simply put, we exist in systems that disconnect us from our true selves, families, lineage, communities, as well as other beings, nature, and the invisible. Navigating dysfunctional and disempowering systems daily can make us feel depressed and anxious as a normal response to this disconnection from life. Mushrooms are intelligent beings who seek to connect us with ourselves, our families, our communities, other beings, nature, and spirit. While mushrooms can remind us of our connectedness and reawaken our compassion, we are the ones who must instigate change. If mushrooms show us our sovereignty within those dysfunctional systems and guide us to connection with all people and living beings, our depression and anxiety can shift. Their purpose is not to make us less depressed or anxious but to instigate us to address and shift the roots of our suffering.

AMANITA MUSCARIA (FLY AGARIC)

Those of us who grew up jokingly saying, "Don't eat yellow snow" probably didn't imagine that at special times of year in certain places, yellow snow was likely to have psychedelic qualities. Enter *Amanita muscaria*, or fly agaric, the classic (and toxic) red mushroom with white spots of Smurf, Super Mario Brothers, and mushroom emoji fame.

Thought by indigenous Siberians to grow from the saliva of the highest god, these fungi were relatively rare and considered very sacred; therefore, they were reserved for consumption on special occasions by special people. Shamans would ingest them, especially when they wished to communicate with the souls of ancestors, contact spirits, give a newborn a name, find a way out of threatening situations, see into the future and peer into the past, or journey or fly to other worlds. Shamans in training could be tested with high dosages to determine whether they could master the mushrooms and thus deserved their future office.

On the eve of the winter solstice, for example, a Koryak shaman would gather several red mushrooms with white spots to embark on a spiritual journey to the tree of life near the North Star (over the North Pole), which held answers to all the village's problems from the year prior. As the mushrooms prefer to grow under pine trees, he'd have already left some hanging on pine branches to dry and offer fresh ones to his flock of reindeer. After donning tall boots of reindeer skin and a red outfit accented by white in honor of the mushroom's colors, he'd go out in the deep snow to gather the dried and fresh mushrooms, returning with mushrooms and perhaps snow yellow from his reindeer's urine in his sack.

At that time of year in that part of the world, the entry to his yurt could be blocked by tremendous snowfall, so he may have had to climb to the yurt's roof with his bag and slide down the center hole that acted also as his chimney. In anticipation of the ceremony, he'd place a stick upright through the smoke hole of his yurt to allow his spirit to exit and enter, and offer some of the mushrooms to his flock from those he carried in his sack.

The yellow-tinged snow – imbued with urine from either reindeer or himself – could then be melted and made into a much less toxic but still psychoactive beverage, as the most toxic components had been metabolized by the reindeer's (or the shaman's) first-pass effect in the liver. Alternatively, the shaman himself would consume the hallucinogenic mushroom to enter a trance-like state of heightened awareness conducive to physical and spiritual healing.

The shaman would share his urine with his community for the same effect. That night, he'd hand out dried mushrooms or the yellow snow beverage to the wealthy and influential people of the village who would partake in the annual solstice ceremony and hang any additional mushrooms to be dried in a sock by the fire.

Don't yuck their yum.

The surge at the onset of the mushroom's psychoactive effect stimulated the animals into prancing and jumping, and in their altered state, humans might have seen this as flying and felt like they were flying, too. The shaman and the reindeer would fly to the North Star (which sits directly over the North Pole) to retrieve the gifts of knowledge, which they would then distribute to the rest of the village.

We all know where this is going, I'm sure. These traditions were carried South by way of the druids, who had adopted spiritual practices from much farther north. The great god Odin was also known to ride at midnight during the winter solstice on an eight-legged horse, chased by devils. The horse's mouth was red with blood and white with foam, and next year's *Amanita muscaria* mushrooms would emerge where flecks hit the ground. Eventually, the stories merged into a red and white–cloaked supernatural figure riding a sleigh through the air behind eight flying reindeer. The imagery caught on and captured the Western imagination in many varied ways, including that in Victorian times, the traditional symbol of chimney sweeps was *Amanita muscaria*. Indeed, many early Christmas cards featured chimney sweeps with red and white mushrooms. To this day, Russian forest workers still report chewing dried pieces of *Amanita muscaria* to withstand physical exertion more easily.

This taste shows how Master Plants and psychedelics have played seminal roles in everything from pop culture, mythology, art, literature, and music to religious rituals and beliefs, our connection to spirit, and even our concepts of God.

Historical records such as cave paintings, wood carvings, and sculptures suggest that the psychoactive effects of *Amanita muscaria* have been known since ancient times on all continents. Similar practices likely occurred in geographically and culturally distant groups for religious, divination, therapeutic, and social purposes.

The first evidence of *Amanita muscaria* use as an intoxicant is based on linguistic analyses of North Asian languages from 4,000 BC, in which the roots of the words *drunkenness* and *Amanita muscaria* appear to be the same. The use of fly agaric mushrooms is deeply ingrained in the folklore and traditions of the indigenous peoples of Siberia. For example, the Evenki and Koryak people of Siberia have a tradition of using the mushroom in their winter rituals to communicate with the spirit world. In 1992, researchers found residue from fly agaric mushrooms on a bowl in a burial mound in the Altai Mountains, indicating that the mushroom had been used in the funeral rites of the ancient Scythians. Viking Berserker Warriors are thought to have used it before combat to instigate a state of rage and indifference to pain.

Varieties of *Amanita muscaria* are not limited to northern land-scapes but are found throughout much of the world, including

Central, South, and North America as well as Japan, and are cataloged in art, pottery, and other ritual objects from those regions.

Archaeological excavations have uncovered artifacts that suggest the use of fly agaric mushrooms by Indigenous cultures in Canada. A copper bowl discovered on the west coast of Vancouver Island was found to have residue from the mushroom, suggesting that it was used in shamanic rituals. Other evidence exists of their use in North America, both past and present, by the Dogrib Athabasca people in Canada as well as by the Ojibwa and Ahnishinuabeg indigenous people in the Lake Michigan area in the United States. Dene people of northern Canada, the Nuxalk Nation of British Columbia, and some Inuit communities in northern Canada have mythology that describes the mushroom's psychoactive properties and its use in shamanic practices.

Physical effects of *Amanita muscaria* include parasympathetic stimulation, shifting between wakefulness and sleep, illusions, hallucinations, and delirium. Most older literature describes the experience as unpleasant. Newer literature, however, states if the mushroom is consumed with the expectation of hallucinogenic effects, then (not surprisingly) the outcomes tend to be more pleasant. Though popularly considered lethal, fatality is very rare. As with many mushrooms, the most significant risk of *Amanita muscaria* is misidentification and ingestion of poisonous look-alike Amanita species.

Amanita muscaria contains a wide array of alkaloids and other compounds; thus, the pharmacology is complex and not fully understood. Once dried, the ibotenic acid decarboxylates and concentrates as high amounts of muscimol, which is thought to be largely responsible for the psychoactive effects. These compounds have also been found in the urine of those who have consumed *Amanita muscaria* mushrooms, and they do retain their psychedelic activity in the urine. In any case, the alkaloids and other compounds imitate normal neurotransmitter function (agonists) and disrupt the catecholaminergic and serotonergic effects causing hallucinations in ways similar to LSD and harmine.

The experience can present in phases, including a first phase of stimulation, increased energy and muscular vigor (but not always), a second phase of tranquility and drowsiness, and a third phase of mystical experiences, a sense of non-ordinary realities, bliss, or fear. Other alterations can include loss of balance, muscle spasms, dizziness, nausea and vomiting, and visual and auditory distortions. Dream-like experiences and sensations of macropsia or microsia (perceiving objects as very large or small)

Amanita muscaria and the other varieties of Amanita are not controlled or illegal in most countries other than the Netherlands and the United Kingdom.

Caution: It is essential to make accurate identifications of fungi, as different varieties vary widely in potency, and other lethal species that can be confused with *Amanita muscaria* and especially with *Amanita pantherina*, as is the case with *Amanita phalloides*.

AYAHUASCA BREW

When a brew carries the name La Purga (Vomit Inducer), we'd expect most people to run in the opposite direction – and fast. Yet ayahuasca use, thought to be as old as South American civilization itself, has only grown by leaps and bounds over the past several decades.

Little early literature describes ayahuasca use before the Spanish invaded, but "witches' pots" used for brewing ayahuasca were found in archaeological excavations estimated to be at least 3,500 years old. Aside from an early account from a Jesuit at the end of the seventeenth century that refers to a "diabolical brew," the first accounts in which the word *ayahuasca* appears in the context of curative and divinatory purposes are those of Jesuit missionaries who, in the 1700s, traveled through the Napo River area of Ecuador.

The first modern and scientific report of the use of ayahuasca was in 1851, in which Richard Spruce documented the use of the medicinal concoction in Brazil. Then, in 1857, Manuel Villavicencio wrote the first known account of a subjective experience with ayahuasca.

The indigenous Tukanos of the northwestern Amazon believe that ayahuasca emerged in the sacred place where the Sun-Father wed the Earth-Woman. They say ayahuasca was created at the very beginning, at the same that those two poles reunited to create humans.

The Amazonian Shipibos are deeply respected for their knowledge of Master Plants, especially ayahuasca. For them and many other indigenous communities, illness results from sorcery that can be of human or nonhuman origin. Ayahuasca is thus used primarily as a form of spiritual detection and hunting – tracking the individual that caused the illness. Many medicos of the "old school" did not even require ayahuasca to achieve this work; the more remote the community, the less likely they were to imbibe ayahuasca. These days, drinking ayahuasca in group ceremonies has become more fundamental to this process, particularly for mestizo (mixed lineage) shamans who live in closer contact to urban life.

Ayahuasca is a Quechua term composed of two words: *aya*, which means "corpse, dead, dead human body," and *waskha*, which means "rope, cord, braided or twisted wire." Thus, it has commonly been translated as "the vine of the dead" or "the rope of the dead." Curanderos continue to imbibe "the drink of true reality" – also known as *daime, hoasca, kahpi, yage, rao, mii, la purge*, Abuela, and seemingly infinite other names – to determine the origins of disease, travel into the invisible world, communicate with the lords of animals and plants, and accompany participants of rituals into other worlds. The goal can also be to allow hunters to purify their bodies and souls and to communicate directly with spirits that control access to game animals in order to improve their tracking and aim.

Many indigenous people refer to ayahuasca's powerful and multidimensional visions in ways that indicate both intimacy and respect: "Amazonian Television," "jungle cinema," or, in some cases, their "university."

The brew ayahuasca is not made from the vine alone. Countless recipes exist to prepare ayahuasca, which only rarely contain only the *Baniesteriopsis caapi* vine. Ingredients added to the vine decoction depend on the region in which it is prepared, the curandero or vegetalista who cooks it, and the desired intention or effects. The stems are boiled, sitting on the fire until it becomes thick, black, syrupy, and very pungent as one or more other plants are added.

Experienced ayahuasqueros have a vast wealth of knowledge of the effects of various plant combinations to achieve their desired outcomes, with over one hundred different botanical species added to ayahuasca brew documented. When the healers want to know more about a plant, they may add it to the ayahuasca brew to experience the plant and learn. The most popular companion is *Psychotria viridis*, a plant from the same family as coffee (also a Master Plant!) known as chacruna, which results in the combination most commonly referred to as ayahuasca. *Diplopterys cabrerana*, *Ilex guayusa*, *Heliconia stricta*, and the deeply intoxicating and deliriant Brugmansia are other common companion plants for the brew, as is tobacco, depending on their availability in the region.

The curanderos who work with this brew guard their recipes carefully – including which plants to use, where to find the vine and other herbs, which protective spirits must be invoked, and how to prepare the brew. For example, the varieties of ayahuasca are important: sky, thunder, lightning, and *mariri* ("magical phlegm"). Yellow ayahuasca, for example, is called sky and is thought to be for medicine or visions. Some believe that other varieties teach sorcery if they're not handled very carefully, or even if they are.

However, they attribute the effects not to active compounds but to plant spirits who reveal themselves as master teachers to humans when under the influence of ayahuasca. The goal of imbibing the brew is not limited to healing illness. Yes, the plant spirits make it possible to see where people need healing, discover origins of disease, and learn recipes for medicines, but they also reveal where their hunters can find game deep in the forest or how to see from the normally invisible perspective of nonhuman beings. In this paradigm, true reality is hidden from the normal eye, and we can glimpse a more holistic worldview through dreams and visions. The curandero is a specialist in dreams and visions, acting as a tour guide in this other reality with the help of ayahuasca.

For example, in *Sound of Rushing Water*, author Michael Harner writes about one journey to cure a sick man with severe abdominal pain. The curandero first saw the anaconda coiled around the sick man's head, transmuting into a crown of gold; then, a giant butterfly hovered above his head and sang to him with its wings. Snakes, spiders, birds, and bats danced above him. The sound of rushing water filled his ears, which connected him to the power of the first curandero. The medico could now see into the stomach of the sick man, which became transparent like a shallow mountain stream, and he could see within it a poisonous serpent coiling and uncoiling, sent by an enemy shaman. Addressing what was seen as the real cause of the illness allowed the sick man to heal.

This "sound of rushing water" describes what is commonly heard at the onset of the full effect of the ayahuasca brew. The experience has also been compared to standing by the tracks as a train or subway approaching.

As areas around the jungle have become more urbanized, more nonindigenous people have come into contact with the brew, leading to a practice of urban shamanism. The rituals mix indigenous and Catholic customs in an attempt to heal the afflictions of urban dwellers and have led to ayahuasca churches, sects, and ayahuasca tourism.

Most foreign participants have no idea what variety of ayahuasca they drink in a ceremony, never mind any other plants or additives combined into the brew. For example, neo-shamans often add significantly more DMT to their brews to guarantee a bigger kick to the experience. While a Master Plant journey may be unpredictable in and of itself, these other aspects create another layer of uncertainty and sometimes danger, particularly for more sensitive people.

Preparation rituals play a key role in many communities. For some, a very strict *dieta* – which is less a diet and more a full-body preparation – is instituted by the maestro (master) who is preparing for the journey. Practices can include no sexual relations for days to months, adhering to special dietary rules including no pork, salt, chili, spices, or fat, and using laxatives or purgatives as well as enemas, libations, and more. All are meant to be ways to purify the body, mind, and spirit before the ritual itself.

Sacred songs, or *icaros*, are a central part of the powerful medicine of ayahuasca, and are considered sound transmissions directly from the spirit of the plant that are equal in healing power to the ingested medicine. *Icaros* are not meant to be beautiful to humans but attractive to the spirits so that the desired and correct ones support the intentions of the maestro. A key component of attaining status as a healer and maestro is accumulating musical and vocal techniques and building a large, powerful repertoire that heightens emotional and sensory responses. Certain ancestors, animals, plants, and other elements have their own songs as well as designs that appear in visions; chanting encourages nonhuman agents to share knowledge, mentorship, and protective powers. The music transcends time, space, and existential aspects of reality.

Smoke plays an essential role as well. Whether smoking and blowing tobacco or burning incense, these are essential as protection and to ward off evil spirits. Chicha, an alcoholic brew, can be drunk, and coca leaves may be chewed as well. Brugmansia leaves soaked in rum can also be drunk as a tonic.

Banisteriopsis caapi contains beta-carbolines (harmine, harmaline, and tetrahydroharmine), and *Psychotria viridis* and *Diplopterys cabrerana* are sources of dimethyltryptamine (DMT). The combination of the plants allows DMT to have an oral effect because in the absence of beta-carboline alkaloids the DMT would be degraded by monoamine oxidase (MAO), which is present in our bodies.

The harmala alkaloids contained in the ayahuasca vine have significant health-enhancing properties. All three harmala alkaloids induce the formation of new neuronal connections; harmine, in particular, also has anti-inflammatory, analgesic, antimicrobial, antioxidative, anti-addictive, anti-depressive, and possibly anti-Parkinson's and antitumor properties.

HUACHUMA (SAN PEDRO CACTUS)

Psychedelic plants and the rituals surrounding them have long captured the imagination of modern filmmakers. And anyone who has watched *Indiana Jones and the Temple of Doom* has had a taste of imagined early rituals involving the San Pedro cactus. The Chavin temple, which inspired the movie's Temple of Doom, has some of the oldest representations of San Pedro cactus engraved in stone, along with textiles and ceramics. Depictions at Chavín show priestly figures with animal-like features marching in crowns and headdresses, including a figure known as the Raimondi Stela holding, you guessed it, San Pedro cacti.

At the time, San Pedro may have gone by any number of other names including aguacolla, hahuacollay, pachanoi, achuma, andachuma, wachuma, or huachuma. The rituals likely began earlier than 1,300 BCE; by 200 BCE, the people of this region likely had domesticated and cultivated *huachuma* along the Peruvian coast. Even earlier than that, the oldest archaeological remains of crops from ancient civilizations in the Andes contained remnants of huachuma in Cueva del Guitarrero (Cave of the Guitar Maker in Spanish, also known by the Quechua name *Kitarawaqachiqpa mach'aynin* with the more expressive and possibly accurate meaning of "get drunk while playing the guitar"), dating back as early as 8,600 BC. Among the tremendous stash, which included peppers, beans, maize, squash, the earliest known textiles, arrow/spear points, rope, basketry, and wood and leather tools, the famed cave also contained an array of ritual items used for ceremony with the cactus.

Due to the aforementioned physical evidence of psychoactive plant material and ceremonial items found in the cave, this site is considered the oldest, strongest direct evidence of entheogenic plant usage in early human history.

Evidence also reveals an image of an owl-faced woman holding a cactus found on a ceramic pot from the Chimú culture dates back to 1200 AD. According to native beliefs, the owl is a patron spirit and guardian of herbalists and shamans. The woman depicted is most likely a curandera (healer) and huachumera.

During the Spanish colonial period, writings of colonizers described the psychedelic effects of the cactus when ingested by native peoples. Just as with mushrooms and peyote, the colonizers and the Catholic Church fought against the religious use of huachuma.

Eventually, Christianity influenced indigenous ritual practices and huachuma was renamed San Pedro, with new traditions blending indigenous elements with Christian ones. The new moniker referred to Saint Peter, who held the keys to enter heaven, indirectly acknowledging huachuma's ability to offer divine access to humans while here on Earth.

The primary traditional use of San Pedro has been for diagnostic reasons – the healer ingests San Pedro to see the nature of the patient's illness. They can also be used for purification through purging and as an anti-inflammatory in the form of a topical poultice.

The San Pedro ritual is known as a *mesa*, generally performed with the purpose of healing a sick person for whom normal treatment has not worked. Others use San Pedro to obtain money or find lost objects or animals. Huachumeros (those who work with huachuma) collect special objects over time to add to their mesas, including swords or machetes, staffs, stones, shells, sugar, tobacco, brandy, candles, and more. These objects confer power to the healer.

Huachuma is called "grandfather medicine" and is often called Abuelo (grandfather in Spanish) because of the ancient wisdom and lessons bestowed upon participants during their journeys. The goal of the huachumero or huachumera is for the participant to bloom during the ceremony – to open as a flower to the divine – just like the night-blooming San Pedro cactus.

Huachuma is typically ingested as a dried powder or a tea made from the cactus. Some huachumeros serve it after soaking the dried cactus powder in citrus juice and water overnight. The effects can begin after 30 minutes and can last 12-14 hours. Traditional huachuma ceremonies take place at night, beginning around midnight. Though the tea can be prepared by boiling the cactus for up to 24 hours to minimize nausea, some can still experience digestive upset. In general, participants prepare themselves with cleansing and fasting in the days leading up to the ceremony.

Depending on the potency and preparation of the cactus, huachuma produces visions and dream-like states that tend to be more gentle or subtle than other psychedelics. Yet the experiences are no less meaningful. People report meeting and receiving assistance from guides, ancestors, otherworldly beings, and sometimes the spirit of huachuma himself. Blissful states, heightened senses, waves of emotions (often including tears), and a sense of being connected with all life are commonly described. Another frequent theme is being in a loving presence and feeling the opening of the heart. The experiences offer guidance, clarity, breakthroughs, healing, and awareness of their divinity.

According to the ethnobotanist Richard Evans Schultes, huachuma is "always in tune with the powers of animals and beings that have supernatural powers... Participants (in ceremonies) are 'set free from matter' and engage in flight through cosmic regions... transported across time and distance in a rapid and safe fashion." An Andean shaman he quotes describes the following effects: "First, a dreamy state... then great visions, a clearing of all the faculties... and then detachment, a type of visual force inclusive of the sixth sense, the telepathic state of transmitting oneself across time and matter, like a removal of thoughts to a distant dimension."

IBOGA

In the blockbuster movie Black Panther, a "heart-shaped herb" thought only to grow in the country of Wakanda plays a central role in a sacred brew necessary to initiate and empower their leader to become protector of the Wakandan people as Black Panther. This initiatory process always follows the loss of the prior leader who held the role of Black Panther. As such, this special herb is associated closely with loss and death and also offers superhuman physical properties (and healing, when needed) – all by way of a plant journey that allows direct guidance from ancestors. In the movie, Wakandans have unique access to another rare and unmatched natural resource of unequaled power, but only partaking of the heart-shaped herb enables victory for the Wakandans. The flip side? The initiate may experience cardiac arrest during ingestion, and die.

Sounds like a fantastical plot for a superhero movie, right?

It turns out that the Central African shrub iboga has qualities not so dissimilar from the heart-shaped herb described here.

The herb – and the film – beautifully point to the question long asked of humans by iboga: How do we as a society midwife our dead and the living who survive them through this journey over the threshold? Not surprisingly, near-death experiences (and perhaps death itself) are thought to activate many of the same mechanisms as psychedelic medicines – and often result in potent mystical experiences that can be even more reliably transformative to someone's remaining life than a psychedelic journey.

Iboga has long been a vehicle to contact ancestors and fairly reliably bring up an objective overview and accounting of autobiographical life experiences. Dream-like autobiographical journeys are more common with iboga than other psychedelics, with minimal open-eye visuals and pronounced closed-eye visions, often with many rainbows and feeling of lightness or floating. Time perception is altered, with time lengthening far beyond ordinary measurable time.

Iboga induces an introspective experience that is thought to have deep psychotherapeutic benefits. It's considered an "oneirophrenic" because it often induces a waking dream state, and the journeyer is usually aware of where they are and what is happening and can observe themselves in the process as though they are outside themselves.

Even at lower, nonpsychedelic doses, the iboga root is also known to confer "superhuman" strength and stimulation, allowing extraordinary physical exertion without fatigue over a very long periods. Warriors and hunters alike hold iboga in high regard as a way to track animals or for long marches, extended canoe voyages, or difficult nighttime watches. Iboga is also a known aphrodisiac.

On the flip side, at journeying (hallucinogenic) doses, there can be a very real risk of death, most likely by arrhythmias leading to cardiac arrest in certain vulnerable individuals.

Iboga is often defined as a person with her own soul who connects humans to the spirit world. Iboga does not heal directly but rather supports healing. According to the indigenous Bwiti healers called Ngangas, iboga's widely healing properties regarding substance use disorders are because this plant purifies and heals the spirit. Iboga does this by opening the door for constructive examination of past experiences, including those on the margins of consciousness. Iboga connects people to themselves, allowing deactivation of spirit-related pathologies, such as substance use disorders.

Bwiti is Africa's best-known animist ritual culture that engages with iboga for healing and rituals for important life transitions. Iboga is incorporated into becoming an adult, losing a loved one, emerging as a leader, and more. In the tradition, an initiate can only be welcomed if they've seen Bwiti, and the way to see Bwiti is by consuming iboga. The spiritual discipline, in which iboga plays a central role, is based on oral traditions that use a large pharmacopeia of plants for physical, emotional, and spiritual cleansing and healing practices.

Bwiti emerged prominently in Gabon during the French occupation, which displaced the coastal Bantu population and created new (not initially welcome) contacts with the inland Pygmy people. The Pygmies, who had a long history of incorporating iboga into rituals, ultimately decided that sharing the practice of Bwiti with the Bantus would discourage the Bantus' ongoing attacks on the Pygmies. As often has been the case for Master Plant practices in colonized areas, French forces attempted to suppress Bwiti iboga rituals. As a result, they grew in popularity. Bwiti practices became an alternative to the colonial system and ultimately symbolized a nonviolent expression of resistance against colonizers. As the use of iboga not only continued but spread, the French couldn't help but notice the benefits. Eventually, iboga emerged in France as a stimulant under the name Lambaréné, after the Gabonese city.

Iboga can refer to many plants, including *Tabernanthe iboga, Tabernanthe manii, and Voacanga africana,* which have been used traditionally for centuries. The iboga brew is made from its root bark, traditionally used in initiatory rituals as a sacrament by the Bwiti as well as other secret societies in the Congo and Zaire. When boys come of age between the ages of nine and twelve, for example, they traditionally ingest large amounts of the root. Once they emerge from their days-long journey, they are considered adult men. During this period, older community members care for them, staying awake by chewing on iboga roots.

Many Bwiti practitioners consider iboga to be the biblical tree of the knowledge of good and evil. They say that the plant brings those who consume the brew into contact with their ancestors and reveals the nature of life and death. More than simply a medicinal plant, iboga is said to act as a portal to truth. The transformations that result in an individual's personality and physical body result from being brought into contact with universal truths. For this reason, it is commonly believed that the uninitiated cannot fully understand this Master Plant's potential.

While no two iboga experiences are the same, they share similar phases. In the first phase, patients close their eyes and see images from the past or symbols that represent past struggles. Some people say they view themselves at various ages as if watching scenes from a film, only faster and more chaotic. Many say that for the first time in their lives, they view their actions objectively, helping them to understand where their desire for drugs originated. In the second phase, fewer memories arise, allowing the participant to evaluate that material in a more neutral way. During the third phase, attention slowly returns to the outside world, though heightened arousal, vigilance, and reduced need for sleep can persist for days or even weeks following treatment.

The stories tend to fall into a similar vein – a single dose of iboga instigates a visual journey, typically of a person's most significant life events, in many cases, enabling them to forgive themselves and others for past traumas.

For the Global North, iboga remains best known for the treatment of addiction. Because iboga experience facilitates a deep review of personal history as well as the person's role in the collective, from family to society at large, iboga goes to what might be considered the root cause of drug use.

In the process, iboga is thought to rewire the brain, eliminating withdrawal symptoms and extinguishing opioid and other cravings within hours – with results lasting weeks, months, and sometimes much longer. Unlike buprenorphine and methadone, two commonly used treatments for addictions, iboga resolves symptoms of opioid withdrawal by a not yet fully understood mechanism that is different from any other addiction medication or treatment.

Iboga has a track record of interrupting both psychological and physical dependence on substances including opioids, cocaine, heroin, alcohol, tobacco, and others. In animal studies, iboga reduced cocaine and morphine self-administration as well as alcohol intake. Humans have experienced reduced feelings of reward from nicotine and fewer cravings overall.

Purified ibogaine, the principal and most highly researched compound in iboga, is preferred by many clinics because the dose can be standardized and still offers a positive outcome for those with addictions. A 2017 paper in the Journal of Psychedelic Studies surveyed eighty-eight people – most of whom had been using opioids daily for at least four years – who had visited an ibogaine clinic in Mexico from 2012 to 2015. About 80 percent said iboga eliminated or drastically reduced their withdrawal symptoms; half said their opioid cravings diminished, and 30 percent said that after iboga, they never used opioids again. Though this Master Plant is by no means a magic bullet, a short-term disruption of the patterns of addiction offers a respite period to make needed changes to a person's environment, behavioral patterns, and relationships.

Ongoing research indicates promising future benefits in many other categories beyond addiction. A 2020 research paper in the journal Chronic Stress found that fifty-one US veterans who had taken iboga in Mexico from 2017 to 2019 experienced profound reductions in symptoms related to every domain they measured, including suicidal thoughts, PTSD, depression, anxiety, and cognitive impairment. The improvements were far beyond typical, currently approved treatments – even if these effect sizes were cut in half, they'd still be almost three times more powerful than currently approved treatments. More than 80 percent of the vets surveyed said their psychedelic experience was one of the top five most meaningful experiences of their lives.

However, it cannot be emphasized strongly enough that iboga carries a notable cardiovascular risk due to as yet unpredictable reactions, including prolongation of the QT interval on EKG, slowing of the heart rate (bradycardia), and death. Though some cardiac and clotting conditions are generally contraindications for iboga, it is not yet fully understood who else may be most at risk. Until more is known about the underlying mechanism, those who plan to partake are strongly advised to be medically assessed and remain in controlled environments monitored by health professionals trained in cardiac emergencies.

Increased demand for iboga and ibogaine internationally is certainly impacting and placing increased pressure on wild plants in Gabon. The regenerative capacity of iboga in the wild, which affects its availability in urban areas, is compromised due to extensive illegal harvesting for sale in international markets, seizure of domestic shipments by police, and deforestation.

In Gabon, iboga is legal and was declared a national treasure in 2000. Yet most of the iboga and ibogaine sold online is derived from plants stolen by poachers from protected forests reserved for the Bwiti. According to conservationists in the area, any noncertified harvest should be considered illegal and likely resulted in extermination of elephants, panthers, and gorillas. In 2019, the government suspended the exportation of all iboga. Wild-harvested iboga is prohibited for export, and the only iboga permitted to be exported is that which has been cultivated and complies with the Nagoya Protocol.

SYRIAN RUE

Lebanese poet Kahlil Gibran noted: "Travel and tell no one, live a true love story and tell no one, live happily and tell no one, people ruin beautiful things."

Nearly every indigenous culture around the world warns against the evil eye. The evil eye is one of many forms of spiritual sickness that's the cause of everything from bad luck and betrayals to mental and physical illness. The person who inflicts the evil eye may or may not be intentionally causing issues – even compliments, no matter what the intention, are thought to make you a target.

In Bedouin folklore, for example, there are three levels of the evil eye: a person who praises something without making the correct blessings, who silently wields their envy, and who purposely seeks out an individual to cause harm through their bitter gaze. Those most vulnerable to the evil eye are the healthy, beautiful, and wealthy, as well as children and pregnant women.

In Iran, those who believe in the evil eye use *esfand* seed, also known as Syrian rue or harmel, and heat them until they pop to protect against *cheshm khordan*, or being afflicted by the eye. The practice dates back to when Zoroastrianism dominated Iran, and the seeds were used to clear away negative energy and invite fortune, whether in new homes, shops, or elsewhere. People burn massive amounts of incense balls made of Syrian rue seeds as offerings for the festival of Nowruz in Iran. They believe the smoke dispels disease, the evil eye, and all misfortune.

Peganum harmala is known as Syrian rue in English, *harmel* or *harmal* in Arabic, *besasa* ("plant of Bes") in Egypt, and *mejnenna* ("what makes you crazy, possessed") in Morocco.

Syrian rue was directly associated with the ancient god Bes, a deity of the Pharaonic Pantheon. Bes was a good fortune deity, a protector of women giving birth, newborns, infants, and people sleeping. He was also the divinity of music and dance, as well as sexual pleasures and wine. He protected dreams – in Ptolemaic times, "rooms of Bes" were used for rituals to cure people through their dreams – with the help of Syrian rue.

Wildly popular across Europe, Asia, and North Africa for thousands of years, *Peganum harmala* is a perennial plant with much in common with ayahuasca. The two entheogens share a similar molecular profile, and both have been associated with many types of healing and spirituality in different cultures.

In fact, this Master Plant has been explored as a possible candidate for the visions of the burning bush and even the receiving of the Ten Commandments and may have been burned to create the fumes that instigated the visions for the Oracle at Delphi.

Avicenna (c. AD 980 to 1,037), the Persian philosopher and physician, was aware of its psychoactive properties. The Koran states that "every root, every leaf of harmel, is watched over by an angel who waits for a person to come in search of healing."

Syrian rue is one of the plants considered to be the original mysterious *Haoma* plant, a drink mentioned in ancient Persian texts but whose identity is not known. People are thought to have used it in spiritual, shamanic, or religious contexts. Because of this, dervishes in Bukhara have been known to worship the plant and may have used it for its intoxicating effects.

North Africans have used Syrian rue as a medicine and a magical tool for thousands of years. Moroccans add Syrian rue seeds to make harmal wine or grind the seeds into snuff to inhale for a "clear mind." In Iran, people use the seeds as incense to ward off diseases and the evil eye. Couples burn a combination of olibanum, alum, and Syrian rue seeds on their wedding night as an aphrodisiac.

In Ladak, India, the seeds are roasted and pulverized to obtain a fine powder called *techepakchìatzen*, which is ingested or smoked with tobacco to obtain intoxicating effects. The Hunza shamans of northern Pakistan inhale the vapors of harmel, which they call *supándur*, to call the spirits during their trance. Shamans in the Himalayas use Syrian rue seeds as a magical incense to enter a trance state as well, where they can make love to divining goddesses, giving them great healing powers.

Syrian rue is also becoming known as something of a medical panacea in nonpsychedelic doses, as an anti-inflammatory, neuroprotective, antimicrobial, and antidepressant. Growing data shows beneficial effects for treating cardiac conditions, cancer, COVID, diabetes, epilepsy, psychosis, kidney stones, numbness, and pain – including joint pain, back pain, tooth pain, and chronic headaches – as well as helping induce labor and addressing unwanted pregnancy.

It's important to note that a handful of papers address the potential toxicity of Syrian rue as well, usually in very high doses or inappropriate use. Fatality is very rare; reports of serious poisoning are most common in pregnant women and also babies who are surrounded with the smoke as a form of protection.

Interestingly, a common vision accompanying overdose consists of seeing flames in the visual field. Many have described seeing doctors and walls of hospitals shrouded in flames.

PEYOTE

Peyote in the wild are not easily seen until they reveal themselves. The cactus top is flat, even with the earth, and blends with dirt and rock. Though spineless, peyote grows next to another kind of cactus with jumping spines that can stab painfully, requiring special care to be taken care with every movement.

The Tarahumara people say that peyote sings songs to guide them in their hunt for the sacred cactus. It's thought that peyote grows in the footprints of Kauyumari, the Deer God or Deer Person

Elder. He is a trickster god who purposely makes peyote very difficult to find, camouflaged by the desert floor.

The use of peyote dates back more than three thousand years, as
evidenced by a ceremonial symbol used by the Tarahumara found in
ritual carvings dating from that era, preserved in volcanic rocks.
The English and Spanish word *peyote* comes from the Nahuatl
(Aztec) word *peyotl*. Huichols call it *hikuri*. To the botanist, peyote is
called *Lophophora williamsii*.

Peyote is not picked but hunted. The Huichol, the oldest-known
guardians of this Master Plant, believe peyote are living beings, each
precious and fundamental to life. The power objects of the shaman,
or *mara'akame* – prayer arrows to hunt the peyote and the sacred
basket to collect them – are also living beings.

To successfully hunt for the body of the cactus, the hunters must
connect with the cactus's spirit. They must call in Kauyumari and
watch where he runs through the desert and note where his feet
touch the ground. There, peyote will grow.

Singing to the peyote – or to Kauyumari – allows him to choose
to reveal himself and the peyote that grow in his footsteps.

One of the most well-known and important rites of Wixarika
peyote worship is the pilgrimage to Wirikuta in the desert of San
Luis de Potosí, a sacred place of the Huichol. This pilgrimage is the
most sacred ritual of their calendar since the peyote collection
provides for all of the celebrations for the year. In this tradition, the
sacred hunt is the only way to find peyote in a good way.

Peyote is considered heart medicine, and finding them requires
quieting the mind and feeling the connection through the heart.

People on the hunt have described the revelation of suddenly
seeing peyote everywhere, all around them, when previously none
were visible. When they connected with sacred intentions, they
were given eyes to see the hidden peyote.

Each discovery and "capture" is followed by a physical offering
of tobacco or something else sacred, as well as a song or prayer of
thanks. Then they are cut, leaving the root system intact, and placed

very carefully in decorated bags to protect them from being bruised or harmed.

No one eats the cactus before the offering is given to Kauyumari and the spirits of the land. Sacred prayer arrows, decorated bowls, small paintings, and other meaningful personal items that pilgrims bring are left as gifts of thanks.

Peyote is a protected and very slow-growing species. To experience any psychedelic effect requires ingesting a substantial amount of buttons, as they're called.

In Mexico, the worldview of the Huichol, also known as the Wixarika, is intimately related to peyote. Their calendar centers offerings, pilgrimages, festivals, and celebrations related to the knowledge bestowed by peyote.

The Native American Church also uses peyote in ceremonial contexts and has around 250,000 members in Mexico, the United States, and Canada. The members can use peyote legally under the United States Indigenous Religious Freedom Act.

The most famous of peyote's alkaloids is the psychedelic compound mescaline, which many are familiar with as a "drug" in its own right. For the Huichol, however, the power of the plant comes through divinity rather than chemistry. For the Huichol, peyote – along with deer and maize – are central to their cosmology and sacred practice. Every ceremony is dependent on all three of these because they make life complete – the deer represents masculinity, hunting, independence, and freedom; the maize is femininity, food, domesticity, and routine; and the peyote is considered both plant and animal, outside of time, a portal to beauty that feeds the soul.

Peyote is regarded differently by various communities. For some, like the Huichol, peyote can only bring benevolence; for others, like the Taramuhara, peyote can be fearsome. Some looka-like cacti resemble peyote but, similar to the poisonous plant Datura, bring terrible visions of scorpions, serpents, and dangerous animals. These reactions are not considered just a case of mistaken identity but also a demonstration of not coming in a good way –

without speaking of your life, cleansing yourself of everything, the false *hikiri* (peyote) will discover it and bring out bad thoughts, that which is evil and frightens the person.

The Huichol people have no fear of peyote. This is largely because they know they come to it in a good way. Though it can be found in markets, that kind is considered no good to them because it was not gathered appropriately with the right offerings. Peyote must never be purchased but only hunted in the land of its origins in the appropriate ceremonial manner. They always plant some of what they gather close to home so it will be available.

Peyote, like maize, is thought to read a person's thoughts and punish falseness or evil. In this paradigm, the peyote rewards or punishes a person according to their inner state or where they're morally wanting. The sanction is just, immediate, and certain.

For these communities, peyote is a panacea. Though only drunk or eaten ritually during the dry season ceremonies, it may be eaten at any time of year. Peyote could also be used for myriad ailments: hemorrhage, cramps, fainting, rheumatism, and fever. It's used topically for wounds and ingested medicinally to alleviate pain, boost energy levels, or bolster endurance or courage. The medicinal dose would not instigate visions.

Even in the 1500s, the colonizing Spanish documented the prophetic properties of peyote, noting that "by eating it they can foresee and predict everything, such as whether they should attack the following day," or even more mundane questions like the location of lost objects through "visions either frightful or mirthful." They observed benefit physically, noting peyote "sustains the person and gives them courage to fight and not to feel hunger nor thirst."

For the Aztecs, Master Plants and their visions were offered as rewards. For the Huichol, peyote visions are gratuitous and are kept personal, solitary, secret, and, most of all, precious, beautiful, and unique. Consuming peyote is part of but also separate from the religion, and very different from any religious experience that is ritualized and impersonal.

Partaking in peyote for meaningful visions is mostly for the *mara'akame*, or shaman, not for ordinary people. For anyone else, any attempt to reproduce or interpret peyote's fleeting visions is to minimize them or disrespect them.

Studies have evaluated cognitive performance and the psychological state of people who have consumed peyote for years in Native American Churches. No evidence of psychological or cognitive deficits has been found among those who have used peyote in the Native American Church for extended periods.

In the ritual known as the Peyote Way, Native Americans eat dried slices (buttons) of the cactus or drink it as an infusion. The experience presents with physical symptoms, including nausea, vomiting, cramps, chest pain, and restlessness. Several hours later, physical symptoms give way to the plant's visionary effects, including depersonalization, visual hallucinations, an altered sense of time and space, and an out-of-body experience. The spiritual guide for the ceremony, known as the peyote road man, leads the participants in prayer and song.

Peyote offers connection to Great Spirit and holds divine power. Eating peyote can offer messages from the gods and is thought to foil sorcerers and evil entities that cause disease. Peyote ceremonies are usually called to heal a specific individual, but they can also be to celebrate life events or offer thanks. Peyote acts as a way to ensure communal well-being – which maintains health both individually and at a broader social level.

SALVIA DIVINORUM

Imagine a ritual that takes place only at night, in the pitch-black of silent darkness. Now imagine being given 26 leaves of a plant, collected with prayers, picked in pairs, and rolled together into a cylinder to chew. To ingest these leaves, there's no swallowing or spitting them out – only chewing and chewing them to elicit the juice. Even the juice of the leaves is kept in the mouth to be absorbed topically through the mucus membranes.

Imagine looking along the darkest, shadiest parts of riverbanks and ravines in the Sierra Mazateca of Oaxaca, Mexico, the only place the plant prefers to grow wild, and discovering the live plant herself thriving in a profound shade that few other plants could survive.

Meet *Salvia divinorum*, a spirit to which the Mazatec people pray and ask for guidance and who they associate with a powerful guiding spirit. They call her Ska Pastora, which means the Shepherdess. Indigenous people are careful to honor ritual guardian spirits who are present in their rituals with the Shepherdess. These spirits serve to guide and protect them during their experience.

Vegetalistas working with *Salvia divinorum* look at their patients in absolute quiet and darkness. Any cloudy or dark areas they see indicate a problem in that area of the body. They will then try to lighten up the dark areas with herbs rubbed on the body and other ritual practices, including the use of Salvia divinorum by the healer, to gain insight into the cure. This traditional practice goes back at least hundreds of years.

The Mazatec people have been used by the Shepherdess for purposes of divination and to treat various diseases such as anemia, rheumatism, headache, stomach swelling, and diarrhea.

Salvia divinorum and psilocybe mushrooms can be used by the same Mazatec healer families, in part because mushrooms are available at a different time of the year. But some prefer this seemingly unassuming plant to mushrooms. The leaves or mushrooms are always measured out in pairs. *Salvia divinorum* rituals are often used for healing and can be led by women or men, alone or together. Altars for *Salvia divinorum* and mushroom rituals often contain images of the Virgin of Guadalupe and other saints.

They say that the needs of the plant act as an indicator of the best ways for humans to engage with the plant. The plant grows in the dark and cannot reproduce by seed, only by cuttings passed down through the generations. So too, are the ability to locate the plant and engage with the specific healing rituals of Ska Pastora passed down through families. Shy and humble in presentation, the effects are considered more subtle, telepathic rather than "hallu-cinogenic" when consumed in the traditional way.

Once the leaves are chewed or infused, effects can emerge within ten minutes, lasting up to forty-five minutes. Some people claim to have experienced effects hours after chewing and describe a total duration of over four hours. However, the doses in these cases usually vary from five pairs of leaves (a non-psychotropic dose for most, traditionally used to treat anemia and regulate excretory functions and stomach swelling) to up to fifty pairs.

The chewed or infused leaves are described as producing a smoother effect, including visions with closed eyes. The silent dark-ness is necessary to appreciate the intensity of the experience, as it may be difficult to perceive the effects otherwise.

The Shepherdess may have very ancient roots. As with many Master Plants, we continue to untangle her many identities, partic-ularly those lost during periods of indigenous persecution. Some think she is the ancient Aztec plant *pipiltzinzintli*, which translates to "the purest little prince," written about and forbidden during the Spanish Inquisition.

The mechanism of *Salvia divinorum* remains mysterious. Unlike other known psychedelic Master Plants, *Salvia divinorum* contains no alkaloids. Salvinorin A, thought to be the primary active compound within *Salvia divinorum*, is the most potent natural psychedelic substance known, about ten times more potent than psilocybin. Because it does not contain nitrogen, however, Salvi-norin A is not considered an alkaloid as most other psychedelic compounds are. Instead, it stimulates the kappa opioid receptors, which differs from other psychedelic compounds that act mainly on the serotonergic system and 5-HT2A receptors. Salvinorin A is therefore unusual and produces psychedelic and dissociative effects even in very low doses, which, depending on the route of adminis-tration, can last between fifteen minutes and two hours.

Salvia divinorum can induce intense changes in both perception and mood. Some describe warmth, pressure in certain areas of the body, floating, a sense of merging with objects in the environment, spatial and temporal distortion, geometric visions, dream-like land-scapes, and extracorporeal experiences. People also report increased appreciation of the environment, feeling calm and experiencing synesthesia, an array of visions, and a deep sense of insight and spir-ituality.

Less pleasant effects can include forgetting a substance was consumed, a sense of loss of control, panic attacks, fear, terror, agitation or loss of motor control, dizziness, anxiety, paranoia, temporary loss of the ability to communicate, and amnesia. Some people describe an array of strange sensations, including a "dou-bling" of space-time, radical changes in perspective of reality, and the sensation of entering other dimensions.

Experiences can be frightening, given their intensity and strangeness. Occasionally people may get up and walk without being aware of it, which can lead to falls and accidents. The frequency of difficult, confusing, or frightening experiences seems to be high enough that many people decide not to reuse Salvia after a single experience.

These effects are more common with potent extracts and less likely to occur when the leaf is chewed. When the plant is consumed by smoking or inhaling the vapors, on the other hand, the effects are established much faster, and the intensity is much greater. The experience begins within seconds of inhalation with a sustained peak of up to 20 minutes, with residual effects for up to one hour.

Having a caretaker present for experiences with *Salvia divinorum* can be key. The setting should be safe, quiet, with minimal stimuli, away from crowds, dangerous objects, or obstacles to minimize the risk of accidents and negative experiences.

Salvia divinorum is also being explored for medical benefits. Salvinorin A may offer analgesic effects and can reduce pain responses in mice. The same compound has also been shown to affect the brain's reward pathways and may have potential as a treatment for addiction. A study published in the Journal of Phar-macology and Experimental Therapeutics in 2006 found that salvi-norin A reduced the self-administration of cocaine in rats. Some studies have suggested that *Salvia divinorum* may have antidepressant properties. A study published in the Journal of Medicinal Plants Research in 2011 found that an extract had antidepressant effects in mice.

Many people find that very, very low doses enhance erotic contact. These doses can still induce space distortions, sounds becoming colors or shapes, and language distortions. A feeling of being loved and cared for is common. People can feel they have become other people or other animals or have moved in time to other eras. Seeing through the eyes of an animal is a typical effect useful for divination.

BRUGMANSIA

Brugmansia, or toé, is considered to be what the angels play to infuse the forest with celestial music. Also known as angel's trumpet, the association with angels could mislead people to underestimate this powerful visionary plant. Don't be fooled. Brugmansia is classified as a deliriant strong enough to lead to madness and death. The names borrachero (inebriator) and cojones de diablo (devil's testicles) may be more appropriate to the most common effects. Indeed, chamicado in Peru – the practice of intoxicating someone against their will – means 'touched by an angel's trumpet.'

Due to their potent narcotic effects, the seeds are thought to have been mixed with coca leaves in pre-Columbian times for anesthesia. Shuar and Achuar people drank this tea, called maikuna, to obtain visions that could help them acquire an arutam wakani, or "visionary soul." Once acquired, the soul is sent forth to make inquiries into the other world. The visions are especially important to warriors to restore their lost power after ritual war killing.

In some traditions, the "jaguar inebriant" – connected to the strongest of all shamanic animals – is only to be produced and drunk on the waning moon. Some believe that even the honey produced by bees from this plant is toxic and inebriating. The blossoms, leaves, or stems can also be added to ayahuasca or San Pedro brews or smoked with cannabis or tobacco preparations to amplify their effects.

Indigenous communities regard Brugmansia as sacred. The leaves were smoked to make prophecies, divine, or diagnose. The seeds can be added to chicha, a maize beer drunk at festivals and religious rituals. Toé is one of the well-known Master Plant teachers used in the initiation of an apprentice during shamanic dietas and may also be combined with the ayahuasca brew to enhance the experience. The drink made of the plant puts the patient into a dreamlike state where it's impossible to discern reality from hallucinations.

Some shamans use this medicine when faced with truly difficult cases because it can cause the shaman to lie comatose for two to three days. An assistant will always be present to keep watch and record any messages uttered. But unlike ayahuasca, toé is usually taken just by the person in distress in a private setting with the accompanying medico. The shaman, healer, or a respected family member must prepare the potion with great care and close attention, and monitor the person for the duration of the experience. The branch of the plant is broken by hand because a metal tool would offend the spirit of the plant, and a small amount of the inner pith is scraped out.

Many consider toé to be the most dangerous and powerful hallucinogen. The effects begin within three or four minutes; the drinker is accompanied by an adult for restraint, if necessary, should the drinker become delirious and try to run off into the jungle. The visions may be terrifying, such as two gigantic animals – jaguars or boa constrictors – fighting each other, a disembodied human head, or a ball of fire. When the vision gets near, the drinker must be brave enough to run forward and touch it, at which point it instantly explodes and disappears.

The visions given by toé are dark and frightening. Animals and humans that might in an ayahuasca vision appear to be potential allies appear in a toé vision to be menacing or terrifying. That is why toé grants such power: it demands great courage; if you can survive the toé vision, the spirit world holds few terrors. Thus, too, toé hardens the body, so as to be resistant to attack by sorcerers. In the Amazon, as elsewhere, courage creates power.

While there are reports of healing incurable states with toé, most approach her with great caution, as she can also be used (or use the user) for black magic. People can also be drugged on purpose, and there have even been some fatal cases after drinking the mix of ayahuasca and toé. In this way, she also helps detect sorcery – those who carry out harmful magic in secret.

A person with an incurable disease may journey for several days. Their visions can be immersive, including healers or even the spirit of toé treating the patient by removing intrusive objects or revealing the sorcerer or evil spirits responsible for the illness. Sometimes people report being taken by car or plane to distant cities where they are treated by "white" doctors and nurses who use modern medicine.

The purpose of the angel's trumpet was to act as a key to open the door to the other world – to establish contact with the gods, animal helpers, or the spirits of the ancestors to ask them for help and to receive their teachings. Only with their help could the next phase of life be shaped in a positive way.

Brugmansia is considered the strongest and most toxic of all known Master Plants. Regular ingestion is thought to lead to death or madness. Brugmansia is a last resort, the most potent reserved for the most drastic cases.

The material is boiled in water or steamed at high temperatures in a plant leaf, always away from the household, to avoid contaminating elements that could harm or kill the ailing person. Doses are measured in drops or small gourds, as even a small dose can last from one night to three days. An overdose can cause weeks or months of hallucinations, instigate lifelong psychosis, or death.

Yet the plant is found everywhere. In Colombia, there are entire boulevards of the aromatic trees; people suffering from sleep disorders walk past the scented trees in the evenings. In Peru, it's thought that anyone who sleeps under the Brugmansia will end up temporarily or permanently insane. Even the scent of the flowers is said to possess narcotic properties and induce headaches and nausea. In Nepal, leaves of this plus Cannabis indica are smoked by sadhus and tantric practitioners for meditation or yoga exercises. In some indigenous communities, unruly children are given some of this drink so they will learn how to behave properly while delirious.

The classic mnemonic for identifying Brugmansia poisoning goes "hot as a hare, blind as a bat, dry as a bone, red as a beet, mad as a hatter," because symptoms include hallucinations (mad), spiking body temperature accompanied by decreased sweat and saliva production (dry and hot), tachycardia and difficulty breathing (red), and sometimes even temporary blindness. The intense psychoactive compounds derived from Brugmansia do have medical uses: hyoscine, also known as scopolamine, which is now usually synthesized artificially, is used to treat nausea and to stem saliva production.

Toé is powerful, but it is also mischievous and sometimes treacherous. Beings may appear armed with knowledge, but they can also play tricks, inducing people to drink sand as though it's water or eat leaves as though they're food. Wide paths through the forest open and then close in a tangle of vegetation. Beautiful vistas illuminate, then vanish. Wise, otherworldly characters appear, speak profound and mysterious words, and then suddenly disappear with a sad gaze, never to return. Jaguars, monsters, evil giants, and witches can become threatening and even make chase. Toé may not offer healing without asking for great sacrifices in return. And when not approached with respect, the plant spirit may tempt the person with dangerous sorcery teachings or entice them with false promises or deadly challenges.

When the effect passes and one returns to the material world, very little is remembered of the fantastical experiences of the spirit world: it all remains a vague nightmare/dream.

TOBACCO

Perhaps one of the best known – and most widely misunderstood – of these plants is tobacco. Tobacco is already one of the most important Master Plants in the lives of people in the modern world, but to indigenous communities, it is a fundamental part of cosmology.

Tobacco was likely the first plant intentionally cultivated in the Americas – even before seed agriculture was widely practiced. Some communities grow sacred tobacco only from seeds passed down ancestrally. They offer songs to the tobacco plants as they grow.

Tobacco is considered food for the spirits. Tobacco can be sprinkled or thrown onto a fire to amplify prayers or offered in gatherings to give thanks or repay the plants. Tobacco is offered by those requesting the help of the spirits. A pinch can be put at the base of a tree to ask for the tree's help or be blown onto an object or person to protect or strengthen them.

Many native people say that humans exist to offer tobacco to the spirits, because the spirits cannot do that for themselves.

The wisdom goes that human intent is part of the sacred power of tobacco for the spirits. Tobacco is considered a megaphone for prayers by amplifying intent. Some believe the only way to build spiritual strength and become a warrior in the spiritual world is by drinking tobacco.

In pre-Hispanic traditional use for prevention or treatment of physical ailments, tobacco might be chewed, pulverized and inhaled, smoked, or macerated to be drunk or for external use in cataplasms, baths, drops, or enemas. The master curanderos used it in rituals because of its psychoactive effects, which granted it the category of sacred plant. Tobacco allowed them to mediate in the contact with the other world and nourish their energetic body with this yang, or masculine, energy.

Tobacco is controversial down to the origin of its name. The Maya used the word cikar to describe smoking, which became part of their ritual and religious practices. In Spain and Italy, the words *tabacco*, *atabaca*, and *altabaca* may come from the Arabic *tabbak*, which refers to medicinal plants with soporific or hallucinogenic effects. The word may derive from Tobago, the Caribbean island, describing a fork-shaped pipe cane that locals of that region used to inhale and smoke various Master Plants including tobacco. Indeed, cave paintings found in the Dominican Republic show Tainos engaging with these pipes, one of whose ends is placed in the nose. The Taino people considered tobacco an exchange object, offered to the mothers of plants as well as to bad spirits to appease them. This welcome gift, their primary medicine and means of relating with the spiritual world, was one of the gifts they offered Columbus when he arrived.

There are sixty-four tobacco species. Only a dozen species contain enough nicotine to be effective in human beings.

Yet practically speaking, any amount of tobacco is considered poisonous and thus tremendously powerful. As a result, shamanic cultures around the world ingest tobacco, with North Americans being the main exception. Even in a pipe ceremony, they hold smoke in their mouths and release it rather than inhaling.

Traditionally tobacco was used to sit with intent, alone or with others, but never to smoke while doing other things. When tobacco is grown and processed and used in a way that comes from greed, the belief is that the tobacco holds the intent of that greed. Anyone who smokes that tobacco internalizes that intent.

Not surprisingly, the spirit of tobacco is said to demand tremendous respect, without which we risk being punished due to not observing appropriate protocol. Peruvian vegetalistas use fresh tobacco leaves to prepare cold water extracts adding other plants or alcohol, which could be administered nasally before ingestion of Huachuma or San Pedro cactus. Tobacco would be first consumed as a raw, aqueous extract (matter and water), then as a cooked extract (fire), and finally smoked (fire and air). These stages are followed in this strict, irreplaceable order. Thus, the northern way of consuming tobacco – directly smoked – could be considered a serious and possibly deadly transgression – akin to claiming access to spiritual knowledge without taking the time to first integrate the strength of tobacco in its material dimension. Indeed, the tabaquero does not necessarily inhale the tobacco smoke but swallows it, directing it toward the stomach, where the energetic forces reside.

Associated with purity, fertility, and fecundity, tobacco plays a major role in curative rituals and important tribal ceremonies. Recreational use – for nonsacred or nonmedical reasons – is uncommon.

This tobacco is virtually unrecognizable from commercial tobacco. It is without chemical treatment and additives. It has a fragrance that the spirit of ayahuasca is said to like.

Native to the Americas as well as Polynesia and Australia, tobacco has made its way around the world. It can be rolled with other local leaves: banana, corn husks, bamboo or ficus, datura or Brugmansia, and spruce bark, birch wood, fir wood, and moss in Siberia. In Europe, tobacco was mixed with hashish in ways that negated the physiological effect of the other. In the pre-Hispanic period, tobacco was thought to be combined with coca powder or plant ashes and licked or mixed with cacao, coca, and chili powder as a snuff.

Thus, tobacco is a common companion to ayahuasca in the Amazon. The vegetalistas imbibe tobacco juice (of Nicotiana tabacum and Nicotiana rustica) or lick ambil (an edible tobacco preparation) with ayahuasca. Tobacco can also be smoked in ceremonies and curative rituals of certain curanderos, who blow smoke over the ayahuasca brew and participants, combined with specific ícaros.

Another word used is mapacho, which refers to the cigarettes made with local tobacco (dried, cured, and chopped Nicotiana rustica) or ampiri, the name given to the ash or tar produced by the final combustion of tobacco. Fittingly, the word ampi means both "medicine" and "poison."

Tobacco is also employed in medical practices. Medicos rub a decoction of the leaves over sprains and bruises or use crushed fresh leaves as a poultice over boils and infected wounds, and tobacco juice is drunk therapeutically for indisposition, chills, and snake bites.

In addition to physical detoxification, tobacco allows participants to connect with their inner world, granting them a feeling of strength, mental clarity, concentration, and emotional stability. This process reactivates the spiritual dimension and favors reestablishing a deep sense of life.

For the many people who hold the tobacco plant sacred, the stigmatization of tobacco results from having reduced tobacco to an object by ignoring the appropriate rules of engagement. As such, we've been paying the long-term consequences of profaning this sacred Master Plant. The indigenous worldview on Master Plants sees the only path to resolution of the destruction of addiction to what we consider "substances" as acknowledging the unconscious or conscious truth of our sometimes monumental capacity for self-destruction and developing connections to the invisible world, including ancestors and spirit.

DATURA

Datura, also known as jimsonweed, is a powerful and enigmatic plant used for medicinal and spiritual purposes for centuries. Its historical and medical importance can be traced back to ancient cultures, such as the Aztecs, Native Americans, and Indians, who revered it for its mystical properties.

In Aztec culture, datura was known as "teonanácatl," meaning "divine flesh." Considered a sacred plant, datura could help connect individuals to the spiritual realm and provide insights into the nature of the universe. The Aztecs often consumed datura as part of their religious ceremonies, believing they would receive help communicating with the gods to receive guidance for their lives.

Similarly, Native American tribes used datura for its psychoactive properties, often in ceremonial contexts. For example, some tribes would use datura as part of their vision quests, in which individuals would seek to connect with their spirit guides and gain insights into their destiny.

Datura has been discovered in various caves with ancient art dating back thousands of years, including the Chauvet Cave in France, the Altamira Cave in Spain, and the Tassili n'Ajjer plateau in Algeria. These caves contained depictions of animals, humans, and abstract forms interpreted as representations of spiritual or supernatural experiences. Datura has been identified in residues found on cave artifacts, suggesting that it was used in shamanic or ritual practices to achieve altered states of consciousness and access the spiritual realm.

In Indian culture, datura has a long history of medicinal and spiritual use. The ancient Indian scripture Atharva Veda mentions datura as a plant that can cure a variety of ailments, including fever, cough, and skin diseases. It is also believed to have antispasmodic and analgesic properties and has been used to treat rheumatism, asthma, and menstrual disorders. In Ayurvedic medicine, datura is known as dhattura and is used in various preparations for treating insomnia, anxiety, and epilepsy.

In addition to its medicinal use, datura has also been utilized in Indian art as a symbol of divinity and spirituality. In Hindu mythology, the god Shiva is often depicted holding a datura flower or smoking a datura cigarette. The flower is believed to represent the goddess Parvati, considered the consort of Shiva and the embodiment of divine femininity. Datura is also used in tantric rituals to achieve spiritual enlightenment and union with the divine.

From a medicinal perspective, datura has been used to treat a variety of ailments, including asthma, fever, and pain relief. Its therapeutic effects are due to the presence of several alkaloids, including scopolamine, atropine, and hyoscyamine. These compounds have antispasmodic and analgesic effects and are used in modern medicine to treat a range of conditions, such as motion sickness, irritable bowel syndrome, and Parkinson's disease.

Datura can have a dark side. The plant is highly toxic and can be deadly when consumed in large quantities. Datura can cause delirium and even coma or death. One of the main dangers is the unpredictable nature of the plant. The effects can vary widely even in any given individual, depending on a number of factors, including dose, method of ingestion, and individual body chemistry.

When used for its psychoactive properties, datura can produce intense visions and altered states of consciousness. The effects of datura are often described as surreal, with users reporting a sense of disconnection from their physical body and, sometimes, a profound sense of insight into the nature of reality. Many find the particular experience of datura to be deeply disorienting.

Datura has long been a vehicle for shamanic initiation, as it is believed to facilitate spiritual experiences and connections to other realms. In South America, the Shipibo-Conibo people use datura as part of their traditional shamanic practices. They believe the plant helps them connect with the spirits of nature and gain a deeper understanding of the interconnectedness of all things.

A FEW WORDS ABOUT WITCHES' OINTMENTS

The true poison plants are, in many ways, the most potent of plants. The ambivalent nature of their potency – medicine or malice – has long been known and led them to be called witches' herbs, devil's drugs, or magical. Poisonous plants are thought to get their power from their closeness to the realm of death. Some of the best known of these plants include tobacco, datura, brugmansia, belladonna, jimsonweed, and mandrake.

Those who made use of them were known *pharmakides* – "witches" or "sorcerers" – derived from the Greek *pharmaka*, which means "medicine, poison, and magical substance." It's worth noting that this etymological root means all three – medicine, poison, and magical substance, not just one – because again, the inner terrain of the person creating a relationship with the plant determines whether these plants inflict damage or offer health and protection.

It was said the greatest magician was one who best knows the secrets of plants – building a relationship with potent plants was considered a gift.

Paracelsus said when it comes to medicine, dose makes the poison. Dose is incredibly important when it comes to any plants or pharmaceuticals for that matter, but especially for these pharmaka. Not infrequently, those who were poisoned, literally or figuratively, did not demonstrate appropriate respect by using an inappropriate dose or did not understand the particulars of the inner terrain – metabolics, genetics, microbiome, nervous system – of the recipient.

Of course, sometimes the poisoning was intentional, which is a whole different can of worms but in a way, demonstrates perfectly how to be in a good relationship with power – our own as well as that of the plants.

The poisonous nature of these plants simply demands respect in a whole different way.

The potentially poisonous alkaloids from *Atropa belladonna* (deadly nightshade), *Hyoscyamus niger* (henbane), *Mandragora officinarum* (mandrake), and *Datura stramonium* (jimsonweed) have long been used to make "brews," "oyntments," or "witches' salves" for witchcraft and other activities. Several of the alkaloids – including what is now known as scopolamine, used to prevent vomiting as well as motion sickness – were discovered to best absorbed through sweat glands in the armpit or via the mucous membranes of the rectum or vaginal area. It turns out that administering a drug vaginally is the most effective route to avoiding the first-pass effect of the liver even more so than rectal drug administration.

The witches were said to absorb the alkaloids in the plant medicines, then fall asleep, and "fly on these broomsticks" in dream states in which they journeyed. Whether titillating lore or truth, the witches' herbs do not just offer magical or psychedelic properties, but historically also medicinal ones, albeit in very low, carefully administered doses.

More than anything, the lore of witches and the witching herbs connect us to the parts of ourselves that are wild, disobedient, uncivilized and ungovernable in a world that demands obedience and submission. And as we'll later see, those parts will become some of the most important in our health and the healing of the world.

Disclaimer: This chapter is for educational purposes only. Some of the plants outlined here can cause harm or death upon ingestion, inhalation, or even topical exposure when not approached in a safe and appropriate way. Further, several are illegal to consume or even grow. I am not recommending the ingestion or cultivation of any of the aforementioned Master Plants or synthetic compounds without guidance of a healthcare provider and exploration of the legal status in your area.

6

PLANTS ARE BEINGS

One of my practices with Master Plants is to grow and care for them – not for consumption, but to build connection and relationship. When I first received the now ten-year-old ayahuasca vine I've been tending, I had put her in my sunroom before going away for the weekend to bring one of my teachers, an ethnobotanist and fourth-generation curandera, to stay with me for a few days. When we arrived to my home, we saw right away that the plant was wilty – and my teacher said to me in a panic, "She's sick! We need to wash her, give her a stick in her pot to wind around, and put a red ribbon on her."

After her resuscitation, the ayahuasca vine visibly perked up.

Later that evening, my teacher took me aside and said ominously: "There's something I forgot to tell you." She sounded serious. "If an ayahuasca plant feels neglected, she will do things to catch your attention."

Anyone who grows plants knows that some are more high-maintenance than others. My ayahuasca vine is a diva. She lets me know she's unhappy in all kinds of ways, by wilting, by pretending to die (but not really dying), by not growing. She never interacted with the beautiful tall sticks I placed in her pot for her to wind around. Instead, she pouted until I brought home a fairly massive living tree as a companion for her – only then did she begin to truly thrive. She always finds her way to wind around other plants that I've learned to place nearby. Because of her, I've created a jungle of sorts in my New York City living room.

Some people talk to their plants. For those who don't, making chit chat with a plant may sound like a practice reserved for crazy plant people. The odds are that if I asked most of the population if they'd ever spoken to a plant – let alone a plant spirit – they'd probably say no. But most of us have knocked on wood or at least referenced it.

The practice of knocking on wood actually comes from the Celtic belief that every tree is inhabited by a spirit. Ancient priests and priestesses knocked on wood to summon this spirit an aid in warding off evil or fulfilling a wish. This practice, like so many others in our culture, has rich meaning that was erased. What if we were to imagine that every time we knocked on wood, we were actually summoning the spirits of the tree? And what if we were to extend an offering or gesture of gratitude in return?

Our deep connection with plants has been largely forgotten, but not entirely erased. Nowadays, most people think of plants as being pretty to look at or healthy to eat. Yet plants have taken care of our nourishment, oxygen, hygiene, beauty, and medication – not to mention providing guidance – since the beginning of time. Yes, guidance. As we've discussed, plants have long been considered to possess great wisdom by way of the spirits that inhabit them.

Throughout history, healers relied on "signs and signatures from the divine creator" to guide them. Traditional healers have always said they know what plants to use for any given condition because they were guided or told by the plants. We were taught it was trial and error, but ancient herbalist texts show otherwise.

One example of this is the Doctrine of Signatures, an ancient principle based on the idea that plants communicate their healing power to us by way of their resemblance to our corresponding body part or the disease that they can help to address. This is considered a universal language – one of many that plants can speak. As one example, dandelion flowers are bright yellow, resembling urine and also bile – a signature for a plant that offers detoxification through urinary and liver support, for which dandelion is well known. The stem of dandelion is hollow, which is a signature for diuretic activity, another medicinal property of the dandelion. The flowers grow in copious amounts easily found almost everywhere in the world, which tells us that this common plant is likely safe to consume in greater or more frequent amounts as food and medicine. And they're considered invasive and difficult to remove, which is a signature for difficult to remove illnesses in the body, like tumors – and believe it or not, several studies have shown that dandelion (yes, the weed we spray with poison to kill!) has potent activity against several aggressive cancers. Each plant carries a unique set of such signatures.

To be clear, these signatures are not thought to mean that plants organized themselves in this particular way solely for the benefit of humans, but simply that encoded into their appearance and behavior, they transmit clues about who they are in a language humans can interpret. Think of it as a doctor wearing a white coat and stethoscope, or a nun wearing her telltale habit. These are ways humans and other beings offer each other a window into who we are, what we have in common, or how we can serve one another.

ARE PLANTS INTELLIGENT?

Science is finally catching up with the complex intelligence of plants.

Yet we are still debating whether plants are intelligent to this day, largely because they have no brain. Researchers have come up with a term to describe the (conditioned) human inability to see or notice plants in our everyday lives; the phenomenon is known as "plant blindness." This term also refers to our failure to recognize the role of plants on earth and believing that plants are inferior to animals, who in turn are inferior to humans. This "cognitivism," as it's called, comes from the fact that we humans have been taught to consider ourselves to be the pinnacles of intelligence – and as we can claim the role for ourselves, we blithely miss the irony that self-appointing ourselves as the arbiters of intelligence implies nothing more than grandiosity and hubris. Think about it – the people who loudly proclaim that they're the most intelligent...usually aren't. In fact, it could easily be argued that we have long been acting much less intelligently than every other species on Earth.

Most people don't realize that plants do in fact possess a "brain," although it is not in the form of an organ, as it is for us. Plants do, however, have a neural network – their root system.

And as it turns out, this idea is not new. There was a scientist, albeit a controversial one, who described the neural nature of plant root systems as being sensing and intelligent in his 1880 book *The Power of Movement of Plants*. A few people may have heard of him. His name was Charles Darwin.

Because humans only deign to conceive of other beings as *beings* when considering them in human terms, it may make more sense to start thinking of plants as being upside down – heads underneath the soil, with their legs and genitalia (yep, flowers!) visible to us.

In their roots, plants store memories, analyze inputs, design responses, and plan for the future. Structurally, plant root systems closely resemble the neural network in our brains and perform like them as well. They produce neurotransmitters. As mentioned in Chapter 4, DMT – a potent psychedelic compounds found in many Master Plants – is also produced in the brains of humans and animals. Plants also produce serotonin, dopamine, melatonin, acetylcholine, and GABA. These are some of the many chemical ways that plants communicate with us – for example, passion-flower, which has been shown to calm anxiety as effectively as certain benzodiazepines (but without risk of addiction), contains the inhibitory neurotransmitter GABA.

Plants are highly active, dynamic and sensitive to the world around them. Like humans, plants carefully and continually monitor their environment holistically for important and relevant shifts, and then rank each of them, make meaning of them, and respond (or not). They use a number of complex languages to do this, including but not limited to chemical ones. As a result of their immobility, plants have evolved many biochemical mechanisms to sense and respond to their environment such as changes in light, temperature, humidity, soil pH, and more. They have photoreceptors to measure wavelengths of light to perceive not just brightness but also color. They perceive gravity by way of grains that shift inside organelles called amyloplasts, which allow their shoots and roots to determine up and down.

Although they are not rapidly mobile as we are, plants do move - as evidenced beautifully with time lapse videos. These videos show what I noticed with my ayahuasca vine: when a seemingly aimless tendril senses a pole – or in her case, another plant– to grab, the tendril becomes motivated and purposeful as it winds its way around. The main way plants move is through growth – rather than walking away, they can change their shape by growing in new directions.

Plants are far from passive.

Plants react immediately to potential dangers to their structural integrity. Some plants are so sensitive to simple touch that they change gene expression within minutes and alter transcription of over seven hundred of the genes measured within thirty minutes. They can distinguish their response based on what is touching them – a raindrop, for example, elicits only a minimal response. When attacked by other plants, on the other hand, a plant can create and release sophisticated compounds that inhibit the attack. Plants can aggress upon one another. Wild garlic mustard, for example, secretes benzyl isothiocyanate, which inhibits the growth of the mycorrhizal fungi that support tree diversity.

Plants create complex tools, primarily in the form of chemical compounds, and use them quickly and precisely in ways that are arguably more adept than humans. If plants are overeaten by insects or foraging animals, they can analyze the saliva and pheromones of that organism and craft an immediate chemical response. The response may make the foraging organisms loopy, which distracts them from feeding, or they craft very specific pheromones that imitate a predator of the insects to frighten them away. Or they call in the predator of that insect to the plant to kill it. They can also create compounds that shut down the organism's reproductive system to limit its ability to procreate. Meanwhile, the affected plants simultaneously emit another set of signaling molecules to neighboring plants in their ecosystem to communicate what organism is feeding on them so the surrounding plants can manufacture their own set of pheromones to protect themselves and each other. Each of these chemicals must be exact – in structure and concentration – to be effective.

Plants notice patterns and trends in the world around them and change their growth and behavior both in short- and long-term ways in response. These are much more complex than simple reflexes – they prioritize, compromise, and make their own decisions.

Plants also demonstrate individuality. Take two white oak trees, side by side, at the start of winter. One may opt to shed their leaves at the first cold snap to protect themselves against potential strong winds and heavy snowfall – and the other holds on to their leaves in the hopes of another warm spell that allow them to store nutrition for the coming winter. Same environment, different decisions. Each tree demonstrates unique will and individual actions.

Plants innovate and exercise free will, choice, self-protection, and adaptation – no brain necessary.

And like any good teacher, plants challenge us to deeply consider where our own intelligence – and consciousness – truly reside.

ARE PLANTS SOCIAL BEINGS?

Most of us are comfortable thinking of plants competing or attacking each other in the context of our "survival of the fittest" us versus them paradigm.

Plants also act as kin to one another. They care for their

offspring and their community. Biologists have long accepted that diverse animal species have evolved means to recognize and interact with other members of their species, often specifically kin members, to enhance their survival. More recently, studies have shown that even various microbes have the ability to recognize their kin. And studies have shown that plants, too, can recognize and interact with their kin.

Plants are part of self-organized, emergent systems that are highly responsive to the needs of their greater community. They sense when any members of their ecosystem are ailing and can produce necessary compounds to help (or isolate) them. If other plants are ill, they send those compounds through mycelial networks to reach the plants who need them. If an animal in the region needs help, they can emit chemical cues through their above-ground structures, directing those animals to the location of medicines they require. Yes, plants and animals communicate with one another through chemical signals, even at a distance.

Ailing chimpanzees, for example, will travel through the forest until they find the plant with the highest levels of compounds they need. To address intestinal parasite infections, they pick a leaf off the plant, fold it, and swallow it whole. The remedy only works if taken in this specific way; chewing the leaf negates the benefit. Stomach acid extracts the compounds from the plant which then disable intestinal parasites. The leaf is also covered with hundreds of tiny hooks, which scrape parasites from intestinal lining so they can be excreted. Many such examples demonstrate that animals understand complex, effective and highly specific ways of engaging with plant medicines.

Scientists decided to name this phenomenon "instinct," mainly because they refused to entertain that this behavior could indicate intelligence or intraspecies communication.

Yet unlike us, plants have no skulls to limit the growth of their neural networks, which means their "brains" can be larger and more complex than that of humans. Their neural networks can extend indefinitely throughout the soil; as an example, take Pando, the 13-

million pound quaking aspen grove in Utah where one tree's root system has generated 47,000 genetically identical trees over more than one hundred acres. Not that this needs to be a competition, but if it were: Who has the bigger "brain"?

And yes, this kind of communication is happening with us too – the trick is for us to be tuned in enough to perceive them.

CAN PLANTS BE OUR KIN, TOO?

I've treated, interviewed, and listened to hundreds of people share their psychedelic experiences to date, and it is nearly universal for people who have experienced Master Plants to spontaneously use the phrasing, "The mushrooms told me ..." "Ayahuasca said ..." "San Pedro wanted me to...."

This is in fairly stark contrast to those who engage with synthetic compounds. Though they may say "I learned from my MDMA journey that I'm worthy of love," people don't typically say, "LSD told me to forgive my mother" or "ketamine said to stop being so cruel to myself." It's not that it couldn't happen, but for better or worse, a journey with a Master Plant is different than a chemical compound or entity stimulating our neurons or even opening a portal to other realities. While both can be meaningful, plant experiences offer an opportunity to establish contact and cultivate intimacy with someone (not something) older, wiser, and greater, who exists outside of time and space – what I can only call a spirit.

Over a decade ago, a respected researcher who was interested in formally studying the effects of herbs, approached me after my presentation on botanicals. He asked which compound I recommended he study first. I tried to explain that plants are very complex beings, as complex as we are, and that studying the interaction between the universe of us and that of a plant by looking at one component could be, well, limiting. From the perspective of an herbalist, plants are complex, responsive beings who happen to produce a full spectrum of ever-changing compounds that all work together within us in nonlinear ways. Think back to what I said to the researcher about "the entourage effect" in Chapter 5: we miss the richness, complexity, and most of all, the *truth* of our interactions with plants when we presume that only one component is impacting us.

I said: "You can't really understand how a plant interacts with our bodies by simply exploring one compound of thousands extracted from that plant. You can learn how that particular compound behaves, as you would a pharmaceutical, but you won't understand the complexity and richness *and personality* of the plant."

The scientist and other researchers who had gathered around us were visibly aghast by my suggestion, and responded: "Well, that's not how research is done."

Yet this attitude is nearly universally held. Most people think of plants as things for us to use, exclusively here for us and our needs – What will they do for us? How will it help us? People consider a plant's fiber or vitamin C content, for example, or whether it has an appealing taste, or whether it will make us gassy.

When we talk about plants, we think about what they can do for us. Will they make us healthy? We ask if the plant is a superfood, medicine for us, or whether it is "useful."

Plants are not simply here to be useful to us. Plants are powerful, likely far more powerful than we can imagine. Consider coffee, chocolate, grass. No, not that kind of grass! Grass, as in the green plants that we grow as lawns. How much time do people spend planning for, attaining, and then maintaining all of these plants, and what are we really getting in exchange?

Plants drive our behavior; they have a myriad of ways to compel us. They make sure we will go to any lengths to do their bidding, and never question why.

Let's talk poisons. What we call phytonutrients – that make apples red or grapes purple and that we consider very healthy – actually act as tiny poisons in our bodies. This news may feel shocking, but in the context of everything already discussed, it tracks that plants don't make these compounds simply for us to be healthier – at some point, they evolved compounds that can poison us if we ate too much of them, because they considered us predators (and we are!). Luckily for us, we've evolved mechanisms that enable those minipoisons to make us stronger. Our mitochondria and cells have grown to experience these small poisons – packaged as they are alongside vitamins and minerals, fiber, stem cells, and glucose – as signals to optimize our function, rather than the other way around. This relationship is called hormesis – when a tiny amount of something harmful that would normally kill us instead boosts our well-being. Some other examples of hormetic stressors include fasting, exercise, sunshine, and...psychedelics, which contain alkaloids or other components that can cause nausea, vomiting, diarrhea, and other unpleasant, sometimes disorienting symptoms, while potentially simultaneously improving our health and well-being.

We have developed synergy with plants, including through their conversation with the cells and organisms in our bodies.

We remain in an ongoing, sacred exchange with plants through the entire cycle of life and death. They feed us with their bodies when we take their lives. And when we die, we in turn feed them with our bodies, which eventually become part of the soil that nourishes them.

We've evolved together with plants. We are kin.

THE WOOD WIDE WEB

As systems biology is exploring and describing more and more the complexity within systems, we're facing the fact, despite ourselves, that life doesn't exist neatly in the boxes we were taught they were.

In Chapter 2, we talked about how the world really is based in "Me and We" – that we live in a series of nested relationships. But those relationships extend far beyond people, plants and even microbes. Any conversation we have about the interconnectedness of life and how everything affects everything else must include fungi, who demonstrate this phenomenon in physical form as a web of life that connects tremendous numbers of organisms. Fungi are the web.

These symbiotic networks and mycorrhizae, as they're called, grow around plant roots, extend out into the soil, and connect multiple plants together. They act as physical connections between organisms.

And, as described so beautifully by Merlin Sheldrake in his book *Entangled Life*, fungi are also emergent systems that are decentralized and self-organizing. The mycelium network has no head or heart – and no known brain equivalent. Yet one fragment of the mycelium network can turn into an entirely new network.

As humans, we're not used to nonhierarchical systems. We have centralized bodies. We design our societies in centralized ways with heads of state and capital cities. But these organisms do not work this way. Mycelial networks explore their surroundings using their sensing bodies. They literally digest their surroundings, and adjust themselves in response to changes in their environment.

Fungi illustrate perfectly the fluid boundaries beings can have between each other. We think they are one thing but they are actually another, even while they still may be the thing we thought they were. This is not so different from our assumption that humans must be made mostly of human cells, when in fact if we were to measure cell by cell, we are made mostly of microbes. These fluid boundaries erode our categories and defy our attempts to put them – and ourselves – in neat boxes.

By virtue of their intelligent behavior, these organisms are challenging our anthropocentric and brain centric paradigms. As a neurologist, I have nothing against brains – quite the opposite! – considering and learning to approach problems from other organisms is exciting. There are many ways to be a problem-solving, responsive, adaptive organism.

For example, in an iconic study, Japanese researchers created a big dish modeled on Tokyo, and placed oats on what would be the urban centers in the Greater Tokyo area. The slime mold explored this dish. Within a few hours, slime mold formed an efficient transport network between the oats that almost perfectly matched the existing Tokyo subway network.

Fungi and mycelium possess skills similar to slime mold. The lives of these organisms depend upon their being able to adapt their networks to constantly changing environments. In fact, people are now working on ways to incorporate them into computing circuits because they outperform our own human-designed algorithms for space searching.

It takes honesty and humility to recognize that fungi and slime molds can act as our teachers. Perhaps it made us feel better to invent a fancy name for this phenomenon, biomimicry, which describes how we learn and innovate based on nature's brilliance. Yes, please.

Plant life is not separate from the lives of their fungal partners. Long ago, algae from water and fungi from land joined together – with fungi acting as roots on behalf of the algae, and algae metabolizing light and carbon dioxide to offer energy-containing carbon compounds to the fungi. Fungi serve as a sort of plant mycrobiome. Yes, plants also have their own complex and diverse microbiomes, which developed over hundreds of millions of years of evolution, just as ours did.

Of course, these ecosystems engage in all sorts of different mycorrhizal relationships (*myco* from fungus, *rhiza* from root). And these networks extend beyond a single plant, because fungi are promiscuous and connect with more than one plant. The plants, too, are promiscuous, and connect with more than one fungus.

The "Wood Wide Web" describes these shared fungal networks, and plants linked together through shared fungal networks – it's a sort of social network of plants. These networks can behave in a variety of ways. Sometimes plants and fungi share resources, where carbon compounds can pass from larger plants to smaller parts as can water and other nutrients. In other systems, larger plants seem to extract excessive nutrients from the networks. In those cases, smaller plants grow better if you cut them off from the network because they're no longer having to compete in this shared pool with larger plants who have more ability to pull the bigger sink strength.

The Wood Wide Web is fascinating because it demonstrates another way that plants are connected to each other. Even bacteria can surf along these fungal hyphae and pass through inside of them, as though they're highways to navigate the obstacle course of the soil. Meanwhile, bees visit one plant, then another, and then another, which creates another shared network of interaction.

These persistent physical connections form a living web, a matrix of interaction.

Mycelial networks also help us learn about decentralized systems, decentralized organization, emergent structures, cooperation between distant parts of a network, and swarm intelligence. Just as plants have sensitive root tips that explore their environment, mycelial networks have growing tips of fungal cells to explore theirs. The "fingertips" of the mycelial network act as a sort of swarm. But then that swarm analogy breaks down quickly because all the tips connect to each other as one single network. What's mind-bending for us is the way it/they switch back and forth between singular and plural. Mycelial life blows apart our comfortable categories.

From just a fragment of mycelium, we can grow an entirely new network. And those two networks can fuse back together again at a later stage. A mycelium network can continue to propagate and even become immortal under certain conditions.

All of this forces us to ask ourselves where the individual starts and stops? Most of us would say that an individual starts and stops when that one person's skin ends, and the next person's body begins where their skin begins. But fungal life demonstrates that the story is not quite that simple. And, as we're learning, it's not so straightforward for us either.

If you aren't *you* without your microbiome – without those organisms that can change your immune system, your behavior, your emotions – when does the you (singular) become you (plural)?

More and more, we are discovering that these boundaries we once felt so sure of are actually not nearly as certain as we thought they were. We see that very clearly with mycelial networks, which constantly change the boundaries of themselves. They are fusing, creeping, shapeshifting selves. And Master Plants show us that in many ways we are, too.

RECONNECTING WITH MASTER PLANTS AS OUR KIN

We've been taught not to see aliveness in the living beings around us but rather to see objects. We've been taught that the world is a thing, and everything in it are resources and commodities. Trees and rivers, mountains and stones, deer and coyote, and mushrooms and plants are all objects. As a result, most people now feel fear of nature. Fear of the wildness of the world. Fear of our own wildness. Fear of ourselves.

Yet plants and fungi are not Other. They are our living family. They long for us. Our family members surround us and we're not getting to know them. Most of us speed by trees and plants and animals on roads and highways without acknowledging how lonely we are for each other. These beings want to be in a relationship with us, but they can't easily connect with us or teach us when we are distracted by devices, running from one place to the next, enclosed in speeding cars. The animals must venture to the borders of the forest to keep their tree kin company.

And we, too, are longing for our kin in return. We feel lonely and displaced and we hardly even realize it – we know it mainly through anxiety, addiction, depression, even autoimmunity – which are not simply a collection of symptoms but an expression of loss and longing in our bodies. We don't feel a sense of belonging because we don't have those family members, and those relationships, and the wisdom that we're missing from our greater than human kin.

This kinship is not difficult to access, but we have to show up in a certain way. All that is required is to be willing to invest in and build that relationship. Some people find that this engagement comes more naturally to them, but the skills are accessible to anybody. It simply takes practice.

When we sit in stillness with the natural world, we become more and more aware of the voices that don't speak in words.

We have been taught to be impolite to plants. It is no wonder we struggle to hear them. The ones we deign to notice are Master Plants and other loud ones – the invasive, the poisonous, the psychedelic. But we have the capacity to hear more subtle communication from quieter plants, too – beginning by seeing past our plant blindness, and simply noticing them or even noticing our longing for them.

We can cultivate our own politeness, reverence, and humility. We can, for example, recognize that pine trees have been here 700 million years and have accumulated more wisdom and experience than we have as a species that's only 1 million years old.

We can (re)learn to respect our elders.

The world is alive. Everything around us is alive. Every being in nature is a *being*, with consciousness. We are not just isolated creatures without purpose or meaning. We are connected to everything, part of a messy and magnificent web of life, which is part of a conscious universe with intelligence and aliveness that deserves our attention and appreciation. And when we do pay attention, we can't help but see that the rich relationship we're in deserves our awe, reverence, and gratitude.

The bad news – and good news – is that we can't really know these things from an expert or a book, but only from spending time with these living beings and experiencing them.

All forms of life are in constant vibratory communion. This communion happens all around us and through us, among the plants, fungi, insects, birds, soil, sun, stars, wind, and waters – all the elemental beings that carry life. This conversation vibrates through our bodies down to our very cells. We are perfectly designed to be a part of it. This is the reality of our lives. No psychedelics necessary, though they can help us remember – if we let them.

Together we and the land and the insects and the birds and animals are singing ourselves into being because the world is alive and filled with mystery, and we get to experience this magic through participation.

Some of this may not feel rational, and that's okay. Maybe it isn't. But if we become curious, we can recognize that it's not irrational but rather *nonrational*.

For those who are struggling to glimpse beyond the rational and logical, try an experiment: Pretend to be four years old and tell this as a story describing the extraordinary, nonlinear, almost magical nature of Nature. Other experiments you can try: Smile at a plant. Hug a tree (yes, a real hug). Notice how you *and the tree* feel before, during and after.

Unlearning takes practice.

And for those who can't otherwise find a way out of the role of disinterested, disconnected, objective observer, Master Plants can remind us. These teachers awaken us, sometimes gently and sometimes rather rudely, to this experience of life and aliveness. In doing so, they remind us we are never alone. Master Plants show us the sacredness of this profound thing that is both indescribably ancient and always emerging anew, and always inviting us to engage as full-fledged, participating members.

7

DOSING AND PREPARATION

I n the mushroom foraging world, there is a saying: There are *old* mushroomers and *bold* mushroomers, but there are no *old, bold* mushroomers.

Catchy, right? But also very instructive and practical.

Those who forage or work with mushrooms – psychedelic and otherwise – have long understood the necessity of cultivating respect and, dare I say, reverence in their relationship with mushrooms. This approach is not a la-di-da spiritual one; it's because they literally put their lives on the line when they consume an unfamiliar mushroom. A lack of reverence and humility – or not knowing exactly who they're dealing with – can mean the difference between poison and prize.

The "poisonous" nature of psychedelics – as well as mushrooms – demand the building of a relationship based in humility and honor.

While many commonly used psychedelic plants and fungi are not physiologically toxic, we learned in Chapter 5 that some certainly can be harmful, especially when not approached with proper caution. But beyond that, most can induce vomiting or diarrhea, and cause physical and mental responses that can include visions, disorientation, and sometimes full-on delirium that exactly mimic the body's response to toxins. A review of the scientific literature reveals papers that refer to these reactions as poisonings – occasionally due to true elevated liver or kidney enzymes or other physiological signs of toxicity – but more often due to an unexpected struggle with these known effects.

Traditionally, psychedelics have been closely associated with death – both spiritual and in some cases, physical. Not to mention that the conditions people often seek to treat with Master Plants – severe addictions, major depression, PTSD, anorexia – can have life-or-death consequences. Iboga, for example, is considered a plant ancestor that can determine whether a person is worthy of life or death. And while iboga is one of the Master Plants that can instigate death in certain vulnerable people (rarely, but it does happen), it's also thought that the comatose state iboga induces enables the initiate's soul to wander with ancestors in the land of the dead. Even iboga visions are often of dead ancestors.

The other side of the coin is that iboga can act as a powerful stimulant that activates nearly superhuman levels of physical stamina and also allow people to emerge from life-destroying addictions. Death and life, closely intertwined.

Modern society poses death and life as opposites, but that approach is new. Since ancient times, life and death have been thought to walk together hand-in-hand. Living our lives with intention prepares us for death, and remembering our eventual death helps us to live our lives with greater intensity and passion.

Accessing the support of Master Plants through journeys to the underworld and back again always requires respect and reverence before, during, and after any interaction.

What are some other considerations?

TAKING OUR MEDICINE

In the modern world, we've been taught that just because we can *take* something (I'm being both literal and figurative here), it's ours to use as we wish – be it a medication, land, a tradition, or a prayer. We've also been led to believe that we should be able to anticipate the process, the outcome, or cure.

However, as discussed in the previous two chapters, Master Plants don't play that way.

In Chapter 5, we learned that indigenous wisdom holders, who are the experts in this technology, clearly state that Master Plants can offer medicine *or* malice. What we get depends largely on us and how we engage: who we are, what we want, how we initiate contact, and what we do afterward. And even then, we rarely can anticipate exactly how any step of the experience will look. In a society that values control above all else, the surrender inherent to this process can feel challenging, to say the least.

Master Plants begin to share their wisdom and lessons the moment we enter a relationship with them. But this relationship may not start at ingestion. As we've already discussed some of the extraordinary ways Master Plants work within our brains and bodies, it should come as no surprise that their mechanisms extend beyond our usual conceptions of time and space in regards to the experience itself.

For example, most people consider their psychedelic experience to officially begin at ingestion and end when their mental state is no longer altered. Not necessarily so. As many discover, the true Master Plant experience begins long before the time of ingestion – from the first moment they enter our awareness – and continues long after. As such, conversations about psychedelic experiences focus on preparing before and integrating afterward, as well as considering set and setting during the experience itself.

The "set and setting hypothesis" holds that the effects of psychedelic drugs depend on set (personality, preparation, expectation, and intention of the person having the experience) and setting (the physical, social, and cultural environment in which the experience takes place). Set and setting are described in the scientific literature as "nondrug parameters of psychopharmacology." Yet current research suggests that the so-called nonpharmacological effects are responsible for a major part, if not the majority, of therapeutic benefits in any number of drug treatments, including psychedelics. Set and setting sound like innovative concepts in a paradigm that assumes the primary effect is derived from a pharmacological compound and its mechanism of action, yet at the same time, parsing them as though they're separate is artificial and misses a major point.

The experience surrounding Master Plants is not separate from their medicine. The experience *is* the medicine.

Preparation, integration, set and setting do not just define what we get out of a psychedelic experience – beautiful visions, a meaningful journey, healing of trauma, and so on – they help us to demonstrate who we are to the Master Plants so the Master Plants offer us the best of themselves.

Think about it this way. If we were going to meet a profound spiritual teacher, we would probably want to prepare ourselves. We'd think about how to present ourselves respectfully and appropriately. We might select a gift to bring. We might attempt to learn protocol for addressing them, to avoid offending them or making a faux pas. We'd probably spend time reading or listening to their words in advance. We would want to demonstrate to them that we were worthy of the experience, of any wisdom, lessons, words, or attention the teacher might offer us. We would likely say thank you and even perhaps write words of thanks afterward to show our gratitude and appreciation.

Similarly, inviting the medicine rather than their malice of Master Plants, as discussed in Chapter 5, requires us to come to the relationship in a respectful, considered, considerate way. While we are not always in control of how we experience the Master Plant (discussed in more detail in Chapter 8), we have a choice in how we approach Master Plants, certain parameters around our experience, and how we integrate afterward.

Moreover, engaging with medicine rather than malice does not refer only to avoiding a "bad trip." We'll get to that. Rather, as in any relationship, our agency resides in the way we show up for others and how we navigate interactions: being considerate in what we say and do; operating with generosity, humility, and respect; expressing gratitude; treating them and their people as our kin; and navigating challenges with extreme care whenever they arise.

It sounds simple. But in reality, those of us who have been raised in the ways of the Global North may find ourselves at a profound disadvantage because we may not have been taught how to operate from the approach of right relationship, particularly when it comes to flora, fauna, or fungi, and the people and land that support them.

Most of us live in a transactional society with transactional relationships. People pay money and anticipate excellent service in return; not surprisingly, they expect interactions with Master Plants to follow suit. Yet this isn't how Master Plants operate.

We can pay money for what we consider the very best of everything, and it doesn't mean the subjective experience of Master Plants will be wonderful. And that's partly because money alone isn't enough to demonstrate respect, reverence, and reciprocity in this setting.

To be clear, I do not believe that difficult psychedelic experiences always result from a lack of respect or appropriate preparation – far from it. But at a minimum, preparatory conversations of set and setting go far beyond our sitter, music selection, whether we have comfy blankets and crystals, and even our intentions or expectations.

We have much more to consider.

WHAT MAKES A POISON MEDICINE AND MEDICINE A POISON?

Let's start with dose.

Sixteenth-century healer Paracelsus famously distinguished poison and cure by dose:

"In all things there is a poison, and there is nothing without poison. It depends only upon the dose whether a poison is a poison or not."

This aligns with the ambiguity of the first known uses of the term *pharmakon*, from which we get the words *pharmacy, pharmaceutics,* and *pharmacology.* In ancient Greek, *pharmakon* can refer to a remedy or a poison.

Remember when we talked about hormesis in Chapter 6? Phytochemicals are compounds made by plants that can act as small poisons, and that make us stronger on a cellular level. They are just some of many stressors that could be toxic or fatal in larger (or too frequent) amounts but are therapeutic and sometimes even necessary in small quantities. Another example is fasting. Many studies indicate that intermittent fasting for sixteen hours a day or even for up to days can be beneficial from time to time. Fasting for a month, however, depletes us – that's called starvation. Similarly, exercise in moderate amounts strengthens us in ways that allow us to go to occasional extremes; running a marathon every day would be damaging.

Hormesis can even translate to ecological health. Forest fires are terrifying and destructive, for example, and can decimate thousands or even millions of acres of wildlife. Yet within controlled areas, forest fires can be necessary to ignite new growth by accelerating the transformation of rotting trees to carbon matter, clearing brush to allow more light through to the forest floor, and activating certain seeds for trees that can only sprout after the immersive high heat of a fire.

What appears to be damaging or destructive in the moment may be revitalizing and generative in the long run.

Poisons – and psychedelics – have gotten a bad rap mostly because, for all of our supposed technological advancements, modern society still hasn't mastered nuance. From a more black-and-white perspective, a compound is either a poison or not. And yet one of the most common causes of poisoning is from over-the-counter and prescription medications in doses that are higher than tolerated.

Don't get me wrong – I'm not arguing that poisons don't exist or that what we consider poisons can't be very dangerous. Certain substances can alter us, sometimes permanently, and even kill us under certain circumstances. But often, there are two sides to the coin. Many lifesaving medications were derived from poisonous plants– the cardiac medication digitalis comes from foxglove, the breast cancer therapeutic Taxol from the Yew tree, even poisonous venoms from animals have become popular pharmaceuticals. In other words, a poison can serve as a powerful medicine under the right circumstances.

As it happens, Master Plants have long been accused of being "poisons" because of the potent way they affect us – and thus have gotten reputations for being extremely dangerous.

And in a sense, Master Plants have the potential to be dangerous in the sense that they alter us in profound ways. They are powerful. And as with anything powerful, most of them have the capacity to cause harm under certain circumstances – physically, mentally, emotionally, or spiritually. As much as we may see their incredible potential and want to spotlight only their benefits, it does no one any good to ignore this important truth. At any given moment, not everyone needs to engage with power of this sort, not everyone wants to engage, and not everyone should engage. And to that end, those needs and wants can change over the course of our lifetimes.

Still, when we come at the right time and in the right way – as beginners who want to learn – Master Plants absolutely have the profound capacity to alter us for the better.

THE DOSE MAKES THE MEDICINE

My inquiry around ways to engage with the Master Plants grew when people began to approach me with interest in consuming them, whether to microdose or macrodose. What I found fascinating was that from the moment they felt the call of these plants, their lives already started to change. Big things began to happen for them – sudden realizations, startling epiphanies, and new life events – that might normally follow Master Plant experiences. But these changes began before they'd ever ingested anything. It turned out that ingesting medicine to have mystical experiences was not always required as the only avenue for the plants to offer their medicine to us.

This understanding became more evident to me as I began to grow many of these plants in my own home, tended them, learned about them, and learned from them daily. I've discovered that each plant has a unique personality, vibration, and set of needs. Tending them daily has changed me. Growing Master Plants has become a potent way of experiencing their medicine.

According to a more indigenous, mystical paradigm, the gifts we receive from Master Plants can present from the moment we've entered into a relationship with the spirit of the plant. Our spirit is communing with their spirit, with no big ingestion or experience necessary.

Understanding this as a way to experience plant medicine spoke to me more so because I have long treated those who are very sensitive – the "canaries in the coal mine." Some of these people, I've discovered, perceive tiny doses in exceptionally profound ways – whether due to lower sensory or metabolic/detoxification thresholds; highly sensitive or reactive nervous systems; or disrupted microbiomes or genetic variations. Some of us may naturally produce higher levels of our own DMT, or "endogenous entheogens."

As it happens, various communities have different traditions regarding dosing. In many Peruvian ayahuasca ceremonies, for example, larger quantities of ayahuasca brew are consumed, inducing nausea and vomiting. On the other hand, some indigenous Ecuadorian vegetalistas drink significantly smaller doses by comparison and regard hours of induced purging with disgust. "Large quantities are not necessary for you to have visions or learn the wisdom of the plants," they said to me.

Philosophies and customs around combining plants vary as well. The blend of plants in a given brew may differ widely, depending on the community, plant varieties available in the area, and the lineage. Some healers may consider particular blends blasphemous or insulting to the Master Plant, whereas others may have specific traditions around mixing.

Just as no one spiritual teacher resonates with everyone, psychedelics are by no means one size fits all. Throughout history, they've always belonged to particular people in particular places with particular lineages that include a Master Plant (sometimes more than one). In the more disembodied, displaced reality of the moment, many of us have been removed from that type of lineage and connection. As a result, we are only at the very beginning of exploring which plant, dose and approach will best serve any given individual or set of individuals.

And as psychedelic tourism grows more and more, we must also consider what will happen to Master Plants like ayahuasca, San Pedro, and many others that may not be meant to be consumed en masse by millions of people repeatedly and endlessly without allowing for the plants to replenish. We are on our way to having ayahuasca farms, San Pedro fields, or psilocybe mushroom growing facilities, not to mention synthetic production of the pharmaceutical molecules we've discussed. Many wonder whether this approach is a good or bad one.

The question is: How can we come into right relationship with these Master Plants as they become further commoditized?

MACRODOSING – FIREWORKS AND CANNONBALLS

Most people hear the word psychedelics and automatically think of what's referred to as peak experiences or "tripping" – experiencing profoundly altered reality, visual or auditory hallucinations, and generally being out of commission for the duration. And most people think that's the only way psychedelics "work."

I call these the "fireworks and cannonballs" experiences. Many people seek those in particular, whether for medicinal, spiritual, or recreational reasons. And indeed, a growing field of research is showing that in the context of appropriate therapeutic support before, during, and after, full-on psychedelic experiences can be profoundly transformative and healing, particularly for people in struggle of some kind.

The terms *peak* and *mystical experience*, used in psychedelic science for nearly sixty years, have been sought after since the dawn of civilization. Humans are thought to be wired for meaning-making experiences of a spiritual nature. They exist at the core of the major religious traditions and indigenous lineages. These experiences can be characterized by a sense of sacredness, awe, humility, wonder, deeply-felt positive moods such as love and bliss, a feeling of unity, and a perception of all things being interconnected or that everything is one.

One powerful feature can be a sense of transcendence. People can have a sense of transcending time and space as we know it, and going beyond the body as we normally experience it. For the person whose body is a source of suffering, whether because of body image or because their body is failing and will soon stop working, this insight that they are more than their body can be transformative. People with terminal cancer describe the experience of seeing that they are more than their cancer, for example. Connecting to the part of themselves that is more enduring, whether soul or spirit or consciousness, can ease their physical, mental, and spiritual anguish as they approach one of the most important transitions of their existence.

As we previously discussed in Chapter 5, taking our default mode network (DMN) offline for a period of time can affect us in a very profound, lasting way. Remember how predictive coding means we constantly apply our lens from the past to each new situation? Much of the time, we only really see a few select details of what's happening in the present moment.

Macrodosing means the dose ingested is large enough to disrupt those old narratives, sometimes very suddenly and profoundly. In ways that may or may not be clear in the moment of the journey, we can have a window into ourselves as we really are underneath all of our experiences, as opposed to what we're carrying with us and projecting onto the here and now.

To be clear, just because these experiences are described as "peak" or "mystical" doesn't automatically make them easy. Quite the opposite. Often called ten years of therapy in five hours, these journeys can be productive, meaningful, and still very challenging. Remember, the DMN also suppresses old memories and emotions like grief and anger. So, when psychedelics take the DMN offline, strong feelings and old memories – ones we've shoved down, compartmentalized, or told ourselves we've "dealt with" but haven't – may arise.

Yikes.

Important, but not always fun.

In a macrodosing experience, we may suddenly see, feel, and experience things we don't usually see or feel or experience about ourselves, our lives, our relationships, the world, and reality itself – and these visions can feel very real and intense. Encountering our interior or our shadow self, the parts we don't show to others or even ourselves, can feel as though we are holding a mirror up to ourselves at a level of uncomfortable detail and truth. At the same time, it's sometimes very necessary to highlight these parts of ourselves because, more often than not, our hidden parts can worsen or even create problems in our lives without our ever realizing it. Sometimes we recognize how we're disempowering or damaging ourselves but feel at a loss as to how to disrupt our patterns. A psychedelic journey can shine a spotlight onto these parts of ourselves, usually because we have demonstrated that we're in some way ready to see – and hopefully address – what we need to address in ourselves.

Visions can also be frightening for other reasons, including seeing snakes, jaguars, or other fierce creatures that are real or imaginary. Some people experience their own death during a journey. With support during and integration afterward, these experiences may become meaningful. It's also important to know that sometimes they do not. Some people experience journeys that are traumatizing or retraumatizing. While people who have had mystical experiences ranked as one of the top five most meaningful experiences of their lives, those who had extremely frightening experiences ranked them as some of the most difficult experiences of their lives.

No official numbers exist to date, but some facilitators have described a range between 3 and 5 percent of the population with almost no response to any dose they receive. The mechanism is unclear at this time. Their receptors may be blunted from long-term use of SSRIs, or perhaps they struggle to let go of control. It simply may not be the right time. Some may decide to pursue working with other Master Plants or psychedelic compounds that work by different mechanisms; others may do additional healing work and try again at a later time. Paradoxically, sometimes these people benefit most in that moment from microdosing or quantum dosing to cultivate that relationship gently. For some, less can be more.

Contraindications for Macrodosing

Certain physical or mental conditions, including cardiac, renal, liver conditions, or a personal or family history of psychosis, might preclude a person from safely engaging in a macrodosing experience, depending on the Master Plant. Certain Master Plants, like iboga or ayahuasca, come with more contraindications than others, like psilocybe mushrooms.

Master Plant experiences may require stopping certain common medications that can cause dangerous interactions, at least for a period of time.

As a result, for people with health or mental health conditions, this decision is best made in partnership with a psychedelics-informed healthcare professional to ensure safety and the most beneficial experience and outcome possible.

Support during the experience is strongly recommended, ideally with someone professionally trained and experienced. Until such professionals are covered by insurance or are affordable, people may choose trip sitters or attend ceremonies of various sorts. Proceed with caution always.

In all cases, whether in a hospital, clinic, ceremony or with a guide, ask questions and always listen to red flags or feelings of someone or something being off, even if there's no apparent reason why. Master Plant experiences can render us tremendously vulnerable, and we should be in an environment where we feel absolutely safe and comfortable in every way possible.

MICRODOSING – WHEN LESS IS MORE

As discussed, macrodosing has not been the only way people have historically engaged with Master Plants. The customs among indigenous communities vary widely and may include different dose levels as medicine and in ceremony – medicinal, aphrodisiac, and shamanic. Shamanic dosing describes a larger amount that profoundly alters all but the most expert healer, taking that person entirely offline and immersing them into non-ordinary reality, sometimes for many hours. Aphrodisiac dosing is mildly altering but allows a person to function. Medicinal dosing is most similar to what we'd call microdosing, and indeed could even be applied topically to address legitimate medical concerns.

Among certain communities, only the healer ingests the medicine in a significant "shamanic" quantity, which allows them to see inside the person needing healing. Sometimes, the person in need of healing may ingest a small amount of the plant, or even none at all, and still fully experience the necessary healing.

Microdosing describes ingesting a subthreshold dose of psychedelics (or mushrooms that are non-psychedelic, or any medicine). Subthreshold means that the dose will not alter us in any profound way that would prevent us from operating in our daily lives. In the case of psychedelic medicines, regular subthreshold are being explored as a way to enhance cognition; boost physical energy; promote emotional balance; treat anxiety, depression, OCD, and addiction; and even address medical conditions like chronic pain, autoimmunity, asthma, dementia, ADHD, or autism.

Psychedelic microdosing was popularized by Silicon Valley

professionals as a way to get to that next level, become more creative, and think outside the box. And in fact, growing research is beginning to show that this approach may offer that and much more.

Those who regard Master Plants as neurochemical compounds that only impart dose-dependent effects often can get stuck in the "more is more" perspective. Yet early research indicates that like tiny poisons that make us stronger, microdosing may also offer hormetic effects. As emergent systems, our complex physiology often responds best to a gentle nudge rather than the blow of a sledgehammer. This should surprise no one, but asks that we expand our perspective beyond the linear, man-as-machine model.

Indeed, growing evidence indicates that microdosing may prove to be more effective for some conditions than macrodosing. For example, animal models show that microdoses confer anti-inflammatory effects. Dosing small amounts over time may offer cumulative benefits that larger doses do not. For example, researchers are finding a profound shift in T-helper cell recruitment, eosinophilia, and mucus production in the lungs of asthmatics with microdoses of psychedelics. Microdoses also can benefit mood, cognition, sleep, pain, autoimmunity, and allergy. This approach still seems to facilitate neuroplasticity in gentle ways over time.

An average macrodose might be between 1 and 5 grams of psilocybes, for example. A microdose might divide that dose up over 10 or 20 (or even more) doses, depending on the starting amount and the individual. The microdose might be taken once every 3 days or so, or for a few days in a row, and then off for a few days. Then that dosing could continue over a month, a few months, or longer.

The reason to space microdosing beyond daily is to prevent building tolerance, which can reduce their benefit. Some people microdose every day, but ultimately, might not experience the full impact and potential transformation without at least occasional "vacations" for a week or several days periodically. On the other hand, some people who microdosed daily for long periods have reported feeling chronically ungrounded or unsettled.

Many people find they feel the effects most potently not the day they ingest their microdose but the next day. They report feeling more productive, creative, or even mildly euphoric. The most potent shifts can also be cumulative over the full span of dosing, whether over weeks or months. Allowing spacing between doses also offer opportunities to tune in and notice the shifts.

For some, microdosing can feel very subtle, sometimes overly so. For others, the shifts are clear – lower anxiety, greater clarity, more creativity, an enhanced sense of wonder and awe, and even mild euphoria. People have reported they feel more motivated to take better care of themselves – eat better, drink more water, exercise more, and less need to rely on other substances to cope. In addition, people have described feeling less awkward, more social and less hard on themselves. Others have reported successfully weaning off psychiatric medications for depression with the help of their mental health professionals. On the other hand, a small percentage of people report that microdosing provoked feelings of greater anxiety rather than calm.

Most importantly, people find microdosing to be transformational but at the same time gentle. The journey happens more quietly, over months. The intention and outcome can still be to experience healing or growth but with more nuance and softness; microdosing can still be effective in terms of insight, quiet revelation, and shifts. For some people – especially those who are destabilized, who struggle with a dysregulated nervous system, who are exceptionally sensitive neurochemically, or who have complicated health or mental health issues or are on otherwise contraindicated pharmaceuticals – find microdosing offers deep healing that feels less risky or traumatic to their systems. They say microdosing allows them to get in touch with how they feel on a subtle level rather than in the midst of big ups and downs of a more intense journey.

Some people feel more comfortable working toward a macrodosing experiences. Perhaps they've already had a profound ego death experience that's taken them out of their comfort zone or experienced potent surrender in some way. In those cases, engaging with quantum dosing or microdosing for integration and processing can be meaningful. Then, if still needed, they can engage in a macrodosing experience.

A growing number of studies on microdosing in humans shows benefit, though to date much of it catalogues people self-reporting on their microdose experiences. The research is largely limited by legal parameters around studying even small doses of psychedelics taken outside of an academic center. Legal authorities and ethics boards demand a carefully controlled setting that people remain throughout the duration of the microdosing. A macrodosing experience has a clear beginning and end that can easily happen in a medical center over a day (excluding follow-up). Microdosing, on the other hand, must take place over weeks or months, and thus cannot be easily contained in a medical setting for the duration.

Imagine having to go to a clinical setting like a hospital every two or three days and sit there for eight hours while microdosing for a month or more – that would be a pretty tough sell to participants! As such, the microdosing research to date in humans remains under-explored. Keep an eye out for carefully controlled studies focusing on specific populations, as for people with ADHD.

Stacking describes combinations of different Master Plants, botanicals or other compounds or nutrients that may amplify overall benefit. One "stack" touted by Paul Stamets for dementia includes psilocybin-containing mushrooms in microdose, lion's mane mycelium, and niacin. Together, this combination is being explored to stabilize or even reverse dementia symptoms.

Some researchers (and others) have expressed concern that the reported benefits of microdosing reflect the placebo effect only. Is it possible that the placebo effect plays some role in these studies?

Perhaps. On the one hand, so what? Placebo does not mean a treatment is ineffective, but that the treatment instigates a profound healing mechanism not measurable with our current approaches. Our concept of placebo requires a significant recalibration.

On the other hand, growing studies show promise for microdosing beyond placebo. Ultimately, we may have to have design studies that measure the more nuanced, nonlinear benefits of Master Plants. For example, studies down the road could take under consideration the indigenous perspective that holds that the spirit of the plant connecting to our own, and determine how plants (and synthetic psychedelics) perform depending on how they're grown, collected or prepared, or taken in a more ceremonial environment.

For the significant number of people who may not (or not yet) be interested in having fireworks and cannonball experiences, but do want to form a relationship with Master Plants to gain healing or insight...engaging with Master Plants through microdosing may be a gentle way to begin that process. The outcomes can include transformations, insight into traumatic experiences, greater resilience, or improvement of physical or mental health issues.

Considerations for Microdosing

Microdosing is sub-psychedelic, which means we can operate as usual while microdosing – go to work, take care of kids, drive a car – without being compromised. However, as with any new therapeutic, we always want to ensure that our first experience is low stakes, without too many activities or heavy demands.

It's important to note that each person's threshold for the psychedelic effect of a microdose can vary based on any number of parameters. One person's tiny microdose is another person's macrodose. It's therefore wise to first engage with microdosing on a day when we can tune in to ourselves.

Microdosing can also soften boundaries. For those who work with clients or patients or who need to be really "on" or in "killer" mode, prepare for the possibility of feeling more open-hearted. Some people feel softer or less guarded. If that could pose a problem in a professional or personal setting, keep that in mind around deciding when to microdose.

To date, most microdose literature is in people who engaged with psilocybe mushrooms. For those who can legally access them, it's important to note that the many strains and cultivars all can have different potency and impact beyond simple milligrams in weight. Each strain can exhibit different personality and qualities. Keep in mind they may also be affected by the person who grows the mushroom and prepares the dose.

Beyond the esoteric, keep in mind that plants and mushrooms are not pharmaceuticals –these living beings are not any more standardized than we are, nor are they meant to be. Even before considering dose, or how the plant was harvested, or any ceremonial aspects, remember that physiological variations exist in nature. Even the soil – or in the case of psilocybe mushrooms, the quality of cow dung (including whether the cow is receiving nutritional supplementation) – influences the potency of the mushrooms. Consider how complex the actions of flora, fauna, or fungi may be as compared to any pharmaceutical and then consider how complex our bodies are – how varied our neurochemistry is, our epigenetics, our microbiome, our nutritional status, our emotional landscape and nervous system regulation.

Master Plants cannot be absolutely predictable. What's more, we shouldn't want them to be. Master Plants are dynamic and wild, which is part of what makes their healing so powerful.

QUANTUM DOSING – BRINGING EXTRAORDINARY INTO THE ORDINARY

What makes a medicine a medicine, and where does the medicine of the plant reside? As discussed, modern science would point to the chemical compounds. But as we're seeing, the story is far more complex and nonlinear when it comes to Master Plants.

Quantum dosing is a way to experience the medicine of Master Plants vibrationally, without ingesting the actual plants.

This concept is not new.

We've already explored that wisdom holders from indigenous nations view both the medicine of the plants and how they cure illness through a very different lens than that of modern researchers. For them, medicine and healing come from the Mother of the Plant, also referred to as the plant's spirit.

All plants oscillate in measurable ways, which creates a kind of music. To date, oscillations in plants have mostly been disregarded by plant researchers, treated as inconvenient "noise" or interference. Yet sonic transmissions of plants are just as fundamental a communicatory expression as the complex chemical compounds they craft that we accept as being "medicine." They are part of an encyclopedia of plant knowledge and communication that we can access under the right circumstances.

For the ayahuasqueros and others, this music is thought to be no less potent than ingesting the plants themselves; in fact, many consider these medicine songs transmitted to them by plants to be equal or greater in power than imbibing Master Plants in physical form. They see them as a fundamental avenue to profound healing without ingesting plant material at all. Not coincidentally, the one who conducts the ceremony around Master Plants is often called Maestro.

As such, quantum dosing takes place in traditional settings through this music, which is thought to be vibrational transmissions from the Mother of that Master Plant. As one example, the Quechua word for this vibrational medicine is *icaro*, which derives from the word for "to blow."

Ícaros are the vibrations of the plant made manifest, transmitted through the healer or vegetalista working with Master Plants in the form of music. These chants are sung or whistled, especially during ayahuasca ceremonies. To be clear, they are not composed by the Maestro, but are considered to be a gift given by the Master Plants to the healer over intensive weeks or months spent training together, known as *dietas*. These ícaros serve different functions at the start, the middle, and the end of a ceremony with Master Plants – to provoke visions, to encourage release and purges, and to return to the physical body. Different ícaros are also thought to invite other plants or animal helpers, protection, and angels.

In the words of the indigenous shaman and artist Pablo

Amaringo: "The ícaro is the sound of the universe, planets, stars, comets, and supernovas. Everything is created by music, by vibration, by sound. When the celestial spirits enlighten us with their wisdom, we receive the ability to sing ícaros and we become part of a divine choir. Music is universal, and we are made of primordial vibration. Ícaros are the music of creation."

The oscillations of Master Plants can imprint into liquid as well, and be consumed. Ingesting these in the form of Quantum Drops are another way to experience quantum dosing. This approach invites Master Plants to become creative partners in the ceremonial experience, sharing their "oscillations" through their songs. This process results in vibrational medicine, made together with plants that tended to with profound care and attention and are never harvested for ingestion. In appreciation for this care, the Master Plants infuse the drops with this ceremonial relationship in the form of sonic medicine.

Quantum dosing is vibrational and, therefore, legal and safe for people who are highly sensitive, sober, pregnant, or have other medical or pharmaceutical contraindications preventing them from larger doses of psychedelics. This approach also can help prepare for or integrate a ceremony, and also serve as an option to partake for those who otherwise cannot or don't feel attracted to engaging with larger doses.

Master Plants can share their medicine and teachings in ways that don't overuse them or turn them into pharmaceuticals or "things." Growing Master Plants and tending them, engaging with their seeds, and even creating or wearing artistic depictions of them are all ways to experience gifts of these plants in quantum doses.

Skepticism may prevent some people from engaging with this modality, but consider: One of our greatest challenges in life is not just to access the spiritual, symbolic, or cosmic, but to incorporate those transmissions and lessons into our daily lives. I often hear people share that they feel transcended, but can only maintain that feeling as long as they don't have to deal with anyone else, like their kids.

That's the tricky part.

Most people macrodose to unequivocally catapult themselves out of linear reality, whether for healing, wisdom, beauty, transcendence, or escape. While macrodosing offers profound pattern interrupts on a fairly reliable basis, a subsequent plant of action after a journey may not be clear or easy. Sometimes Plant Teachers do all of this work for us, but more often they do not.

Quantum dosing of all kinds supports us through the tremendously challenging task of translating the nonlinear or ceremonial into practical actions and ways of being in the world. They help us integrate Master Plant experiences – including our expectations – into the reality of daily life. They help us cultivate intimacy with the ancient plant wisdom, with ceremony, with the sacred, and with the non-ordinary.

In other words, quantum dosing allows us to bring the extraordinary into the ordinary on a daily basis. Deepening our relationship with Master Plant wisdom enables us to cultivate richer relationship with ourselves, each other, and all living beings by enhancing within us a sense of greater awareness, presence, and aliveness.

WHO COULD BENEFIT FROM MASTER PLANTS?

Master Plants offer the possibility of significant improvement for people suffering from medical or mental health conditions that have not responded well to conventional and even integrative approaches. Some of those conditions include major depression, PTSD, OCD, addiction, eating disorders, traumatic brain injury, and the depression and anxiety experienced by people with terminal illnesses like cancer. Studies are underway to explore the benefit for conditions like Alzheimer's, Parkinson's, ALS, bipolar disorder, autism, ADHD, asthma, and chronic pain conditions. Also, many people may benefit who do not qualify for an official diagnosis, but are struggling. Diagnoses may serve a purpose, but are also artificial and limiting, and should never become a barrier to receiving treatment.

Still, Master Plants may not be for everyone at any given moment. Not everyone needs them or will benefit from them in any dose at a given juncture of their lives. There's no need to consume Master Plants just because they sound good, or everyone says it's the "right thing" to do.

When we feel that call, however, it's worthwhile to research, investigate, and really listen.

One of my ethnobotany teachers believes that plants and humans can fall in love and each release "chemicals of love" that change both parties. And remember, transformation begins simply by pursuing the relationship. Consider this as any relationship in which we feel magnetized: "Ooh, I noticed someone over there. I feel attracted to them, and want to know them better." Simply based on that attraction, we may begin to shift how we behave, take care of ourselves, and make changes in our lives (hopefully for the better).

When we feel drawn to a Master Plant – we are drawn to their consciousness, personality, lineage and wisdom. The relationship is beginning. We are forming an alliance. We are considering falling in love.

Then we start releasing certain endorphins and experiencing other hormonal shifts that change our bodies exactly as though we've entered a new, scintillating relationship. Again, the transformation begins long before – and sometimes without – ingesting the Master Plant.

GUIDANCE: YOU DON'T HAVE TO DO IT ALONE

Whatever the dose we're engaging with, a coach, guide or therapist can hold us through the process and be a really important and meaningful part of the overall journey. Before, during, and after, that guidance can help us see what might otherwise not be apparent, offer a container for our reflections and awakening, and facilitate integration.

In the right setting, coaching can facilitate the process of learning to squeeze the juice not just out of the Master Plant experience, but also of our lives. We may not even realize how many opportunities – for growth, beauty, joy, and success – pass us by because we're not in the right mindset (or heart-space) to detect or appreciate them.

Coaching offers us an opportunity for support through this spiritual journey. A major lesson of Master Plants is that we don't need to do everything all by ourselves. Life is much better when we have help, support, and guidance. As someone who trains coaches and guides, the goal first and foremost should be to hold space non-judgmentally and without expectation, create a sense of safety, and facilitate our ability to tap into the inner and outer support that we may not recognize. A guide can hold a light for us while we're walking through the dark, so we can find our way to a life of greater purpose, meaning, and joy.

Working with guides for a macrodosing experience begins with vetting them. Review their training, experience, reputation, and most importantly, philosophy, approach and ground rules. Don't be seduced by notoriety or accolades – as with healthcare providers, we don't necessarily need the best of the best; we need the best person for us. A person's bedside manner, personality, and ability to answer questions openly and without defensiveness all matter. Ensure they easily agree to boundaries around touch, dosing, and any sensitive topics. Feeling respected and heard in a preparatory conversation with a guide is a good predictor of feeling respected and heard during a journey.

Cultural competency is another important consideration. For example, one guide decorated the space with Hindu statues, which a Hindu client found tremendously disrespectful. One person's spiritual décor can be a show of disrespect to another person's sacred deity. Sometimes having a guide with similar experiences or background can feel valuable, and less necessary at other times. For those navigating racial or religious trauma, or sexual or birth trauma, for example, a guide who is fluent in or at least comfortable around those issues can make all the difference.

Especially because guides can be costly, many people opt for experiences in a group setting. Obviously, young people in particular have long experienced psychedelics together in groups. Being potentially vulnerable and compromised with other people in a similar position can carry any number of additional considerations and safety concerns, but can also offer benefits. Being in circle is part of a longstanding tradition, as are experiences of revelry and celebration. Many people describe deep and positive transformation in such settings.

As always, preparation and ground rules are paramount. And again, integration after an experience matters. An online or in person group experienced with psychedelics can make all the difference in a smoother and more successful integration.

If any red flags arise at all, attend to them. Becoming familiar with our inner voice – and listening! – is a critical part of this process. We should never force an experience that doesn't feel right. Having a deep sense that it's the right time, place *and* guide is paramount.

PREPARATION FOR A MASTER PLANT EXPERIENCE

Though no amount of planning gives us absolute control over the quality or outcome of an experience, the process of preparation is one way for us to exercise agency. Preparation begins by asking ourselves if the time is right for a journey, whether it's the first time, or the second, or the hundredth time. What is the motivation or expectation, if any?

Feel into whether an experience is aligned *at this time*.

Oftentimes a particular Master Plant may call to us, and it's worth spending time doing a deep dive to learn about that plant, the place where they have been traditionally grown, and who the wisdom keepers have been for that plant. Is the plant endangered or overharvested? What might be an offering to the plant, the place, and the wisdom keepers that could be meaningful and supportive for them?

Consider legality: Is the plant legal or are you planning to travel to a place that sanctions journeying with that plant?

Consider the experience itself: Which feels more aligned - a clinical or research setting, or a ceremonial one? Being in a group setting or 1:1? What qualities are most important in a guide, and how can we best vet them? Where is the Master Plant being sourced, how will the medicine be prepared, and in which combinations? Will they be tested to ensure no contaminants or additives?

Ideally, anyone planning a Master Plant journey will prepare physically, mentally, emotionally, and spiritually.

Physical preparation is critical but often undervalued.

As mentioned in Chapter 5, traditionally people change their diet in advance of certain Master Plants like ayahuasca – no salt, no spices, no sugar, no fats, no beef or pork, no fermented foods or drinks. This diet may begin two weeks to a month in advance and would continue through the experience(s), which can last days or weeks, and continue sometimes for up to a week or two after. Some may even water fast for several days in advance or in between experiences if they are doing a series of journeys.

Abstaining from mind-altering plants or substances such as alcohol, cigarettes, cannabis, and others is a common practice before ceremony. Although tobacco may be used as a sacred Master Plant, most medicos are clear that the ones that are sold as cigarettes do not qualify. Oh, and no sex. Abstaining for days or weeks before and after is another common way to prepare the body.

At the cutting edge of preparation and integration is preparing and supporting the gut microbiome in advance of an experience to be most receptive to the Master Plant. While we need not bring a Type A approach to this experience, Master Plants interact with our bodies by way of our gut, microbiome and serotonin system when ingested. These factors likely impact the experience itself as well as longer-term outcomes on physical and mental health.

Some studies have measured microbial diversity in the stool of indigenous people in the Amazon, which not surprisingly showed exponentially greater diversity than any stool from so-called modern society. Most of our lifestyles lack sufficient amounts of fresh food, sleep, sunshine and time in nature, and have been subject to antibiotics and other exposures that negatively impact microbiome. Our inner terrain is thus not remotely comparable to those in traditional communities that engage with Master Plants. Burgeoning research suggests that building microbial diversity with diet, herbs and other means may play a critical role in health outcomes during and after psychedelic Master Plants.

Supporting detoxification through practices like sauna, limited fasting, and even red-light therapy can optimize processing alkaloids and other components of the Master Plant.

Supplements that support mitochondrial and neurological metabolism can be helpful, so that the experience itself can allow for more resilience during and less depletion after. Some of these include but are not limited to B complex, L-carnitine, alpha lipoic acid, and CoQ10.

Physical preparation

- Diet
- Nutrients
- Probiotics
- Sauna
- Fasting
- Abstaining from sex (in some traditions)
- Medication vacation (with medical supervision)
- Grounding
- Quantum dosing

Mental Preparation

- Research

- Planning
- Nervous system regulation practices like humming, chanting, gargling, singing, embodiment

Emotional Preparation

- Noticing and accepting emotions that present themselves rather than suppressing them
- Journaling
- Creative practice
- Embodiment practices to tune in to the way emotions express themselves in the body

Spiritual Preparation

- Meditation
- Building an altar
- Dream journals
- Ancestor practices
- Nature walks
- Earthing

CONSIDERING SET AND SETTING

Famed LSD guru Timothy Leary once argued that 99 percent of the effects of psychedelics are set- and setting-dependent.

Setting refers to the physical environment of the experience: in a clinical setting, during a ceremony, in a bedroom, or at a festival. Setting includes music, light, pillows, candles, eye covers, talismans, or anything physically in the space at the start of a journey. Some other basic preparations can include taking care of overdue paperwork, cleaning our rooms, washing dishes, and decluttering. During an experience, keep in mind shifting the setting can sometimes shift the quality of an experience.

Set is more nuanced and has to do with personality and mental state when entering into the experience. Leary divided the set into two subcategories – long-range and immediate. Immediate set includes attitude and expectations. Long-range set has to do with the established characteristics of "the kind of person you are – your fears, desires, conflicts, guilts, secret passions," as well as the environment and society that we return to afterward.

Per Leary, "Session preparation is of critical importance in determining how the experience unfolds. People tend naturally to impose their personal and social game perspectives on any new situation. Careful thought should precede the session to prevent narrow sets being imposed." In other words, Master Plants depend largely on the person having the experience – personality, life experiences, expectations, and willingness to engage with self-knowledge through psychotherapy or spiritual practice.

Master Plants have no single effect that recurs with every person or across all societies. What they have in common is that they dissolve boundaries by way of ego dissolution, depersonalization, and a sense of cosmic unity. They can create hyper-associations – leading to a sense of re-enchantment through the discovery of synchronicities, synesthesia, novel creativity, and innovation (and, at the extreme, paranoia and magical thinking).

No matter the quality of the experience, intensity is considered an essential part of what makes an experience psychedelic. Colors are brighter, sounds more resonant, revelations more miraculous, emotions more potent, and relationships – especially with nature – enhanced.

Most of all, they create a sense of meaning and significance. People are given the capacity to see meaning in what's in their minds with a perspective and level of detail they didn't previously recognize.

For two-thirds of the people who have had psychedelic experiences in a therapeutic setting, for instance, they regard it as the single most meaningful experience of their lives, or in the top five most meaningful experiences. Simply put, psychedelics can reliably elicit subjectively meaningful experiences.

Not surprisingly, there's another side to this. A group of Johns Hopkins researchers conducted an online survey of almost two thousand people who had had a difficult experience with psilocybe mushrooms. Of this group, only 2 percent of the respondents took them in a setting that resembled a controlled clinical environment. For 39 percent of the respondents, the "bad trip" ranked among the top five most challenging experiences of their lifetime.

By definition, revelation can be ecstatic or terrifying – especially depending on the context and variables. By amplifying previously buried emotions and memories, people are forced to confront their inner demons – which can then instigate change in their own lives.

The society we live in leaves us woefully unprepared to confront and alchemize our own trauma, dark sides, never mind the darkness of the world. Our primary treatment for people struggling to deal with their pain is to pathologize it and medicate it away. This approach may feel easier in the short run, as coming face to face with the darkest, most terrifying parts can be indescribably difficult. Yet when we have avoided these painful parts of ourselves for years or decades, and haven't been prepared to encounter them face-to-face, they may become even more overwhelming. Often, this is the very material we will encounter in a Master Plant Experience.

There's no real way to map out exactly what will present during the experience itself. We confront whatever arises and respond to what is needed in the moment. Anything can happen. Some people may feel excitement; most people find that this entry into deeply unknown terrain elicits fear and anxiety. People may shake, have diarrhea, or feel nauseated and throw up. They could struggle with difficult memories that ultimately integrate and move them into a greater sense of wholeness. They could have a moment of connecting to the cosmos or the divine, or go to really dark places because there's something that they need to integrate there. Some people encounter entities of various kinds. All of this is normal.

Obviously, not everybody has a joyful experience. Sometimes people struggle for the entire time. They can come in with expectations like "I want my twenty years of depression to heal in one journey." When people have cancer and crippling anxiety or are going through a divorce, they want relief as soon as possible. They want to feel better right away. Those expectations can be unrealistic, unfair to themselves, and a lot to manage for the guide or therapist or facilitator.

For example, someone with severe daily migraines may discover in a journey a root cause of their migraines. They could be shown an old, very painful memory that they can accept and integrate, or they could be shown their spouse and the codependent way they've been together that's expressing through daily physical pain.

With the right facilitation, guide, and setting – most of the time, but by no means 100 percent of the time – the experience ends up feeling beneficial whether difficult or ecstatic. It's not uncommon for someone who has suffered with depression, PTSD, OCD, or other problems that have plagued them for decades to experience a shift practically overnight. Life becomes different for them going forward.

CAN WE AVOID DISAPPOINTING OR BAD TRIPS?

Expectations can also pose a challenge. Some people come in saying, "I want to have a mystical experience." But no matter how much preparation, intention setting, and planning any of us do before the experience, nobody gets to control what will happen in their own experience, particularly when it comes to macrodosing. This is the dance between expectations and surrendering to what happens. Mystical experiences may not happen every time. Even after multiple journeys, some people do not experience them, for whatever reason.

One of the biggest misconceptions is that healing is a nice, yummy experience. Healing may bring to mind going to a decadent spa and signing up for a "healing massage" or a "healing soak." If only healing always looked like that.

In reality, true healing is rarely pleasant or fun; it's often pretty painful. Sometimes, it's hell.

Most often, we embark on a healing journey because we have to. We're suffering and vulnerable. Our choices are (a) work like hell to regain some part of what we've lost or feel is missing or (b) adjust to a new reality where things are different from what they were. Either way, we have to summon our courage in a big way.

Master Plants like ayahuasca are referred to as "ten years of therapy in five hours," which should be a hint that the process may not always feel delightful. Some lucky few may find the entire process pleasant. For others, the majority of their experiences are hour upon hour of struggle. A difficult or even gut-wrenching experience can become an instigator of positive improvements in our lives just as a joyful one can.

Let's take a moment to discuss bad trips. Not surprisingly, bad trips have become a fundamental reason that many give (especially older generations) for avoiding psychedelics and keeping them illegal.

On the one hand, referring to a trip as "bad" is no longer in vogue. People say: "You have the journey you need." Yes, maybe. But to me this is a bit disingenuous.

Just because an experience offers medicine or meaning doesn't make it unequivocally "good." Experiences can be terrifying, confusing, dysregulating, or retraumatizing. And some may have difficulty seeing any benefit or making any meaning at all, even after processing and integrating.

It's unclear how common bad trips are. One 2010 analysis of studies done with psilocybin in 110 people between 1999 and 2008 found that they weren't common and seemed dose-dependent, with larger doses of psilocybin being associated with higher rates of adverse reactions. In the study, all short-term adverse reactions were "successfully managed through interpersonal support," required no interventions, and seemed to have no lasting effects, based on follow-up interviews.

Negative effects during an experience can include frightening visions, disturbing hyperawareness of physiological processes, troubling thoughts or feelings concerning personal life, and troubling thoughts or feelings about evil forces. This may lead to erratic and potentially dangerous behavior if people aren't properly prepared and supervised. Other negative, typically short-lived effects can include paranoia and, even as aftereffects in the days following an experience, temporary depression, mood swings, or increased psychic instability.

No matter how fervently we may want to believe Master Plants only bring love, unity, and enlightenment, it serves no one to deny or gaslight those who have lived through incredibly difficult experiences. Some also make assumptions that people who have difficult journeys are in some way losers or inferior to people who have positive experiences. This is spiritual bypassing at its worst.

CLINICAL ENVIRONMENT OR CEREMONIAL ENVIRONMENT?

Some people feel drawn to the sacred, authentic quality of ceremony. Yet in many if not most cases, even ceremonies in Peru, Ecuador, or Brazil are not "authentic" or what the local community would experience. Still, they may feel more communal and focused on spirituality than the medical, clinically-focused, or even solo experiences.

There is no one "authentic" environment required to experience the healing elements of Master Plants. Some people feel most comfortable in a medical or clinical setting. We cannot underestimate the power of that particular brand of ceremony. Decades ago, pediatrician Dr. Robert Mendelson described the medical system as a sort of religious parallel with doctors operating as priest equivalents, speaking a mysterious, difficult to understand language (medical jargon), wearing ritual robes (white coats), using ceremonial objects (machines and monitors), with the Temple (hospital) as the center of power.

For those who feel safest within the healthcare system (for any number of reasons), an experience in a more mainstream clinical setting with doctors and nurses steps away may offer more potent healing power than traveling to the jungle for a journey in a circle on the floor of a hut.

Ceremony can happen anywhere: the jungle, a hospital room, our backyard, on the side of a road, and in beautiful nature. Ceremony becomes available to us when we enter non-ordinary seeing, feeling, and knowing.

As we navigate the medicalization of Master Plants, new and hybrid approaches will likely arise. What's most important is that the place and space feel safe, comfortable, aligned, and that options are affordable.

HARM REDUCTION

Harm reduction is exactly what it sounds like: acknowledging the importance of reducing the harm associated with substances that are illegal.

The excitement about psychedelics and their potential therapeutic benefit is driving many to try them on their own, which sometimes blurs the boundaries between recreational and therapeutic use. For some, particularly those with unprocessed traumas who are dealing with many issues in their personal lives, Master Plants can bring up too much and feel overwhelming.

Some existing projects offer gentle, in-person support. The Zendo Project assists people who are suffering from challenging experiences at festivals like Burning Man. They provide harm reduction that is informed around the psychedelic experience, which is an alternative to being surrounded by semi-panicked medical professionals who are unprepared to handle such a situation with sensitivity.

The Fireside Project is an online service that also has anticipated this common outcome of being overwhelmed or overstimulated, and offers real-time virtual support during and after a challenging psychedelic trip. While callers may not be physically held or supported, volunteers can "hold them in conversation" and guide them through practical steps, as necessary.

WHEN THE REAL WORK (AND PLAY) BEGINS

Many people think they're entering the unknown by embarking on a Master Plant journey. It turns out that the encounter with the Master Plant is just a portal, a window into what could be. It's afterward that we really begin walking in the unknown.

We have entered a non-ordinary relationship with an ancient, potent Teacher, regardless of the dose, ceremony, therapist, if we were alone or with a group. We're learning – or unlearning – new things. Maybe we're learned that we know nothing. All of it is normal and fine.

The first thing to remember is we're going to be okay.

A Master Plant experience is the start of a liminal, in-between period. We are no longer who we were, and we're not yet who we're becoming. The integration period describes reentering the world as a newborn of sorts. We have to get to know ourselves all over again because we're no longer experts, even – especially – in ourselves. We are absolute beginners. It's important to take time to find the way we want to walk in the world. How will we bridge the old and the new in an intentional, meaningful way?

This is the period when people are known to spontaneously get divorced and move to Mexico (or Costa Rica, or Bali, or Tulum), walk away from their business or family, or announce to everyone that they're the next messiah meant to save the world (yes, all of these things happen, and not infrequently). It's important to take a little time to settle back into ourselves, preferably with a support person or group and before we make any sudden movements (unless we are in immediate danger).

Landing fully back into ordinary reality takes weeks, at least. In the period, we may think we need to run like hell when really we need to first stand our ground and discuss things. We may think we should stay and discuss when really it's time to walk away. Remember – we are at the very beginning of reorganizing our inner terrain; it's in chaos right now. And our inner terrain is the filter through which we perceive the outer terrain. We must find our way to criticality, the sweet spot between structure and chaos.

It's not uncommon for people to become enchanted by the relationship with the Master Plant or the "messages" received in nonordinary reality and to return repeatedly. Yet just as we wouldn't run after a high-level spiritual teacher yanking on their robes asking every mundane question we had because it would be disrespectful to them, it's worthwhile to sit with the discomfort of not knowing. Embrace the questions without needing immediate answers. Showing up in right relationship begins with engaging with the gift fully before returning to ask for more.

The process takes patience. It isn't always simple. Each step calls us to live more boldly, honestly, joyfully and with greater reverence.

8

SURRENDER AND CEREMONY

As a physician, I was not taught about ceremony. After our so-called White Coat Ceremony where we were presented with our white coats on day one of medical school, the word was never mentioned again.

Not surprising, I know.

What I was taught instead was evidence-based medicine. It sounds good – to make decisions based on science, aka truth, and not, as it was put, our own biases. But the result was that any experience we ourselves observed with a patient being met with a certain amount of derision: "That's just an anecdote."

What this meant was, "What you observed with your own two eyes isn't valid and lacks real meaning until it has been published, preferably in a large-scale, multimillion-dollar study of fifty thousand people or more that confers statistical significance." To this day, if something hasn't yet been published in the right reputable journal, then what we personally witness or experience is thought to lack merit and taken to be untrue. Like all attempts to standardize our complexity and nuance, this approach has led to a sort of bullying of (and by) doctors, particularly against those who say or question anything outside of the mainstream. There is now a reluctance among doctors and other experts to share individual experiences or observations that counter the "standard of care" based on what the research shows. As if funded, approved, and published studies are free of bias? LOL, as they say.

All of this to say: we've been taught not to believe our own eyes.

We also have been taught to adopt the lens of inherent cynicism built into modern science, and without any self-awareness that this attitude of cynicism is a bias in and of itself. The nature of this point of view is that somehow our very skepticism and separateness makes our modern lens superior, smarter and more valid than the otherwise prevailing view of the world as relational, compassionate, and connected.

This cynical lens directly influences the treatment we receive when in the role of patients seeking help for physical or mental suffering. In this most vulnerable role any of us can inhabit as humans, countless people are not believed by their doctors or told "that's impossible" because "there's no evidence to support that" or "that's never been shown."

The impact of being told "I believe you" often brings people to tears and goes a long way in helping their healing process. Being believed – and most of all, realizing we can believe ourselves – recalibrates our sense of inner and outer safety. As discussed in Chapters 1 and 2, that seemingly simple but elusive shift can transform our cellular trauma response underlying illness and set us on a path of well-being.

Another element of the cultural mythology of the moment is that science is the only means by which something can be considered valid or worthy. While science can offer a fascinating window into what is not yet known, such a narrow approach is one of hubris. As we've already discussed, even at its best, science is one of many languages that we use to describe mystery.

Science as it is practiced does not produce absolute certainty or magically turn everything it touches to truth. What it does, momentarily, is reduce our own sense of uncertainty, like a game of Twenty Questions.

Any given study rarely answers more than one question at a time, and often raises countless new questions as it answers a prior one. Like everything in life, science is a process rather than a way to obtain definitive answers. Much as we long for certainty, every perceived answer is provisional and subject to change in the face of new evidence. Science simply increases or decreases our confidence level.

Moreover, science as it's currently disseminated has become a constant deluge of information with little guarantee of truth. One day we hear walnuts are healthy, for example, but the next day we may hear they can kill us! Consider how often we learn that big industry spends billions of cloaked dollars to wield science as a weapon to manipulate policy to their benefit (at the expense of ours). The impact of science depends entirely on the intention of the one who wields the science and the nature of their relationship with the information.

Given the power it holds, science has very much become an instrument capable of medicine or malice.

Social media, with its daily onslaught of dopamine hits disguised as "education," has become another landscape we must navigate. There, algorithms and censorship are designed to present a curated set of facts as "true" science, without acknowledging that the science of any given moment always represents a distinct (and often political) point of view. Influencers and bots only further contribute to crowding our minds with "content," amplifying our sense of overwhelm, and disrupting our own very necessary skills of discernment.

We're drowning in endless information and simultaneously parched for imagination, inspiration, and, most of all, wisdom. The stress that ensues promotes black-and-white thinking, polarization and divisiveness, and makes us feel more different from one another than alike. And as discussed throughout this book, this sense of separation manifests on every level – physically, mentally, emotionally, and spiritually – leaves us in a state of existential orphanhood.

We've lost trust in each other. And we've lost trust in ourselves. We are distrustful of our bodies, hearts, minds, and experiences – never mind our intuition. All of this can make us feel disconnected, confused, and literally lost. It's no wonder we feel so alone.

Many indigenous healers describe this as a state of ongoing soul loss – as though we are walking around missing fundamental parts of ourselves that keep us from feeling whole.

The problems we face right now are unique to this moment, but as humans, we have navigated countless problems unique to any given era over many millennia. And since the beginning of time, ritual and ceremony have served as remedies to these and the many struggles of being human. Here, ceremony is not simply synonymous with celebratory life events like graduations or weddings. Ceremony traditionally has served as a kind of spiritual cauldron that offers an opportunity to safely fall apart – to alchemize all of our seemingly disparate parts, the information and inputs, the inner confusion and chaos – and in the process, allows us to locate our inner compass.

And these days, we need our inner compass more than ever.

SURRENDER – THE PATH TO A MORE CONNECTED WAY OF BEING

We consider our society very advanced and our technology and methodology superior, yet there's still so much that we don't yet know. Some things, we likely will never know.

For example, we don't yet understand why we have visions when we engage with Master Plants or psychedelics. Though there are theories, the mechanism is not known. Yet as discussed in Chapter 3, indigenous people have long shared that all of the advanced science they've learned come through visions during ceremony, which are often (though not always) associated with Master Plants.

The Global North has taken the opposite stance of visions. The fundamental view is that visions are akin to hallucinations, which are the very definition of psychosis. Hallucinations are considered inherently false. Any deviation from these ground rules would mean we are delusional and regarded as a possible danger to ourselves and others. And since our brains are thought to be the source of any visions or hallucinations, any visions from psychedelics are acceptable only insofar as they're considered a temporary result of molecules disrupting pathways in our brains.

But wait, it turns out we don't even fully understand exactly how ordinary vision works. When we look at an apple, let's say, most people don't realize that we are not actually seeing the apple in front of us as it "truly" appears. Photons reflected by the image of the apple strike the retinas of our eyes, which translates them into an electrochemical signal that the optic nerves deliver to the visual cortex. There, the signal stimulates nerve cells that categorize the image into specific inputs. Then the image is reproduced in our brains and we "see" the apple.

We still don't quite know how.

Unsurprisingly then, we understand even less about the images we perceive that aren't stimulated by an obvious external source. To get an idea of where the current research stands, a recent study showed that traveling waves of electrical activity shift in the brain in response to eyes-closed administration of DMT, and that the waves increase as the DMT dose increases. We are at the very beginning of our understanding, and likely have a long way to go before truly understanding why that's happening, let alone the veracity of what we're being shown during visions.

EEG changes also don't tell us very much about the content or veracity of visions. In his book *The Cosmic Serpent*, anthropologist Jeremy Narby deep dives into the almost universal visions of serpents, especially twin serpents or snakes, described by ceremony participants and *ayahuasqueros* under the influence of Master Plants throughout the Amazon. Serpent dreams are found all around the world, as commonly in New York City as in Mumbai. He traces these visions and dreams to indigenous snake-based creation myths and art – as well as twisted ladders, trees, or vines – from around the world to the appearance and science of DNA, and asks the groundbreaking question: could human visions under the influence of Master Plants reflect direct communication with DNA?

Sounds far out, I know.

Yet from the Aztec serpent Quetzalcoatl, who symbolizes the sacred energy of life, and his twin, Tezcatlipoca, to the twin braided snakes illustrated in 2,200 BCE in a Mesopotamian seal ... from the cosmic Rainbow Serpent, whose powers were symbolized by quartz crystals described by Australian Aboriginals, to the cosmic serpent described by the Desana in the Colombian Amazon ... Cosmic serpents are found in creation myths and images from the Amazon, Aboriginal Australia, Sumer, Egypt, Persia, India, Greece, Scandinavia, the Pacific, and arctic Siberia where such reptiles are not even found. Many of these cultures were very isolated from one another both in time and space – as well as from the modern world – yet all share remarkably consistent overlapping themes, from creation myths to visions to dreams, that describe the origin of life – and all happen to resemble what we know about the structure of DNA.

As in the serpent myths, DNA is a single chain comprised of twin strands of base pairs soaking in the salt water of our cellular fluid. DNA itself is infinitesimally small and at the same time almost infinitely large, as the DNA lined up from just one of our bodies could wrap around the earth 5 million times. And we now know that the 98% of our non-coding DNA – previously thought to be useless (and literally referred to as "junk") – emits biophotons. These ultraweak photon emissions, which are 1000 times lower than the sensitivity of naked eye, are quantum particles of light that act as an important form of ultrarapid communication between cells and DNA. What's most exciting is that newer studies show that simply imagining light in a very dark environment increases these biophotons significantly. In other words, they are important not just in the physical eye, but in the mind's eye.

As such, one compelling working theory is that photons emitted by noncoding DNA may be the source of the visions we have during psychedelic experiences.

With this information in mind, should we be reconsidering

whether information critical for our survival has come through psychedelic Master Plant visions and compiled by way of myth and mystics?

Keeping in mind that myth and image was an indigenous extra-literate way of encoding information about science, history, and more, it's certainly fascinating to consider psychedelic visions as a modality of wisdom transmissions about (and possibly directly from) DNA. It's even more fascinating when we consider that Francis Crick – half of the duo Watson and Crick who won the Nobel prize for discovering the double helical structure of DNA – admitted that the image of the structure came to him in a vision under the influence of LSD.

The double helix structure of DNA also strongly resembles a twisted ladder or staircase. Since time immemorial, shamans have described (and created art reflecting) this spiral based on their visions. They consider it the link between earth and the divine realm. The spiral design also appears in creation mythology the world over, from Tibet and Nepal to Africa, Australia, and ancient Egypt. Many scholars consider these winding images to be the first to describe the Axis of the World (Axis Mundi) that appears as a winding World Tree in many creation myths. Interestingly, art created long ago in these very same communities resemble microscopic images of chromosomes, molecules, DNA and more. Yet none of these could have been imitated.

What if indigenous shamans were entirely literal when they said that their visions taught them all they needed to know about advanced botany, pharmacology, geology, and virtually everything necessary for survival, and all from the beings that literally created life? Their visions may have allowed them to directly communicate with – and "see" – what we would now understand to be DNA.

Oh, and Francis Crick was not the only celebrated scientist who accessed professional inspiration through visions or dreams. Countless scientists throughout history could be considered closet mystics who were shown their great discoveries through very similar means, even if they never called themselves mystics or worked with Master Plants or psychedelics for themselves. Friedrich August Kekule saw the structure of benzene in a dream of a group of snakes (!!) swallowing their tails. Dmitri Mendeleev, who created the periodic table, received the entire arrangement of elements in a dream. Dr. Kary Mullis, the inventor of PCR, said: "Would I have invented PCR if I hadn't taken LSD? I seriously doubt it...I could sit on a DNA molecule and watch the polymers go by. I learnt that partly on psychedelic drugs."

Whoa.

Albert Einstein himself related a dream from his teenage years in which "I was sledding with my friends at night. I started to slide down the hill, but my sled started going faster and faster. I was going so fast that I realized I was approaching the speed of light. I looked up at that point and I saw the stars. They were being refracted into colors I had never seen before. I was filled with a sense of awe. I understood in some way that I was looking at the most important meaning in my life."

Indeed, Einstein was often quoted about his insistence on the importance of imagination, inspiration, and intuition: "One woman wanted her child to become a scientist, and asked Dr. Einstein for his suggestions for the kind of reading the child might do in his school years to prepare him for this career. To her surprise, Dr. Einstein recommended 'fairy tales and more fairy tales.' He added that creative imagination is the essential element in the intellectual equipment of the true scientist, and that fairy tales are the childhood stimulus of this quality." Einstein understood that engaging with imagination is far from "playing pretend"; but rather, the first step in manifesting the next, new version of reality.

It turns out that this position has not been a very easy sell in a world educated to, in the words of John D. Rockefeller, become "a nation of workers," not thinkers.

Yet some of the greatest scientists of modern times do not see imagination, dreams, or even visions as "pretend" or false – but as a potential vehicle to epiphany, great discovery, and truth. To many physicists, the invisible is a deeper and more primary reality that underlies our ordinary reality. And these scientists are in exceptional company – that of great poets, musicians, ancient mystics, and indigenous elders. In a very real sense, the nonordinary moments they describe reflect their conversation with the invisible.

There's neuroscience behind these ideas. Psychiatrist Iain McGilchrist theorized that the two hemispheres of our brains each serve a predominant function in the way we see the world. While each hemisphere is in most ways similar to the other, they retained certain differences and never evolved to become one unit. Instead they exist side by side, with a corpus callosum to connect them. The ways they differ may have developed in response to how we are intended to experience – and craft – reality.

The left hemisphere is in charge of linear, detail-oriented, rational, reductionist, and abstract tasks and ways of thinking. From a more primal standpoint, as potential hunters, we must ensure we can track, capture, and kill our prey. And over the last few thousand years, it's been responsible for language – particularly when we developed a written alphabet that required linear scanning and replaced images and symbols with abstract words that had no literal resemblance to the thing it was describing.

The right hemisphere, on the other hand, favors holistic, big picture, out-of-the-box thinking, excelling in connecting dots, appreciating nuance, music, poetry, and perceiving the nonlinear and non-ordinary. Though these skills contribute to hunting as well as foraging, these reflect the skills we need as potential prey.

The left hemisphere facilitates a mode of "knowing" in which everything can be systematically broken down, analyzed, and known. From humans to experiences, all can be dissected into fragments, and abstracted and analyzed without consideration of the "whole." The left hemisphere is responsible for taking a dualistic approach. Think Us versus Them.

Each hemisphere brings into being a world with its own unique qualities. Left brain creates a world of things – inanimate, fixed, familiar, isolated, and disembodied, items that are reducible to their parts. When this view is dominant, everything makes up cogs in a machine.

Right brain, on the other hand, creates a world that is alive, interconnected, embodied, animate, and always changing. When this view is dominant, we live in a world of relationships –where we're not alone, but always operating from a sense of "Me and We."

For millennia, the right hemisphere was considered the big sister to the left hemisphere. In other words, we saw left brain perceptions in the greater context of our right brain worldview. But the demands of our linear, achievement-based, action-oriented culture have created the reverse – a left-brain dominant reality. Through this lens, plants, animals, land, water, sun, stars, soil, and even humans become things.

On the one hand, we absolutely need the strengths of the left hemisphere. But while left brain sees everything as either-or, right brain wants to include both either-or *and* yes-and. When we focus too much on understanding parts, details, and abstraction, we can miss the greater whole entirely – the aliveness, beauty and mystery of the world within and around us that resides in the realm not knowing.

Currently, we're missing the forest for the trees – on many levels.

And as psychedelics have become more medicalized, we've more and more applied our left-brain lens – we talk more about the compounds within Master Plants rather than how they're sourced, grown, harvested, and prepared, and what we must offer to the plants and the communities who hold their wisdom in exchange for the experience. We break down the Master Plant experience into set and setting in very left-brain ways, which is not wrong – but it can become easy to forget that from the indigenous point of view, ceremony *is* the medicine.

We begin to engage our right brain lens by asking: Are we coming for deep healing with humility, appreciation and gratitude, and curiosity? If so, we're on the right track to healing. If not, if we're coming for recreation or escape with no reverence, we may miss the medicine (although sometimes we receive it in spite of ourselves).

This is why many indigenous healers see ingesting the Master Plant as almost secondary.

For example, as discussed in Chapter 7, indigenous people around the world consider music as an necessary way to establish connection with the world of spirits. It would be unthinkable to enter the world of spirits, even with Master Plants, without song. Some songs, known as ícaros, are considered direct transmissions from the spirits of the Master Plants, three-dimensional sound visions that become sacred plant medicine through melodies. Many people can attest to the potent effects of these melodies within our bodies during ceremony, transforming even people who haven't ingested the plants. When it comes to Master Plants, their medicine can take many forms.

Still, Master Plants have always served as a profound vehicle that returns us to this wider, more mystical perspective by opening a portal into the right-brain way of seeing. The right hemisphere opens through the Master Plant Experience by offering openness, interconnectedness and empathy, and enabling genuine contact with the world through a softening or even dissolving of boundaries between ourselves and what we understand to be outside of us. The right hemisphere enables us to perceive our supposedly separate selves and, simultaneously to recognize the profound interconnection shared between all beings. Ultimately, this lens allows for loosening or transcending rigid ego boundaries and perhaps, for some, experiencing nonduality or that we all are one.

What is it about the Master Plant experience that allows us back into this ancient, more connected way of being?

We find our way there by entering a state of spiritual surrender.

The left-brain world tells us that everything can be predictable. But trying to navigate the inevitable unpredictability of life can be bewildering and deeply discouraging when we expect nearly everything to be predictable (because we've been told it should be). When we expect that everything is meant to be changing, evolving, and co-created as we go, we can come with curiosity and interest rather than dismay or despair.

Mystery is a natural, even desirable part of life. Engaging with this not-knowing – through ceremony and Master Plants – activates right-hemisphere ways of operating that allow us to see the changing nature of the universe not as random but as responsive.

Master Plant experiences allow us to activate different perspectives of reality that challenge our preconceived ideas and dogma. This broader approach offers us new skills a different way of engaging with what we call "reality." We can discover where we do have agency instead of getting derailed by resistance or despair when we come up against difficult day-to-day moments or life events that challenge our expectations or sense of normalcy.

Master Plants help us take an eagle-eye view and come from a place of greater trust in the process. Instead of saying, "No!" we can instead pause and take that moment to say, "Wow. Hmmm. Fascinating."

And then: "What can this moment teach me?"

Ultimately, we recognize we are no longer only an actor automatically playing out the script we've been given; we get moments to take a seat in the audience and watch ourselves in action. But this is not like passively watching a movie on a screen. Because we operate from both the lead role and the audience, we discover a greater capacity to influence the plot and the outcome.

The right hemisphere is always seeking this bigger picture, the whole before whatever it is gets broken up into parts in our attempt to know it. Instead of attempting to control reality, we find our way into this process through the practice of surrender. Here, surrender means letting go of what we think we control or even know in order to become more open to what really is.

Most of us are not familiar with an intentional practice of surrender because we think of it as losing or giving up. In ancient and indigenous paradigms, however, surrender is considered not defeat, weakness, or submission, but liberation. Though the spiritual practice of surrender can occur in the presence of another –

like a guide – it cannot be "to another" as in the case of submission. Surrender does not put you at the mercy of another person

Surrender is also not voluntary. We can create conditions for our own surrender – like psychedelics, breathwork, regular meditation, and ceremony – but our only choice is not to resist. Think of it as a water slide – we can put on a bathing suit, stand in line, climb the ladder, and sit down at the top, but once we let go, there's little we can do to control the process. We can have faith, put ourselves in the hands of something or someone greater, and try to enjoy the ride (or not).

These days, talk therapy is seen as the most important step to healing our psychic suffering. And it certainly can be helpful. But consider: the original meaning of therapy was "to serve the gods." It has long been understood that there is something undeniably therapeutic about letting go of our ordinary ways of being and allowing ourselves to engage in a reciprocal conversation with the invisible. It brings to mind a Haitian proverb that states: "When the anthropologist arrives, the gods depart." We will not find magic only by becoming anthropologists studying our stories but by living our lives fully, passionately, and authentically.

Surrender experiences can look any number of ways. They can be accompanied by a feeling of dread and death, as well as clarity, relief, or ecstasy. The key is that surrender allows us to experience being "in the moment" outside of ordinary time and space. And these moments guide us to discover our identity in all of its complexity – sometimes we find our inner Superman hiding beneath our everyday Clark Kent, and sometimes we find an archvillain. Our job is to be in conversation with all that exists within us.

What's most important is that we discover a richer sense of self, wholeness, and unity with our past, present and future selves – and see ourselves as part of the tapestry of all living beings. Moments of surrender plunge us into a process of unlearning that helps us rediscover this sense of integration and connection.

CEREMONY FACILITATES SURRENDER

Ceremony is intended to facilitate surrender – of what we think we know about ourselves, our identities, our beliefs, our goals, our plans, our relationships, and our purpose. Part of participating in ceremony of any kind is to understand that we are letting go of control.

This is the agreement.

Ceremony offers a sense of entry into the world of mystery, where we can let go of needing to understand why everything happens, and helps us to value the practice of unlearning and not knowing. Instead, we come back with exactly as much as we need to know in that very moment to move forward with a sense of guidance and being held.

Does this mean that ceremony (or dreams or visions, for that matter) always offer a direct portal to truth, and we should never question them? No. As we'll see, oftentimes the messages or guidance we receive comes through signs, symbols, and synchronicities. Integration – preferably with the support of a guide or circle of people who can help facilitate interpretation – is as critical to the process as the ceremony and visions themselves.

Because surrender means letting go and is therefore very vulnerable, feeling absolutely safe with the people holding the space – from guiding the experience to the integration – is of the utmost importance. Whether guide, shaman, or therapist, make sure they are trained, experienced, and the right person to create the sacred container necessary for the unique needs of any given individual. We each have individual, familial, ancestral, cultural, and societal stories and experiences that bring us to a particular point with the particular set of needs we have at that time. With few exceptions, such people should be able to describe exactly how they trained and their medical, mental health, emotional, and spiritual backgrounds and practices.

We've come to believe that we must travel long distances to exotic places to find our way to ceremony and that sense of reconnection to the invisible. But there are ways to open those doors wherever and whenever we need that connection, beginning with rituals.

Rituals

Rituals are an age-old way to develop intimacy between ourselves and the invisible world. They're ways to acknowledge and participate in the larger order of things.

Rituals are a predictable, prescribed set of actions enacted at particular times and time intervals that lead to an expected outcome. They generally help us attune awareness to the specialness of any given day or at particular times of the week, month, or year. They offer structure and discipline in the midst of the unpredictable nature of life.

Modern-day rituals can include enjoying a quiet cup of coffee every morning or bringing home an evergreen tree to decorate for Christmas. Older rituals involved acknowledging the new and full moon monthly, and spring and autumn equinoxes and summer and winter solstices seasonally. Even the days of the week guided us to the necessary rituals associated with particular deities and what they represented - Sun Day, Moon Day, Mars Day (Tuesday is Mardi in French), Woden's Day (Odin is the Norse Mercury), Thor's Day (the Norse equivalent of Jupiter), Freya's Day (for Venus), and Saturn's Day. Rituals have long been woven into the fabric of our lives to guide us and help us find meaning in our daily lives.

Everyone knew what to do and when (with individual, familial, communal, and national variations) because rituals were associated with predictable cycles of day and night, week, month, season and year. Rituals give us a sense of participation and belonging in the visible and invisible order.

A DOORWAY BETWEEN WORLDS

Ceremony, on the other hand, is less easily defined or predictable. A ceremony can consist of a set of prescribed rituals designed to create the right circumstances – a predictable quality that invites an unpredictable outcome. But even a particular set of rituals doesn't guarantee ceremony. We could travel to Peru and sit for an authentic ceremony, and we may not experience it as such. And we could be in a hospital or clinic, in our home, or by the side of a road somewhere and suddenly discover it's become ceremony.

When we enter into ceremony, any moment can become sacred and deeply meaningful because we touch a world beyond that which is linear and everyday. In these moments, we can envision life beyond what we could ever have imagined in ordinary time and space. And when we are with others holding the same sacred space and intention, these experiences can be that much more powerful (for better or sometimes worse).

And though we can experience ceremony without Master Plants, the reverse is not true. The indigenous mode of engaging with Master Plants always requires ceremony. Yet for many, Master Plants have become the primary vehicle available for ceremonial experiences in modern life.

Ceremony can happen anywhere and at any time because it typically happens *outside* of time. This is not just a poetic cliché.

Considerations around time are a fundamental underpinning of ritual and ceremony. When we hear the word *time*, most of us glance at our watch or phone to ensure we're not running behind. Time makes us think about our daily agenda, tight schedule, and looming deadlines. All of these betray our left-hemisphere dominant approach to life – linear, structured, and measured in seconds, minutes, days, weeks, months, and years. Chronos time is quantitative – how we live our lives toward a fixed future, knowing that it will eventually end.

Chronos represents our attachment to certainty.

But for the ancients, there has always been another kind of time.

In ancient Greek, it was referred to as *kairos*, which describes the experiences that liberate us from the ordinary business of life. It is auspicious, the perfect moment, serendipity, the time of fantasy, and that which lacks limiting boundaries. We've all had those moments that felt like they lasted for days or days that have passed in what felt like a moment. In kairos time, anything is possible.

Kairos can be seized as it approaches but is lost once it is gone. Behind the idea of kairos is an understanding of the universe as only predictable up to a certain point, and full of uncontrollable factors that can affect the likelihood that human action will succeed or fail. By extension, seeing time in terms of kairos makes human action a defining factor and encourages a multiplex view of time, as different circumstances favor or require different kinds of action. Time is thus a qualitative rather than a quantitative phenomenon. We could think of this as time as defined by the right hemisphere.

Kairos can rarely be planned or forced, but we can cultivate ourselves to be receptive to it. We make ourselves an invitation for these magical and auspicious moments through ritual and ceremony. Indeed, the Hindu word *ritu* describes the time equivalent of *kairos* and is the origin of the word ritual.

During these moments, ordinary time and space don't exist. The usual rules don't apply. The self-limiting stories can become quiet. The world becomes magical. As with psychedelics, anything is possible.

Rituals and especially ceremony allow us to step into a doorway between worlds. Liminal space comes from the word *limen* and describes the period when we're no longer who we were and not yet who we're becoming. In any number of ways, we inhabit in-between identities that defy categorization throughout our lives. And by intentionally allowing accessing liminal spaces, we can incorporate transformation into our lives regularly and also mark or even celebrate particular experiences. These experiences keep us more present and aware.

We've been taught that control is one of the most critical skills in life. We have to hold on tight, be decisive, develop a plan, and adhere to it. And of course, it follows that the more we are in control, the stronger/tougher/more successful/more of a survivor we will be. And maybe sometimes that's true.

Ceremony reminds us that yielding is just as important as control. Strange as it may sound, temporarily letting go allows us to discover what is possible. We can let go of thinking, of being in control, and of whatever we thought we were going to do. We can let go of being the "expert." We can let go of needing certainty and a plan, of always having to know, of being civilized and important and normal. We can let go of old stories and of people that are no good or no longer good for us. We can let go of things. We can let go of what we thought we were going to do so we can find and follow what feels more alive and exciting for us.

We can liberate ourselves from the mandate to figure everything out and instead open ourselves up to discovery.

Deep breath. Feel that sense of relief in not always having to know.

Surrender is powerful. In releasing control, we find courage, strength, curiosity, insight, guidance, and purpose. When we experience letting go, we can see that holding on tight is mostly wasted effort. More space becomes available for what is real, what we love deeply, and what really belongs to us. And it allows us to begin again, to craft a new roadmap for finding balance – between holding on and letting go, order and chaos, past and future, human and divine, individual and communal, light and shadow, good and evil.

Unity has its place, but the peculiar magic of paradox ignites our aliveness like nothing else.

This mystical place of surrender feels unbelievably light. It is a place of allowing, unfurling, revealing, and discovering. We see everything in front of us with new eyes. We recognize signs and synchronicities, and we can make meaning of the messages. We can track seemingly magical opportunities that were otherwise invisible to us.

Most importantly, ritual and ceremony help us navigate the

challenges inherent to being human in style. They allow us to tend our pain, compost our despair, reconcile ourselves to big changes, and connect, heal, and offer gratitude. They are poetic soul maintenance that allows us to tend to ourselves and be in community with the seen and unseen world.

LIVING AS OURSELVES

Ceremony reminds us that we are part of a participatory universe and that everything exists as a means to experience encounters with each other, and we are always changing as a result. We remember that being alive is a reciprocal process: I am meant to change you, and you are meant to change me. We both leave the encounter different and new, and we are always richer for the experience.

It's no wonder that so many people leave the Master Plant Experience – the experience of psychedelic plants taken in ceremony – questioning the truth of what we call ordinary reality. After being in an immersive, mystical environment that strips away the illusions crafted by our left-brain reality, the world we live in daily feels more like an illusion than the visions experienced in ceremony. And while some people think there's a danger of losing ourselves to psychosis permanently through psychedelic or ceremonial experiences – and that can be true, though it's relatively rare – another, perhaps more prominent danger is the despair that takes so many people as they navigate the heartbreak that exists in ordinary reality without ceremony, sacredness, reverence, community, and the ability to sense the kinship and aliveness of the world around us.

Remember when we discussed ubuntu in Chapter 2? In each moment, I am because we are. Again and again, we both emerge as something new all because of how we interact with everything within us and around us, as part of a giant web that is both microscopic and cosmic. And remember that in a twist of rather delicious irony, quantum physics has demonstrated that we are always part of the experiment. We are both the observer and the observed. We are inescapably entangled with each other in a giant invisible web that exists outside of time and space, whether we realize it or not.

With the right support before, during, and after, a Master Plant experience is a journey back to what feels really, really true for us – not just for Me but for We. It is the journey into our own place in the myths that hold all the information and wisdom and guidance from all beings over all time and space. In doing this, our human selves get to glimpse the aliveness of everything. We can hear the invisible calling to us, and we begin to understand. We can learn to ask questions and be spoken to in languages of signs, symbols, and images that ancient traditions have endeavored to catalog since time immemorial. We start to see what's possible without distortion of our ego or biases, and that motivates us to do the hard work that helps us pull away our masks, sand down our rougher edges, and open our eyes and hearts more than we ever could before.

Simply put, these experiences allow us to live more fully as ourselves and as part of something bigger and more beautifully complex and mysterious than we could ever conceive of without them. We are no longer refugees; we all belong to this place. We are no longer orphans; we are all kin.

9

INITIATION AND THE MYSTICAL EXPERIENCE

As we discussed in Chapter 8, psychedelics in the context of ceremony can help us find our inner compass. And like the witching herbs, psychedelic Master Plants can help us find our way back to ourselves by embracing disobedience and allowing us to connect to the parts of us that know the non-ordinary.

Why do we need to find our way back to ourselves?

According to Bruce Lipton in his book *The Biology of Belief*, the majority of our lifelong programming takes place between the ages of zero and seven. And depending on whether or not we receive a sense of belonging and true acceptance during that period and beyond, we live our lives primarily in either protection mode or growth mode. Protection mode means we direct our energy more toward isolation and preparing ourselves for crisis. In growth mode, we reach out, make connections, and build community.

Protection mode focuses on "Us versus Them." Growth mode promotes "Me and We."

This makes a lot of sense, if we think about it. During this early period, we learn how to be human, mostly from our parents or caretakers. In those periods, we become little sponges absorbing all the nuances required to operate within our families, communities, and culture, which is essential for our survival above all. As very young children, when we learn the rules and follow them, life tends to go more smoothly. And the opposite is true: when we don't adhere to the rules of our family and culture, our childhood experiences will tend to be far more negative. During childhood, internalizing this programming in order to be obedient confers safety and a sense of acceptance.

During that period of conditioning and thereafter, we realize that parts of us – desires, interests, characteristics, behaviors – don't invite that sense of acceptance in our family (or community) of origin. Maybe we are emotional, and our family's culture is not to express emotions. Maybe we are LBGTQ+ in a family with conservative beliefs about heterosexuality. Maybe we want to be an artist in a family of Wall Street titans who find that unacceptable or vice versa.

And when we receive a strong, unpleasant response from a parent, caretaker, someone else in authority, or even a sibling or peer – anger, coldness, mocking, sadness – we can feel unaccepted, unacceptable, unloved, and, ultimately, unsafe. And for a child especially, the deepest core of feeling unaccepted is survival – the worry that we will be sent off into the black night all alone without food, shelter, protection, or love.

Acceptance at all costs therefore feels non-negotiable, even if it means shutting down parts of ourselves that really matter.

And this problem is perpetuated in school environments. Any disordered family dynamics or traumas experienced at home are amplified by sitting still at a desk all day with minimal recess; without art, music, or creative activities; eating processed foods and soda for lunch; and doing hours of homework at night (sometimes even in kindergarten!). It's no wonder so many kids are sick, sad, and stressed. They are square pegs being shoved into round holes.

These are real underlying problems that aren't due to one thing. They can't be fixed with interventions, medications, or legislation.

The problem is, in short, empire.

Empire is not "fixable." In empire, curiosity, creativity, and capacity for play are not considered strengths. Empire isn't particularly concerned about individual needs. Empire values obedience: schedules, sameness, and submission. While many of us may remember the traumatic experiences we endured at the hands of particular individuals in our homes or institutions, most of us struggle to see the machinery behind the person or people who inflicted it, which is empire.

From early childhood, the systems most of us navigate are designed *not* to accommodate our unique needs or appreciate our unique gifts. And many people, especially more sensitive ones, carry an array of neurological and mental health diagnoses that reflect why they don't function well within the system of empire. In a sense, these conditions describe the limitations of the overarching system more than a deficit in the individual.

A hallmark of empire is that it normalizes what's pathological and pathologizes what's normal.

In Chapter 8, we explored how the right hemisphere was designed to act as the big sibling to the left hemisphere. Well, in order to succeed and be accepted in these systems, we suppress right-brain functions in favor of our left-brain abilities like reading, analyzing, and understanding abstract concepts.

What falls by the wayside?

Our right hemisphere is responsible for all forms of attention other than focused attention, as well as perceiving information that comes from the edges of awareness. Some call this intuition. Remember, an active right brain helps us understand that the world is animate, alive and interconnected. Yet as right-brain dominant function has come to be regarded as a disability, we are conditioned on a daily basis to deny our most fundamental nature: that we are participating in a constantly unfolding, visible and invisible, reciprocal exchange.

As a result, we also vastly diminish our ability to perceive and sense.

We are each born with a series of sensory gating channels

distributed throughout our nervous systems that can both reduce and amplify our ability to perceive the world around us.

When narrowed, they effectively shut out all nonrelevant sensory stimuli. When selectively opened, we can perceive more acutely, whether music, bird sounds, colors, light, or other more subtle stimuli. When profoundly open, they can flood us with the nearly infinite stimuli that we are swimming in but otherwise wouldn't detect. Most of us would find the experience so overwhelming we couldn't function.

For most of us, our degree of sensory gating is learned. Our unconscious or preattentional mind analyzes sensory inputs and determines which stimuli to let through and which to block. Whatever this unconscious part of us deems most important – whether out of interest or fear – allows the input to reach our conscious awareness. Whatever it deems unimportant remains beyond our awareness.

As an example, think of what happens when we hear our name in the midst of cacophony. The moment we hear it, those preattentional areas of our brains allow for certain channels to open more widely so we can listen more intently to that particular conversation and notice who is mentioning us.

For the most part, newborn babies have minimal to no sensory gating; they are awash in stimuli. And children's sensory gating is wider than those of adults, meaning they perceive more input.

Our ability to tolerate and maintain wide aperture of sensory gating depends in part on our level of safety in infancy and childhood. In a busy and sometimes too intense world bombarding us with nearly infinite stimuli, gating allows us to prevent sensory overload. We engage them as we focus our attention on what is most important to us, in school or work settings, for example. And when all goes well during sleep, they act to prevent us from perceiving outside inputs so that we are not disturbed.

Musicians, artists, writers, the gifted, and those who engage with psychedelic Master Plants can have more profound sensory perception, along with those who have been exposed to profound trauma.

Many psychedelic Master Plants temporarily expand the aperture of sensory gating as well, offering a portal into an experience of reality that offers dramatically more input.

The more widely open our sensory gating channels are, the more likely we are to experience "sensory flooding" and be diagnosed with a pathology. At an extreme, this state can manifest as what we call psychosis, or schizophrenia, in which there can be breakdown in the ability to distinguish self from non-self. Indeed, blowing open these gates of perception or losing the ability to modulate them can be a risk for people with psychosis or a family history of psychosis who engage with psychedelics. We also see increased sensory flooding to a more moderate degree in those who walk around with labels like sensory processing disorder, ADHD, PTSD, bipolar disorder, migraines, and autism.

While these conditions of enhanced perception are quite common to varying degrees, our society suppresses them to the greatest extent possible through medication and other means.

These are some of the very sensitive people I cared for in my neurology practice for almost two decades. I called them the ones who could hear a butterfly sneeze three miles away, the ones who knew things no one else knew with absolute certainty – they're acutely aware of their senses, their dreams, and their inner voice. In some indigenous societies, those with profoundly wider sensory gating than average may have been trained to master and perceive valuable, nuanced information and guidance that others in the community may have been less equipped to perceive.

Once a minimally verbal autistic man came to my office for the first time. He walked over to an altar space I had built, stood there for a moment, and announced to his family: "We're safe here."

Are these conditions really pathologies or powers? As with everything, context matters. The answer requires nuance. People with more open sensory gating channels are aware of an array of inputs that other people may not notice, and thus can assign implications that others cannot. If we consider the above example of hearing our own name in the midst of cacophony, we can understand that *not* hearing the details of those other conversations doesn't mean they aren't happening. As a result of their perceptions, these sensitive people can experience suffering that cannot be underestimated, particularly in a world that does not acknowledge their gifts. Yet with mentoring, these people can embrace and locate the skills and strengths in their sensitivity.

With few exceptions, our society expects outliers to take all steps possible to present as average, rather than finding the gifts in being an outlier. But these people are not average; they are unique.

My indigenous Siberian friend from Yakutsk considers our approach to what we call mental illness absurd. In her community, a person who experiences a psychotic break is thought to be chosen. Though their life may not be easy, their increased perception is considered an exceptional ability, a shamanic gift, and they are trained to cultivate those gifts as a healer. From that moment on, they belong to the community and the community belongs to them.

This example may sound extreme, but can we even imagine a value system that honors somebody's profound individuality, needs, and gifts in our society?

Instead, we've all trained ourselves to live our lives perceiving a tiny fraction of what's happening around us rather than cultivating the ability to process a wide array of sensory input. Is what we call ordinary reality its own version of psychosis?

The question is, what have we been missing?

This is a gift Master Plants can offer us. Indeed, some of the very same skills are cultivated by the shamans, medicine people, and vegetalistas who journey with the help Master Plants.

ARE YOU CLARK KENT OR SUPERMAN?

The vast majority of our early childhood programming resides in our unconscious minds, running about 95 percent of our brain's operating systems. What this means is that from our conscious mind we may say "I want to do XYZ; this is my mission" – but somehow things can go sideways again and again. This is because we – our conscious selves who we believe run the show – are trying to take the necessary steps to accomplish goals and achieve success. But often that's just 5 percent of our minds at work. At the same time, our vast early programming may be unconsciously resisting those goals in all kinds of ways, keeping us in protection mode. Then we wonder why we are getting in our own way, and feeling "stuck."

Yet we may merrily follow our programmed trajectory for years or even decades – maybe even very successfully – before we notice that we feel stressed, depleted, depressed, anxious, awkward, self-conscious, and disconnected from ourselves.

Think of it this way. Many of us emerge from early life as Clark Kent, Superman's alter ego. Clark Kent is seemingly a straightlaced, conventional guy living his straightlaced conventional life. He's awkward. He aspires to be successful, but always gets outplayed. He's trying to date Lois Lane, but she's not really interested. He's nothing like the guy he really can be, who is Superman.

When he's Superman, he's living into the truth and fullness of who he is. He's charismatic, compelling, and imbued with power, and he's helping people by expressing his unique gifts.

We were all born as a Superman of sorts, with our own unique superhero qualities. None of us are ordinary creatures.

Many of us struggle to recognize this truth about ourselves – especially if we were told otherwise – much less fully embrace as the gifted beings we are. This goes back to predictive coding. Based in our neuroscience, the more we consciously or unconsciously believe something will be the case – about ourselves, the world around us, or even the future – the more we prove it to be true by expecting and enacting it. We therefore can't find true belonging until our old ways are disrupted (by choice or otherwise), and we are forced to chart new territory.

Breaking through our "empire" programming requires disobedience, but it must be purposeful – breaking the rules not for the sake of breaking rules but to find our way out of empire and back to our authentic selves.

Master Plants are one of many ways that can help us jump-start this process. There is a reason their reputation has always been so subversive. They encourage us to become subversive.

It turns out that individuals who defy cultural normality are considered healthier. As discussed in Chapter 2, the psychologist Abraham Maslow was fascinated by achieving authentic inner satisfaction, known as self-actualization. In his book *The Farther Reaches of Human Nature*, Maslow said, "A study of people healthy enough to be self-actualized revealed that they were not well adjusted in the naive sense in approval of and identification with the culture. These healthy people had a complex relationship with their much less healthy culture. Neither conformists, nor automatically reflexive rebels, such men and women expressed their unconventionality in ways that kept them true to their inner values without hostility, but not without fight, when that was called for."

Disobedience of this kind usually begins with a provoking event that some refer to as an awakening.

OPENING OUR EYES

Several times over the course of our lives, we find ourselves expelled from our seemingly comfortable existence. Rarely would anyone willingly commence such a journey, even if their prior existence wasn't particularly pleasant. But we rarely get to choose moments of coming to consciousness. These moments choose us.

Even though we're encouraged to "step out of our comfort zones," more often the world starts squeezing, pushing, and closing in on us as though we're in some existential birth canal. Other times, it feels more akin to being maniacally thrown from a cliff. These periods can feel chaotic, unsettling and confusing, not to mention lonely. So lonely. We may feel like we don't know ourselves anymore or where we belong in the world. And we may be extra hard on ourselves because we think we should "have our shit together."

The paradox, of course, is that in these moments we learn the most about truly having our shit together. This new place outside of our comfort zones provides space to expand and try new things. As the familiar falls away, we begin to discover the parts of ourselves that are true no matter what. In the process, we find out more about our unique gifts – our medicine, our integrity – to live by. In short, this is some of the most important work we do.

Often, this process involves a loss or at least what feels like one. It could be of a loved one, a job or career, our home, our health, or even simply a key part of our identity. Sometimes this happens to us as a community or collective – like being hit by a hurricane or seeing entire cities shut down for fear of a virus spreading. Sometimes, these events embed themselves into our minds and bodies in the form of trauma.

We would never choose these experiences voluntarily. But these can be deeply spiritual moments in their way – when routine is in some way disrupted and normal life is completely upended.

Somehow, that loss and the resulting pain allow us to transform. It is a kind of death of our prior selves. But in dying and being reborn, we emerge into a world in which everything becomes clearer, more acute, and filled with possibilities that our old self couldn't see or even have fathomed.

The good news is that we are programmed to go through these sorts of transitions – psychologically, biologically, and spiritually. According to ancient mystics, we are hardwired to be disassembled and reconfigured by these experiences, and especially at certain points in our lives – typically around adolescence, and later around twenty-eight to thirty (entering adulthood), forty to forty-two (midlife), forty-eight to fifty, and again as we enter our sixties (approaching elderhood).

Most people who engage with plant medicines are typically at just such a crossroads in their lives. The inclination may exist only underneath the surface – a longing for something not quite yet known – or be public and obvious, such as divorce, change of career, or coming out of the closet in any number of ways (not just in terms of sexual orientation or gender). It could just be a decision not to remain stuck anymore. Whatever the instigator, psychedelic Master Plants typically accelerate the change.

Often when undergoing an initiatory experience, we are treated as though we have pathology. In one way, this assessment may feel comforting – or at least hopeful – because our first inclination is to fix whatever is wrong so that we can return to our ordinary lives and everything we had planned there. Indeed, very real physical symptoms, mental "breakdowns," or panic attacks can come along with these periods – but they tend not to be easily treated by the standard approaches, because something deeper is happening to us. We think our problem is psychological (which can be a part of this provoking process), so we go to therapists, who diagnose us. We seek doctors because we worry we're physically ill (and sometimes that's part of the provocation too), who tells us we need to be medicated or, worse, concludes that "nothing is wrong."

But pain is not always pathological when we recognize it as a message with meaning. When we were kids, the discomfort of growing pains and growth spurts were accepted as normal. Yet from the moment we hit adulthood, we are taught that we should never feel uncomfortable – or, at least, not admit that we are. If we are sad, angry, depressed, grieving, or suffering in any way, we are expected to keep it to ourselves. And those who can't are called hysterical, sensitive, dramatic, intense, or told that something is wrong with them. Expressing discomfort is a liability.

Yet just as with childhood growth spurts, adult growth spurts are often painful. They're strange, awkward, difficult, and sometimes downright terrifying. They're almost always deeply uncomfortable. And all of that is normal.

Our society pathologizes our discomfort. But discomfort itself – even when it reaches the level of pain – isn't pathology. Pain is a language, albeit one that sometimes grabs us by the throat, that alerts us to the deeper forces that are out of balance within and around us. Our pain acts as a portal through which we can discover where we need to focus our attention, and perhaps heal. Discomfort and pain are an inherent part of our growth process.

Mythologist Joseph Campbell said: "When looking back at your life, you will see that the moments which seemed to be great failures followed by wreckage were the incidents that shaped the life you have now. You'll see that this is really true. Nothing can happen to you that is not positive. Even though it looks and feels at the moment like a negative crisis, it is not. The crisis throws you back, and when you are required to exhibit strength, it comes." And Friedrich Nietzsche wrote: "Only great pain is the ultimate liberator of the spirit....I doubt that such pain makes us 'better'; but I know that it makes us more profound."

When we recognize that even existential discomfort is not a flaw, problem, or weakness but a normal call to growth, evolution, and purposeful disobedience, we can yield rather than resist and become curious rather than run. With practice, we can learn to navigate these periods with greater ease and even joy. And unless we really, really resist – through addiction, suicide, or another dramatic shutting down of some kind – this process of provocation can offer a portal to spiritual awakening.

Most of us have not been educated to recognize the mystical or spiritual component of crises. Oftentimes, whether in the context of very real physical and mental symptoms or solely spiritual ones – these periods offer a necessary change to refine the course of our lives.

FALLING APART TO COME TOGETHER

It turns out that all that compartmentalizing we did to fit in was an illusion. Our egos (the personas we present in the world) unceremoniously sequestered the parts of ourselves that we were ashamed of – those parts that made us feel as though we were unworthy or unlovable. Let's call them our monsters. We thought we could shove our monsters away into attics and closets deep within us – our unconscious - and that then we'd be safe. The problem is that going forward, we take all steps possible to avoid those monster-filled attics and closets. We're terrified to see (or worse, for someone else to see) our monsters. Essentially, those parts run the show in real time from those attics and closets, only we don't realize it.

Ego dissolution allows all of these suppressed parts – childhood memories, emotions, shame, fear, guilt – to emerge from the closet and attic and be seen in the light of day for exactly who they are. Even for just a little while, our unconscious becomes conscious. And then we can discern which monsters need to be addressed, and which are just shadow puppets that we thought were monsters but actually aren't.

Such an experience allows us to become more honestly acquainted with ourselves and embrace the full spectrum of our parts, even those we feel are weak or shameful. In those moments, we can offer every one of them a seat at the table.

Psychedelic Master Plants are one way to instigate a persona-dissolving, ego death experience, which can feel shocking, challenging, disorienting, expansive, and transformative. A psychedelic-induced ego dissolution is most difficult when we are not prepared to relinquish protection mode. Such an experience is often compared to its own kind of "death and rebirth."

Ego death often goes hand-in-hand with what are called mystical experiences. Although such events are each unique, they share a set of common characteristics such as intensity, a loss of "self," a sense of interconnection, accessing the "sacred," and sometimes encounters with spiritual entities. Though these experiences have come to be stigmatized and even pathologized, historically they have been the underpinnings of epiphanies in science, art, and religion since the beginning of time.

These moments offer a greater sense of connection and community – both to us and our neurons. On the neurological level, psychedelics facilitate neuroplasticity. New connections spring up in regions that would normally not communicate. Our neural networks operate with greater flexibility and interconnectedness. Distinct neurological networks become less distinct. The brain as a whole becomes more integrated.

The notion of oneness that is among the criteria psychedelic scientists use to qualify mystical experiences correlates with higher rates of recovering from conditions like addiction or depression. Remember how neurons in a person suffering from depression demonstrate fewer connections to other neurons? Through glimpsing mystery, they begin to reach out and make new connections again.

Practically, we become more able to think outside the box and access new ways of thinking that were previously inaccessible to us. We develop more empathy and open-mindedness, phenomena that are unusual to acquire in adulthood but that are an avenue to feeling less alienated and lonely. This greater sense of connection and interconnection by way of the mystical is a neurological outcome of right brain activation, wider sensory gating, and our neurons finding their way out of protection mode and into growth.

Mystical experiences are not rare. Though they occur commonly with psychedelics, more people have had mystical experiences than we might imagine. From 1962 to 2009, for example, the number of Americans who reported at least one mystical experience in their lifetime more than doubled to half the population.

It's important to note that psychedelics are not the only route to mystical experiences, and experiencing the mystical is not a guarantee for those who engage with psychedelics. Anything that instigates a shutdown of the default mode network (DMN) – quieting left brain functions – can enable us to engage in what has long been called ego dissolution or ego death, including long-standing meditation practice, breathwork, sensory deprivation, near death experiences, and moments of profound wonder and awe.

We can feel more bewildering and awkward than we've ever felt before when we merge from a mystical experience. Small talk may become more difficult. Being around people may feel taxing; silence can be preferable. At times, we can feel like strangers in our skin, and can adopt drastic changes in our preferences around appearance, clothing, music, and activities, not to mention relationships. Expressing ourselves more authentically becomes nonnegotiable, no matter the cost. And while shedding old ways that no longer resonate can feel lonely or scary at first, pretending becomes impossible and true connection paramount. We want to be seen for who we really are.

It's also important to note that pattern interrupts are not required to be difficult or challenging, though they're nearly always intense and emotional. Experiences of wonder and awe can serve a similar purpose in a completely different way. Imagine unexpectedly seeing a bright red feather on the ground, magnificent blossoms covering a tree, a double rainbow, or a hawk taking off with its prey in its talons.

The idea is to allow ourselves to be pulled out of ordinary reality into a different realm of awareness in which we meet the unexpected. Periods when we are not in control nourish us. These moments show us the magnificent possibility in letting go and trusting the intelligence of the universe.

Imagine never noticing the feather or looking up to see the spectacular sunset. We'd be depriving ourselves not only of the beauty that's all around us, but also of opportunities to transcend the ordinary and expected – which is our connection to the essence of what it means to feel alive.

For many, the experience of psychedelics creates a major shift that amplifies the way they experience the world around them. Emotions become clearer, beautiful things are more exquisite, music more poignant, and life more deeply felt. Being pulled out of ordinary reality allows for transformation to happen – and it's usually for the better.

When we let Master Plants or other portals to mystery have their way with us, we suddenly become beginners again. Contrary to what we may think, that's not a bad thing.

In Zen Buddhism there's a concept known as *shoshin*, or "beginner's mind." Shoshin refers to the idea of letting go of our preconceptions and becoming completely open in our approach, even to what's very familiar to us. We no longer assume or expect that we know the answers, but instead let ourselves consider all sensory input as though we're discovering the content for the first time. As the Zen saying goes: "In the beginner's mind there are many possibilities, but in the expert's mind there are few.

Beginner's mind describes a deconditioning from empire narratives and all associated limitations therein.

Neurologically, beginner's mind means our sensory gating has greater capacity to open more widely according to our intention, so we can see, hear, and sense what we never could before. Our cells become more connected and communal. Our nervous systems become more plastic and flexible. Our right hemisphere becomes more prominent and active. And again, as we carry this open state forward into our lives, we are no longer operating from protection mode, but from a place of growth and opportunity.

MAKING MEANING OF CHAOS

Rites of passage used to be an inherent part of most major life transitions – and they were meant to consciously engage with the cycles of death and rebirth within our lives. Not infrequently, the spiritual pain of the transition was acknowledged in some way by intentionally inducing physical pain. The goal here is not to brutalize, but to supersede – to let go of what is thought of as a lesser identity through sacrifice.

The term sacrifice derives from the Latin *sacer*, meaning sacred, and *facere* meaning to make or to do. Sacrifice therefore means to make sacred – the giving up or destruction of something of great value in exchange for something more valuable in return. Ritual is necessary for the pain to be transformative.

Joseph Campbell considered loss of these communal rites of passage, even with their associated pain, to have left a huge hole in our culture. Many young people create a pale version of these pain rituals – think of a group of college kids getting matching tattoos or secret fraternity hazing.

Many indigenous communities include coming of age rituals that induce pain (and even mutilation). When I was in Australia, for example, I had the privilege of learning from an indigenous teacher about the traditional initiatory rites of passage for the Eora Nation, made up of twenty-nine clan groups in the Sydney Coastal area. In general, initiation ceremonies were secret and only attended by initiates and the initiated. Women's ceremonies took place for women only and men's ceremonies for men only. The Eora Nation boys participated in a "tooth ceremony" in which their front tooth was knocked out. The absence of that tooth indicated to others that the young man had become a man. He might have his ears or nose pierced as well. Girls had the tip of their pinky fingers tied so tightly with a string that it fell off. In ritual, they sacrificed that fingertip to the ocean as an offering, in the hopes that in return, they would receive the knowledge and fortune to live from the abundance of the ocean. During this process, elders trained the initiates in the skills, beliefs, and knowledge needed for their roles as adults in Aboriginal society. And when they successfully completed these rites of passage, they were officially considered adults.

These rituals likely sound primitive, brutal, and even abusive to most people who live in modern culture. And they are brutal. Yet ritual pain in some form exists fairly universally across cultures around the world – and is even reliably known to be an important way to reach a mystical, transformative state. It forces us to ask a difficult question – have we demonstrated in our society that we are so evolved and aware as to know better than, or condemn as ignorant, what so many in the world have done until now? I want to say yes, but when I look at modern society, I can't claim we're necessarily superior or kinder. So the answer is: I don't know.

It posits other questions – are some of the self-destructive behaviors so many teens and young adults engage in alone and together an unconscious way to re-create these painful, seemingly brutal communal rites of passage? Is sacred pain – a limited experience of pain imbued with collective societal meaning – necessary for our spiritual development? And without those rituals, are we replacing communal physical pain with existential pain – loneliness, anxiety, depression, even suicidality?

At a minimum, most of us can acknowledge that at least some

amount of pain – physical, mental, emotional, and spiritual – is inherent to being human, and part of the human experience is to learn how to navigate, process and grow from these inevitable periods. Of course, pain is not automatically sacred or by definition a "teacher" (or at least we cannot say that to a person in pain without running the risk of being punched in the face).

We can, however, find meaning in pain when we do experience it for whatever reason, and through that meaning-making, engage with the sacredness – or "medicine" – of the experience. It's the difference between having our tooth randomly knocked out by a person and understanding we are part of a communal ritual indicating we've become adults, ready to share in the privileges and responsibilities therein.

UNCERTAINTY OR MYSTERY?

In ancient times, it was well known that the Universe speaks to us in signs, symbols, and synchronicities. Most of us have at some point or another experienced a moment of synchronicity that some like to call a "sign from the Universe." Today, we have a name for such events – we call them coincidences. What we mean is that we've experienced meaningful events that occur simultaneously in ways that seem greater than chance. These are the moments when it feels like the Universe gets personal.

At a conference I once attended regularly, a friend and I decided to run to the drugstore to get a repair kit for my sunglasses. Though I loved the community of people there, the conference had become crowded and loud, with a frenzy of people trying to sell to the audience with promises of wealth and success, and the audience shoving each other out of the way to buy. As I entered the drugstore, I said to my friend, "This conference makes me feel like I'm surrounded by a pack of piranhas." Moments later, the salesperson handed me a glasses repair kit from behind the counter. The brand was written in big letters across the package. The name? "Piranha."

My friend and I were astonished as we gazed at the kit. What were the chances that I'd use that uncommon word to describe a professional community that I had previously held dear? I experienced a strong sense of validation. No matter how important the connections and information, it felt clear I was meant to shift my professional course so that I didn't become part of the feeding frenzy.

When people experience this phenomenon, they tend to feel a sense of "being guided." These events offer clear signs in the form of course corrections, often in moments of need. They instruct us to stop, go, head this way, beware of dead end, and so on. Sometimes we perceive messages through more complex symbols, such as an eagle circling overhead or a butterfly landing on us. Apparently ordinary activities acquire special significance, revealing deeper meaning by bringing together what we know with that which we don't yet know. In these moments, daily life becomes colored by elements beyond our limited perceptions.

When my own life journey went sideways, what was most disorienting was letting go of the story I'd had for myself and my life. I was a mother, wife, doctor, author – all things I had worked hard for. Who would I be now? As it turned out, I wasn't exactly relinquishing those identities – but more reconfiguring and reorganizing. No part of me was left behind, but some parts that weren't previously at the forefront were now being called front and center. I had no idea what was next for me. After being taught to live with schedules, goals, and milestones – and having hit those things that told me I was successful – I realized that much of it may not have been what was best for me anymore, at least not as it had been. But there was no roadmap. Everything was uncertain. I was navigating unknown terrain.

But remember how criticality is the sweet spot between certainty and the unknown? Without structure, we can accomplish nothing. But without a certain amount of chaos, we miss out on inspiration and opportunities that allow us to recognize that we need to change the course of our lives. We are most able to access our brilliance at the critical edge between what we know and what is unknowable, between science and sacred.

What if mystery is the very medicine we need? What if we are being called not to rush to answers but to ask better questions? What if we allow the ordeals in our lives to become an exercise in unlearning: around our identities, relationships, health, life, and even death? What if we are being asked to slow down and engage with the magic of the world, of ourselves, and of our relationships?

And perhaps then we can begin to discover beauty in the not knowing, the uncertainty, or perhaps we just call it mystery, because...what's the difference between uncertainty and mystery?

Uncertainty is just a pejorative term for mystery.

Master Plants teach us that humans – like plants, mycelium, slime molds, and other organisms – can make and remake ourselves. Master Plants offer a sense of wildness in the truest sense of the word – by showing us that we are intelligent, flexible, emergent systems in constant conversation with emergent systems within and around us, discovering and responding exactly to what is needed in any given moment.

Master Plants give us permission to be disobedient with a purpose, for the sake of true belonging – not to somebody else's narrative but to our own, not in service to empire but to the aliveness of ourselves and every being.

Master Plants show us that we can best disrupt empire by living truthfully, fully, as we really are.

10

RE-ENCHANTING OUR LIVES

"Instructions for living a life.
Pay attention.
Be astonished.
Tell about it."
—Mary Oliver

There was a time when we all spoke the same universal language of plants, animals, water, wind, sun, seed, soil, and ancestors. The invisible world was very real and tangible. In this enchanted world, we were able to experience great pleasure, delight, and wisdom through our relationship with a world filled with intelligent beings with whom we considered ourselves kin. Myth was a repository of this language and held lineages of wisdom from both the seen and unseen collective.

When intuition became taboo, the "spell" was broken. We no longer saw trees, rivers, mountains, bears, and deer as wise, ancient teachers and guides. We saw *things*. The world was considered a dead thing, and everything in it became "resources," "property," and "commodities."

How do we restart conversations with the visible and invisible world around us? Can we regain fluency in the universal language that has no words, a language that we once knew but have forgotten? Is the living world trying to talk to us? Can we find our way back to the part we play in the greater order of things?

This conversation is important – maybe the most profound one we can have. We have lost that line of communication and with it, a fundamental sense of guidance and support. But we can remember our way back if we are willing to reengage.

As with any good relationship, our relationship with mystery and the invisible requires cultivating.

Master Plants are demonstrating for us how to bridge between science and the sacred, even if it feels awkward at first. They show us how to think differently, embrace nuance, gently hold opposing ideas together, and surrender to the many kindred relationships – and to the oneness – that support us. And they remind us of how much is happening beyond our rational, linear ways of knowing.

Indeed, the language of the natural world is communicated quite differently from the one humans typically use – not with words but through our senses and other perceptions outside of time and space. To become aware of the messages of the earth requires us to unlearn the cerebral, detached approach we have been taught and embrace our beginner's mind. We must learn to practice recalibrating our sensory gating channels to welcome greater input. As our subtle perception heightens, so does our ability to access unlimited connection – to ourselves, each other, the natural world, and universal consciousness. Through this, we develop a sense of deep belonging and safety that allows for transformational healing.

Master Plants offer us access to new ways of knowing. What we know that we know is only a tiny fraction of our knowledge. And frankly, what we know that we don't know is also quite small. And what we don't know that we don't know is profoundly more than that.

What's most interesting, though, is what we don't know that we know. Our capacity for perception is far greater than we realize.

For example, we've been taught that our brains are in charge of the entire body and are the home to our consciousness. But robust research using EEG and EKG shows that, in fact, it is our hearts that perceive and anticipate our environment a full 1.5 seconds before our brains.

Might the heart have capacities beyond what we normally attribute to it?

ELECTROMAGNETIC LANGUAGE – OUR FIRST MOTHER TONGUE

The heart historically has held a much more important role in our ways of knowing than we recognize today. Telltale remnants still exist. For example, we often acknowledge the heart quite literally through the words we use. We call people good- or kindhearted to describe compassion and generosity. People who are strong and resilient are hearty. We talk about being heartfelt when people are earnest and fully present. We ask others to share their heart's desire or encourage them to listen to and follow their hearts. On the other hand, people who demonstrate a lack of compassion or empathy are described as heartless or hard-hearted. We even ask them to have a heart. And when we are sad, we are heavyhearted, heartbroken, or experiencing heartache. Our hearts run the show more than we realize.

Perhaps this shouldn't be surprising. Our hearts produce and release their own neurotransmitters, as well as hormones and other communication molecules. More than 60 percent of cells in our hearts are neural cells, many of which communicate directly with our brains – especially the amygdala, thalamus, hippocampus, and cortex – related to emotional memories, processing, sensory experiences and their meaning, spatial relationships, and problem solving and learning.

Could it be coincidental that these areas are also thought to be central to the actions of psychedelics?

Consider: Heart cells themselves store memories, particularly emotional ones. Our hearts perceive our environment and are in continual communication with our brains, and our brains are in constant communication with our hearts. Research even shows that our moment-to-moment experience of time is synchronized with, and changes with, the length of a heartbeat. The heartbeat is a rhythm that our brain is using to give us our sense of time passing. And it's not linear; it's constantly contracting and expanding. Our heart determines how we experience ordinary reality.

All of this comprises our heart-brain axis.

This information exchange is physiological and neurological, in addition to being more intangible – for example, we can receive knowledge about events like earthquakes before they happen, even at great distances, or with people we haven't spoken with in years – all seemingly outside of linear time and space. A meta-analysis that measured physiological responses occurring before a future unpredictable event, called prestimulus responses, revealed statistically significant results in over one thousand subjects. Heart and brain activity changed four to five seconds prior to the event – with the heart activity changing 1.5 seconds before that of the brain.

What this means is our hearts can predict the future. There is no known explanation of the mechanisms for these findings, but there are practical applications – they've been shown to play a role in repeat entrepreneurial success. We call this category of knowing intuition, or even extra-sensory perception, and the resulting insights can sometimes offer us a more rapid and complete understanding than years of accumulated knowledge.

Our hearts emit measurable electromagnetic fields thousands of times more powerful than the brain, to which all organs, including the brain, synchronize. Beyond the neurotransmitters and hormones released by our hearts, this field is a primary mode of communication that comes directly from our hearts – delivering information to the body in response to what they've perceived from our inner and outer environment. All of our cells, organs, and systems, including blood cells traveling through our vessels, synchronize – or entrain – to this frequency field, amplifying the one primarily and powerfully set by our hearts into a larger field.

Within us, the synchronization is measured by cardiac function, respiratory rate, and autonomic nervous system function. Outside of us, the collective field of the body is called a biofield, and can be measured up to 6 or more feet away. Our biofield influences (and is influenced by) the biofields of other people as well as those of animals, plants, trees, rocks, and even the Earth.

Indeed, our hearts are far from simple pumps; they are also organs of perception and communication. Just as our eyes perceive waves and frequencies as colors and our ears perceive them as sound, the heart perceives waves as frequencies as emotions. Just as we decipher street signs to learn how to get where we need to go, we gain information about our experiences – and ultimately, our life journey – as we decipher the clues within us and around us. By way of these shared electromagnetic fields, we are in a never-ending, always-evolving relationship with every cell and even microbe within us, as well as with all beings around us.

Conversely, we are also transmitting information, consciously and unconsciously, to others and the environment around us all the time. In the presence of another person, our fields combine and become something different and unique that we both perceive simultaneously, called entrainment. Think of when we pluck one string on an instrument, the other nearby strings automatically come into a harmonic vibration.

Practically, this dynamic exchange of invisible information is how we know our partner had a bad day as soon as they enter the room, before they say a word or we even lay eyes on them or hear the heavy sigh. Or when we meet someone and automatically say, "I get bad vibes" or "I don't have a good feeling" about them. Or why a friend ranting to us about something that angered them can leave us feeling agitated, upset, and dysregulated. This is not to say that anger (or sadness or really any emotions we experience as unpleasant) is bad per se. However, they are very real communications that temporarily alter us and can require processing and a certain amount of intention to eventually re-regulate. Being able to regulate ourselves is key.

And we don't entrain only with people. Scientific literature shows we also entrain to animals, and they entrain to us – for example, our pets, the birds in the bushes or trees nearby, insects, horses, and more. And independent of humans, animals rely heavily on these electromagnetic fields to communicate with one another and the world around them: to eat, to mate, to find their communities – in short, to survive.

This electromagnetic language begins when we're in utero, literally as our first mother tongue. Our hearts form and start beating before our brains begin to develop. The fetus's heart bathes in the already developed electromagnetic field of its mother, and that immersion can even continue for months after being born. The immersion in this information field is one way that we are initiated into our familial and ancestral wisdom as well as potential traumas of our lineage. And because we are born into a situation in which the first information we perceive is part of this electromagnetic field, we continue to be very sensitive to that information for life.

The very rhythm of our hearts also comprises a kind of communication. Most of us believe that our heartbeats are meant to be like metronomes, regular and exactly even. It turns out that's the opposite of healthy. In a healthy heart, the space between our heartbeats should vary ever so slightly. In fact, heart rate variability (HRV) is a major measurement that reflects the well-being of the fetus before being born and continues throughout our life cycles. We tend to lose variability as we age, for example.

HRV has also been shown to reflect our emotional state with impressive accuracy. Variability patterns communicate the difference between feelings of anxiety, frustration, anger, joy, excitement, or surprise – all of which may be associated with an increase in heart rate but clearly do not indicate the same emotional state.

The very rhythm of our hearts and space between each beat transmits our emotional, physical, and spiritual states both to our brains and bodies and to those around us. When we are angry, our nervous systems become more chaotic and dysregulated – and we are less likely to make decisions we'd experience as positive. The people around us experience the anger through a shared biofield, and it dysregulates them as well. The opposite is also true – experiencing joy, and especially appreciation, regulates us and helps us make better decisions.

Gratitude is also "contagious."

Simply by comporting ourselves with intentionality in our own lives, we automatically create shifts in coherence and therefore a field more conducive to healing around us. And there's a ripple effect – the more we shift our own heart rate variability to coherence, the more others can entrain to us and, sometimes, experience a similar shift. As they comport themselves in greater coherence, those around them can entrain to coherence and on and on.

Master Plants, and especially psychedelics, influence these fields very particularly. As discussed in previous chapters, psychedelics allow access to the mystical, promoting a sense of unity, compassion, and connection. This experience, in turn, can also increase heart rate variability, which helps us remain in our zone of safety, flow, and resilience.

And when we engage in gratitude and appreciation, our heart rate variability settles into a highly organized, sinusoidal pattern called coherence. It turns out we drop into a state of coherence when we shift from linear analytical processing to a state of sensing, which boosts our skills of intuition. Coherence also predicts improved physical, mental, and emotional health according to many parameters. Physically, blood pressure decreases, cortisol (a stress hormone) is lower, memory improves, and DHEA (dehydroepiandrosterone) increases. The effect on mental health is also impressive – studies have shown that an increase in states of coherence ameliorates symptoms including anxiety, depression, hostility, phobias, obsessive-compulsive disorder, and even paranoia and psychosis. On all counts, coherence feels good.

Not surprisingly, dysregulating experiences knock us out of a state of coherence. Traumatic experiences of violence, abuse, or war - that lead to conditions like PTSD – tend to limit heart rate variability. Even simulations like playing violent video games (as opposed to nonviolent video games) lower coherence levels and increase aggression levels.

Gratitude is not necessarily a difficult state to achieve, though it can take practice. Part of that practice is to remember that allowing ourselves to enter that state doesn't require us to bypass or negate our difficulties. The process asks us to spend moments of time focusing on what around us – however large or minute – brings us to a place of appreciation in that moment. One of my friends easily achieves a state of coherence, measured by a device that chimes when coherence is reached, simply by *thinking about* his beloved dog. His dog has now passed away, but he still experiences coherence when he thinks of him. Heart experiences can transcend time, space, and realms. For him, that is one of his go-to most coherent states because his body, brain, and heart remember.

Bacteria, animals, and plants also communicate by way of electromagnetic fields, which influence our HRV.

Plants and trees maintain contact with Earth's magnetic field and contain the very same protein that allows birds to navigate. In fact, trees charge the atmosphere. Ion concentrations above forests are twice as high as grasslands. Remember all the way back to Chapter 1, where we explored that when trees die for any reason, humans die in greater numbers. That may be related to electrical nourishment – and communication – that we invisibly receive from trees, perhaps without even realizing it.

Even mycelial networks communicate electrically. Recently, researchers put electrodes into mycelial networks and measured the rhythmic pulses of electrical activity that emerged from them. The electrical impulses are similar to the electrical impulses that pass along our nerves. Even fungal networks can use electrical impulses to communicate information about what's happening to different distant parts of themselves.

The perceptions of our hearts may show up in part as emotions but also feed into other forms of knowing, best described as intuition and imagination. As discussed previously, both have been downgraded in modern society. But as systems philosopher and futurist Buckminster Fuller said, "We have all heard people describe other people, in a derogatory way, as 'full of imagination.' The fact is that if you are not full of imagination, you are not very sane."

Indeed.

Perhaps recognizing the intelligence of our hearts – and the intelligence of the beings around us – can begin the process of "coming to our senses." We can begin to attune to the countless sentient beings within and around us - from mitochondria and microorganisms to plants, animals, rocks, water, even the Earth. This return to enchantment permits us to reclaim what we have been missing for so long and perhaps remedy some of the suffering that has manifested as the "diseases of civilization" that are epidemic.

How did we become so afraid of the mystical? And how can Master Plants help us reclaim it?

THE HISTORY OF DISENCHANTMENT

In some ways, we can begin by looking at language. When we've come through a spiritual awakening and are recalibrating our perceptions of reality – we often lack adequate words to describe our experiences.

In part, this is because we have no shared lexicon to discuss spiritual experiences outside of organized religion.

Language has been systematically disenchanted. As discussed in Chapter 3, myth has come to mean falsehood, magic has become synonymous with sleight of hand, and even the word enchantment connotes deception. Imagination is something we fabricate; imaginary means pretend. Old wives' tales are spurious, superstitious, and misleading advice coming from older women.

And as we've discussed, the term hallucination in its current use equates the visions of psychedelics as false, delusional, or psychotic when they may not be when explored through the proper lens.

Yet old wives' tales originate in the oral tradition of storytelling. As spiritual teacher Yeye Luisah Teish says, we should think of them as old WISE tales. As with myth, the stories were a way that extra-literate women could share their wisdom to instruct younger people and each other. The stories were designed to teach lessons and make difficult concepts like death or coming of age accessible even to children and to act as a general guide for younger generations navigating their own difficult situations.

Over the years, the tales were often collected by literate men and turned into written works for which the men received credit. Famous fairy tales by the Grimms and others have their roots in the oral traditions of women. These male writers took the wisdom stories that women shared freely with one another and tweaked them into morality tales for children.

Can we reclaim the wisdom that exists in myth, mystery, and magic? And how did we lose it in the first place?

This forgetting began millennia ago when we lost the wisdom of the Goddess but was accelerated over the period of the European witch hunts.

Yes, these events took place hundreds of years ago. And yes, we are still squarely in the post–witch hunt era.

This apocalyptic period changed the course of history. It turns out the European witch hunts weren't really about hunting witches. They weren't just about attacking women, though as many as one million women are thought to have been tortured or killed. They weren't even just about the church gaining control, although that happened too. The witch hunts were about sustained control, conformity, and, most of all, obedience.

All of this served an agenda of disenchantment.

Capitalism required workers to be reliable, dependable, and consistent. They needed to live solely in chronological time - keeping track of hours and minutes, schedules and deadlines. There was no room for kairos, that time outside of time that exists in ceremony. Performing rituals around phases of the moon, gathering for festivals on the equinox and solstice, or taking auspicious days to perform ceremonies was inconsistent – not to mention that these practices were vehicles of self-empowerment and awareness. Empowered workers were not likely to be obedient workers.

Goodbye, ritual and ceremony (outside of the church).

Who were the first targets? Disobedient women, naturally. The ones who marched to the beat of their own drums. The unofficial lay leaders and rabble-rousers of their communities.

These women became targets when the commons, or established communal land, were made private. Sounds like some boring detail from a dusty history book, I know, but hear me out, because the impact was massive.

The commons had always been shared public land, a sort of park, but better – for people of all means to produce food, make money, and gather. Commoners could grow gardens, hunt, graze animals for dairy, meat, or fleece – all for free – and then sell what they didn't eat or need. Most importantly, the commons were communal spaces that allowed people to come together and connect.

Goodbye, communal gathering and access to public land, food, and being your own boss.

Capitalism was rising, and it reframed society. Everything and everyone now looked like potential commodities. Land was a commodity and people became commodities. The lower class were potential workers, and lower-class women could make countless more workers.

See where this is going?

The first problem was that communal land was empowering this massive pool of potential workers to be independent, self-sustaining, and self-organizing and to do as they pleased. So it was eliminated. Without it, many – especially the nonconformist women – became impoverished, hungry, and angry.

Not coincidentally, the witch hunts coincided with the Age of Reason and Enlightenment. Good old Francis Bacon is mostly known (and venerated) for his famed modern scientific method. Less well known, however, was that the scientific method was modeled on the interrogation of "witches" via torture.

Through the lens of science, he portrayed nature as a woman to be conquered, unveiled, raped, and, ultimately, dominated. And the torture and destruction of women and others were not just supported by the intellectuals and scientists of the day – they actually collected their corpses for experimentation. In Bacon's words, this experimentation could allow mankind to "penetrate further" and "find a way at length into her inner chambers." Since "the dominion of man over nature rests only on knowledge," the key to man's mastery over the world lay in organized scientific research.

Bacon promised that his new method would lead to genuine progress in every field, usher in the "truly masculine birth of time," and render nature the "slave of mankind."

Starting to sound familiar?

The mission extended as an attack on the feminine. It was no accident that the witch hunts coincided with the enslavement and genocide of indigenous communities across Africa and the New World. Yes, non-European land and people (and wisdom) were potentially valuable commodities, but indigenous societies were deeply rooted in the celebration of the feminine: Earth-based religion, ceremony, connection between all living beings, and mystery.

The feminine encompasses more than biological women. The archetype of both feminine and masculine exists within each of us. If the masculine archetype within us savors achievement, being in control, competing, conquering, and glory, the feminine represents stillness and being receptive, listening and witnessing, intuition and inner wisdom, ritual and ceremony, community and collaboration, the sacred moment before creation and the celebration of beginning and end of life. The feminine, in all its glory, is in the not knowing and in mystery.

The feminine represents our ongoing conversation with mystery, what is not yet known, and what may never be known.

In this pivotal period of control, connecting to the mystery of the natural world through ritual and ceremony were seen as insubordination. It was the potential resistance of grassroots to power. "Woman as witch" represented the persecution of the wild side of nature and all in nature that seemed disorderly, subversive, unpredictable, and antagonistic to the goals of the new science.

In short, it was the unfettered goal of certainty, control, and domination that directly led our society astray.

The sacred feminine was once symbolized by the snake or serpent. In fact, snakes, coils, and spirals have long been considered direct representations of the Goddess, symbolizing her feminine power of regeneration. The earliest Egyptian hieroglyph for Goddess is the same as that for serpent – the raised cobra. In India, the Goddess is the sleeping kundalini that becomes Shakti upon awakening. In the pre-Celtic British Isles, the goddess Brigit was intimately connected with the serpent. When St. Patrick drove the "snakes" out of Ireland, as recognized on St. Patrick's Day, it was in fact the Goddess people he was persecuting.

Worshiped for more than seven thousand years, the serpent represented the beginning of all cosmogonies before being toppled by monotheism and "reason."

It was the biblical story of Adam and Eve that marked the transformation of serpent as Goddess and Mother of All Life to a more insidious, duplicitous depiction. The story contains all of the same elements as other origin myths up to that point, including those discussed in Chapter 8 – the twin beings, snake, the tree – common symbols that also long represented the Goddess. But here, the snake is evil and the tree is forbidden.

Forbidding trees may sound absurd at first. It may make more sense when we consider that the Semitic tree cults who worshiped the World Tree were likely worshipping a disguised version of the Canaanite representation of the Goddess, or Asherah. Asherah sheltered, protected, and nourished the animal world and whose temples were in sacred groves, and later linked to Eve as the "mother of all living." The prohibition of fruit from a sacred tree and the stigmatization of the serpent as leading Eve astray in violation of a masculine, abstract version of God launched the deep, longstanding repression of Goddess culture and worship. Eve, linked to Asherah as the "mother of all living," was depicted as gullible and disobedient in the bargain.

Telltale clues of the Goddess remained. Tree-like pillars called Asherim described repeatedly throughout the Bible were thought to represent the Goddess. The Kabbalistic Tree of Life was another link. Even the Shekinah, depicted as a feminine nature of God, has been considered by some as a devolution of Asherah.

Thus began a culture that found divinity in domination and obedience rather than interconnectedness, creation, and aliveness.

As a result, we've been living in a state of profound alienation – separated from our physical bodies, emotions, and spiritual selves, as well as from nature, from each other, and from the divine. We are still operating from that ruptured place of trauma and disenchantment. Simply put, we're lonely.

PSYCHEDELICS AND RE-ENCHANTMENT

Master Plants can offer a remedy to our sense of rupture. When we think back to the common Master Plant visions and even dreams of snakes, trees, vines, and spirals explored in Chapter 8, could it be a coincidence that we are being shown images associated with the Goddess?

The impact of the European witch hunts is embedded in our epigenetics, those environmental and situational influences that determine how our otherwise very stable DNA is read and manifested. But remember, the beauty of epigenetics is that while they are inherited from generation to generation, they are also reversible based on what we do in the present moment.

If certainty (and obedience) has led to the disenchantment of the world, embracing relationships, ceremony, mystery – and purposeful disobedience – may be exactly what we need to heal.

We abandoned the paradigm that acknowledges that rich wisdom emerges from uncertainty and change, and instead vowed to uphold a world in which as much as possible is certain. What sustained all humans through challenging periods since the beginning of time – namely, ritual, community, celebrating cycles of life and nature, and connecting regularly with ancestors and the invisible world – was now called wild, primitive, and uncivilized.

Rather than embrace questioning and new ideas, we "burn at the stake" those who journey back from the unknown with theories that challenge the status quo.

At its core, the modern approach to science (and medicine) still is rooted in a desire for obedience, compliance, and control – of both scientists and the greater population. And science – not inherently but as it has been practiced and applied, has become dogma – a way to deny the unknown rather than explore it.

We are reenacting the trauma of the witch hunts that is imprinted in our society on an epigenetic level. We learned that nonconformity is undesirable, that the unknown is dangerous, and that "settled science" is the road to safety and security and never to be questioned. Science, in all its linear, rational certainty, has become the only acceptable lens through which we are permitted to understand ourselves. If we can't see or measure it, it doesn't exist, we are told, yet by its nature, science is incendiary and insubordinate and creates more questions than answers.

Yet science is never settled. Scientists constantly make discoveries that break the rules of everything they thought before. A new generation of scientists are now demonstrating the existence of what we have long dismissed. Quantum physics uses rigorous approaches to show that there is no separation between the observer and the observed and that many timelines can exist simultaneously.

Systems biology is showing the limitations of our reductionist approaches, which have long ignored the value of interrelatedness in complex systems within our bodies as well as in nature.

And it is no accident that many great scientists – Pythagoras, Maimonides, Tesla, Einstein – were also mystics in their way. Remember, science is but one language we use to describe the mystery of the invisible world.

We think of ourselves as the most technologically advanced

society in history. We have access to dictionaries, encyclopedias, documentaries, thought leaders, and the entire TED talk library on the phones in our pockets. We can access infinite data and ever-improving algorithms that help us predict probabilities for the future, and yet the unpredictability of the world is always greater than all of our tools.

As we acknowledge the stigmatization of myth and "old wives' tales" as unreliable or fabricated, we can offer legitimacy to different ways of knowing, and embrace knowledge as a process of revelation rather than a reductionist, black-and-white approach to truth. Indeed, truth is multilayered, not black and white but filled with nuance and contradictions, because many things can be true at the same time.

And of course, unpredictability and uncertainty are not enemies, but simply signals for us to engage with our nonlinear ways of knowing, navigating, and wayfinding.

The mystic Caroline Casey says that not knowing is an accomplishment because the invisible world celebrates when we say we don't know. That's when we're finally available for mystery to find us.

Our newfound perception that comes from initiation by way of Master Plants or ceremony does not come from merely changing our minds and thinking – quite the opposite. Once our minds have been broken open and our mental constructs broken down, that's when we can begin to access the real magic of the world.

Master Plants give us permission to step beyond the wisdom of our mental constructs and into our physical, emotional, and spiritual bodies, where we can access a whole world of new sensation and information. This is the how-heart-head-hands approach. We start with how - making an offering of some kind as we ask for help from the visible and invisible. Then, we move to our hearts, leaning into a sense of gratitude and appreciation as we attune our sensory gating and intuition to receive from the numinous. Only then do we rely on our heads, discerning, making meaning of the messages, and formulating strategies. Finally, we engage our hands, by taking action.

Then, as we operate in this new, greater way, we become beacon holders, demonstrating for others how to do the same.

As we shift our paradigm from "Us versus Them" to "Me and We" we cultivate relationships with our inner and outer terrain – from the microbes and mitochondria within us to the people, animals, trees, wind, water, seeds, soil, and sun around us – that both feed our need for joy and meaning *as well as* physical essentials. Deep connection – to ourselves, each other and the invisible – requires reverence, reciprocity, appreciation, and gratitude.

Master Plants can expand our awareness beyond the linear and rational to light up these connections. The warmth of a hug. The sound of wind moving through beach grass. The magic of a close encounter with a hummingbird or an eagle. Recognizing that sense of joy – the yes! the wow! that is uniquely ours – comes only through carving out moments to step outside of ordinary time. In those moments, our intuition speaks to us and guides us where we need to go.

Re-enchantment is the light that allows us to find beauty, joy, divinity, and sacredness in the seemingly ordinary by meeting the world directly with our hearts. This is what allows us to survive and even thrive in our lives, day by day and year by year – even in the face of pain, loss, challenges, disappointments and the suffering of the world. And it begins by slowing down and creating spaciousness, cultivating kairos moments, engaging with our imaginations to create offerings of gratitude and appreciation.

Relearning this language is part of a homecoming to ourselves and to the invisible relationships that sustain us.

11

WHAT NOW? TENDING OUR INTEGRATION

I t has long been known among indigenous cultures that people must remember their place in the web of life. If we forget and don't take the time to reflect and renew our connection with the sacred, illness and imbalances arise. We've dived deep into the loss of enchantment in the modern world and begun to find our way back from existential loneliness. Now it's time to consider integrating what we've learned in non-ordinary reality – in ceremony, dreamtime, or the initiatory experience of grief, loss, or wild joy – into the everyday.

Simply put, how can we re-enchant our lives?

First of all, re-enchantment is not magic as in the magician's sleight of hand or spell work à la Harry Potter. Re-enchantment describes our conversation with the visible and invisible world. It's the act of attending to the world, and acknowledging how the world responds. The more we notice this conversation, the more we engage in the aliveness of all things and delight in them.

Re-enchantment is an owl feather floating to the ground in front of us that brings wonder and gratitude in a moment of despair. It's palpably missing our beloved, long-deceased grandmother as we're driving and, a moment later, hearing her favorite song on the radio.

It's waking from a dream about a beloved friend we haven't talked to in years and receiving an email from her an hour later. Re-enchantment is when we recognize that we are part of an invisible web infinitely larger than ourselves, and can tap into those connections at any moment.

A doctor friend of mine experienced this firsthand. She was told by a spiritual teacher that her sister, who had died young, wanted to support her in her present life more. She wasn't sure what to think but decided to try a simple experiment. She asked for her sister to help her son win an athletic competition and specifically asked for a sign that her sister was helping him win.

Her son did win.

After winning, however, they got word that the next level of the competition would take place in the town her sister had lived and died in, on her sister's birthday.

There was the sign of help.

This is but one person's story of synchronicity. Yet most of us have any number of such stories, often written off as coincidences. While discernment can serve as a helpful lens to apply at times, why are we so afraid to trust the sense that our experiences have underlying meaning?

At a minimum, finding meaning is what makes life feel, well, meaningful. Through meaning-making, we find choice in a sea of chance, and purpose in what otherwise can feel pointless. And if we consider that synchronicities serve as the first indicators of new emergent systems forming, noticing them may offer even more than living with greater ease and trust. Attending to these transmissions can provide necessary landmarks and guideposts that point us toward co-creating.

This ability to perceive and connect is not limited only to a select few. We are designed to access enchantment. It simply requires our presence and practice.

A ROADMAP FOR HUMAN-ING

An experience with Master Plants can often be life-changing and initiatory. Maybe we've confronted our deepest and darkest shadow parts. Maybe we've touched the divine and beyond, or seen ourselves vulnerable and naked in a way we may never have done before. Whether it felt like visiting heaven or hell, we're back. We've experienced something profound; as a result, we are different – physically, mentally, emotionally, and spiritually.

We've glimpsed a more enchanted world where our senses perceived far more than we'd ever imagined.

We've located our inner compass and engaged with something greater than us.

The grand question is, What now?

Now, we begin to create the semblance of a roadmap for human-ing. And we can gain clarity on the first step on this roadmap by considering the Mayan word for human, which means "one who owes the gods."

What have we brought back from non-ordinary reality? How do we honor the gifts and the calling within the experience? How can we cultivate a life of greater reverence, appreciation, curiosity, and authenticity?

When we have an experience with Master Plants, one of the trickiest parts is trying to fit ourselves back into a life familiar only with the prior version of us. We will likely feel something (if not everything) in our lives is utterly incongruent at first. Everyone around us hasn't made the quantum leap that we have. Allowing our people and circumstances to shift in response to our new operating frequencies can be helpful. There will be time to make significant changes.

Often, we have shed our hard, protective shells and feel more sensitive, empathic, softer and startlingly more tearful than before. How do we maintain this wide open sensory gating while remaining safe?

This process of integration is where we practice. How do we

allow this latest update of ourselves into the old version of our lives? What does collaboration look like?

Behold one of the trickiest practices of human-ing – bringing our non-ordinary transmissions into ordinary, everyday reality. Integrating what's invisible into the visible. Making sacred our places, relationships, and ourselves while still brushing our teeth and paying our bills.

The pain is real.

This chapter offers a small sampling of ways to integrate and connect to the invisible within and around us. To go deeper into everything discussed in this section and much more, see the Thank You page at the end of this book or go to https://drmaya.com/resources.

CULTIVATING A RELATIONSHIP WITH OURSELVES

Rest

"I do not particularly like the word 'work.' Human beings are the only animals who have to work, and I think that is the most ridiculous thing in the world. Other animals make their living by living, but people work like crazy, thinking that they have to in order to stay alive. The bigger the job, the greater the challenge, the more wonderful they think it is. It would be good to give up that way of thinking and live an easy, comfortable life with plenty of free time. I think that the way animals live in the tropics, stepping outside in the morning and evening to see if there is something to eat, and taking a long nap in the afternoon, must be a wonderful life. For human beings, a life of such simplicity would be possible if one worked to produce directly his daily necessities. In such a life, work is not work as people generally think of it, but simply doing what needs to be done."

—Masanobu Fukuoka, *The One-Straw Revolution*

I know, I know. This approach to life sounds extreme. It is diametrically opposed to the way we live. But consider the degree that most of us are prisoners of urgency culture. Texting and emailing, seized with the sense that we need to know everything as soon as it happens and that everything needs to be dealt with immediately. Feeling like we'll somehow be too late if we don't comment, opine, or come up with a quick fix in the moment. Worrying that we'll miss the boat if we're not on high alert every moment. We are in a permanent state of FOMO – fear of missing out – that rarely serves us. Urgency culture has become its own form of enslavement to a world of distractions.

As a result, most of us live in sympathetic overdrive. Remember the sympathetic, fight-or-flight response that keeps us in a state of fear, meant to save us if an unfriendly tiger is chasing us? Our parasympathetic response acts as a balance to the fear response, modulated largely by way of our vagus nerve.

Nature loves to show us what we need to know with direct illustrations. As such, our vagus nerve is a very long nerve that is quite literally meandering – as if it's demonstrating that we need to amble and take detours to be in the calm place necessary to rest, digest, and receive. The vagus nerve is responsible for slowing our heart rate and breathing, improving digestion, and enhancing social interactions (yes, that means feeling less socially awkward!). A lesser-known response of the vagus nerve is to modulate inflammation, just as with respiratory or heart rate. Decreased vagal activity leads to inflammation and cell danger, which in turn contributes to many epidemic conditions, including depression, autoimmune conditions, cancer, and virtually every neurological condition.

These are ways our bodies, minds, hearts, and souls are crying out in very real ways: We've had enough.

Even if we engage with psychedelics and perceive immediate benefits, Master Plants are not a magic fix in and of themselves. No mystical experience is. Yet they open the portal for transformation. The time is ripe to make considered, meaningful changes.

At an absolute minimum, the pattern interrupt can show us where we have agency in the constellation of responsibilities and systems in which we're unconsciously enmeshed. Tempting as it may be to quickly and dramatically restructure (because "that's what

Grandmother Ayahuasca told me to do"), this period offers an opportunity to recalibrate the "do, do, do" approach first and foremost.

Sometimes the ideal move is to pause. The best remedy can be to claiming spaciousness for ourselves wherever we can in an ongoing way.

Our capacity for spaciousness is comprised of priority and also privilege. For those who work eighteen hour days just to make ends meet, for example, less time and fewer resources are available for this process. Yet we begin with dedicating minutes here and there to daydreaming, play, building an altar, taking a walk, or taking a few deep breaths. I am far from glib about the challenges we may face. I'm also not suggesting meditating for five minutes or even five hours daily will solve all our problems. But it won't hurt us either. Any intentional time and space we create to cultivate sensitivity and attunement to the intelligence and guidance around us can be worth its weight in gold.

Many people are blocked by their busy-ness. This can look like an addiction to "shoulds": "I should see this friend in town," "I should spend the weekend at my in-laws' house even though I don't want to," or "I should really get started on this next project." Another common one is "My work is my passion." We are crafty when it comes to concocting strategies to uphold our conditioning to avoid being present in the here and now.

Life is always a balance between what we want to do and what we have to do. Most of us think responsibilities should always take priority over what we love doing because that's what we've been told. Growing up, my mother's constant refrain was: "That's why it's called work, and that's why they pay you to do it." This approach is so ingrained that we take it for granted. Many of us never even ask why.

To intentionally cultivate a love affair with mystery, we must learn to glide. Slowing down takes practice. We practice remaining present rather than checking out. We liberate ourselves into the full experience of the moment instead of repressing our longings. We bring more depth to whatever we are doing. We develop intimacy with the invisible world by cultivating subtle awareness. Slowing our operating speed directly determines how sensitive, aware, present, and responsive we can be to ourselves, others, and the sentience of the world around us.

As we engage, new questions begin to arise: What if we are here to enjoy the beauty of the world and pursue what makes us feel most alive? How would our lives, communities, and society change if we consciously embedded ourselves in this paradigm?

Play

We've come to believe that play is an activity for children and not for adults. In reality, everyone benefits from play. For adults, play reduces stress, promotes relaxation, activates our reward systems, as well as helping us build relationships, enhance communication, strengthen social skills, and have fun. (You remember fun, right?) Play promotes neuroplasticity, creating new neural pathways and improving our ability to adapt and change in response to new experiences – these skills are beneficial always but are especially important to prevent cognitive decline as we age.

Being silly is productive. Fun is valuable. Laughing releases endorphins that reduce pain and promote pleasure, increasing our blood flow, relaxing our muscles, activating our brain reward systems, and flooding us with serotonin and dopamine, which amplify positive emotions.

Play itself leads to greater heart rate variability and coherence. As a result, the neuroscience of play (yes, there's a whole body of research) demonstrates its role in remaining flexible, adaptable, imaginative, and successful and happy in our adult lives. And by play, I mean low-stakes activities of many kinds. Here's a hint: Playing a pick-up game of flag football with some friends counts as low-stakes; playing for the NFL does not. The key is to encourage imagination, role playing, problem-solving and being a beginner, as well as experimentation, curiosity, humility, kinship, and reciprocity.

The wisdom of Coyote, the Trickster, reminds us that we are at our most wise when we can laugh at ourselves and not take life too seriously. According to the lessons of the Fool archetype, humor, lightness, and fun help us to confront the most serious truths and to discharge any accumulated heaviness, making life more bearable.

Pressuring ourselves to be perpetually productive is based on the Cartesian concept of Man as Machine. But humans aren't machines. Our bodies work in cycles: daily, weekly, monthly, seasonally, and yearly. Wake and sleep. Activity on some days and rest on others. Gestation, manifestation, and even more existential cycles of destruction, being in the void, and rebirth. These cycles take place on an ecological level and reflect in our physical, emotional, spiritual, and ecological bodies.

Each phase offers value. Alertness cannot happen without sleep. Manifestation cannot occur without gestation. Activity cannot continue without rest and recovery. The most meaningful words emerge from a backdrop of silence.

Sometimes downtime isn't avoiding work. Downtime *is* the work. Rest, spaciousness and play are sacred. Each nourishes us – mind, body, heart, and soul.

Consider work as something we can do to make our play more effective. Most people play in deference to work rather than designing work to serve our ability to play. And then we spend our lives performing an endless series of tasks that feel like obligations, give us no juice, and don't feel like a *yes*. What can we eliminate from our lives except that which enables us to do what light us up?

No matter our circumstances, we begin by prioritizing what makes us feel alive, starting with as little as a few minutes each day.

Embodiment Practices

Nowadays, the vast majority of people are sitting in front of computers doing mental work. As a result, we spend a tremendous amount of time in their heads. Whether we are driving ourselves to accomplish physically or mentally, caring for our bodies tends to get the short end of the stick. When we feel uncomfortable in our bodies, our conditioning is to quiet or suppress those sensations until they can no longer be ignored rather than attending to them in the moment.

Orienting to our bodies starts with noticing – taking a few moments to attend to our posture, any tension we feel in our bodies, our breathing and heart rate, and any sensations that are pleasant, painful, or simply calling our attention. This may be easier with eyes closed. When we notice a part of the body that feels different or strange, we can place our hands or focus breathing into that area. Sometimes emotions arise. Notice those as well, without fixing or changing them. The experience may initially feel unsettling and require practice, especially if "being in our bodies" is unfamiliar.

We can begin by noticing and promptly responding to physiological urges like thirst or the urge to urinate, for example, rather than ignoring the sensations until they become urgent. Going to bed when we feel sleepy is another practice that is often disregarded. Moving every day – whether meandering, running, dancing, gardening, or hopscotch

As we become more attuned to our bodies, we may notice our physical bodies communicating information to us about us. Sometimes these messages can be surprisingly literal. We may meet someone and suddenly feel as though our lungs are constricted and we can't breathe. Our digestion may become disrupted when we can't "stomach" something. We may experience shoulder pain when we're "shouldering" too much responsibility or back pain when we remain rigid in the face of change. Though not every physical problem presents with this level of clarity, our bodies are sentient, intelligent systems that offer symptoms as a language that can inform us (or usually confirm) what we're struggling with.

Embodiment practices can range from simple and gentle to more complex or vigorous. Deep, slow breathing at the rate of 6 breaths per minute acts as a love language for our nervous systems. Gentle rocking of the hips or massaging our arms down to our hands can be gently regulating. Lying down on the Earth, sitting on a rock, or leaning against a tree can help us feel more grounded in our bodies and connected to the land.

Practice: Hip Figure Eights: See Thank you page

Contemplative Practice

Coping with stress and uncomfortable emotions is a learned skill that many of us lack because our families of origin modeled poor emotional regulation. Yet as discussed, when we don't have the skills to process our emotions, they can control our lives far more than necessary, keeping us reactive and in survival mode.

Whether through prayer, meditation, yoga, mantra, journaling, or others, daily contemplative practices help us become more acutely aware of our inner life, and connect with that which is greater than us. While they are all part of great spiritual traditions, this self-witnessing also can create space for uncomfortable thoughts and feelings to arise and be acknowledged without judgement so that we can metabolize them.

It's not infrequent that people tell me: "I can't meditate," or "Meditation makes me uncomfortable." Exactly. Sometimes, that's the point. Most of us are not accustomed to regularly offering ourselves undivided attention. Sitting quietly with ourselves can sometimes feel excruciating because uncomfortable feelings or thoughts arise that we'd rather not confront. Being with them even for a few minutes, however, can feel like we finally had that difficult conversation we've been avoiding with someone. Keep showing up and keep coming back. Presence and practice are paramount.

When meditation (or journaling, or any practice) feels like a sweet, relaxing journey into ecstasy, wonderful. When we spend ten of the most torturous minutes we can imagine, also fantastic. Both offer benefits.

These practices become indispensable when we are in a place of

THE MASTER PLANT EXPERIENCE

confusion or struggle. At the most basic level, we are "practicing the pause," allowing ourselves to tune into our inner compass. We can close our eyes and ask ourselves: What (or who) makes us feel more alive? What (or who) makes us feel drained? Is this a yes or no for me?

Practice: Release meditation: See Thank you page

Nervous System Regulating Practices – Engaging and Regulating with Your Vagus Nerve

Simple practices, including humming, singing, chanting, gargling, breathwork, and even massaging right in front of our ears, can activate the vagus nerve and expand our for calm. Engaging and balancing the vagus nerve can profoundly impact our overall health and well-being by reducing stress and anxiety, improving digestion and sleep, and even boosting our mood and social connectedness. Practicing one or more of these daily make us to feel safer from the inside out, even in the face of stress.

The word enchantment comes from Latin *incantare, in* meaning into, and *cantare* meaning to sing. 'Singing into' ourselves and the world is a way to literally re-enchant our lives. And the more we learn about the vibrational nature of our cells and the world around us, the more sense it makes that singing can entrain us on every level as a form of sonic medicine.

All of these widen our ability to experience life without getting derailed by interactions and situations that thrust us into dysregulation. That expanded capacity allows us also to access flow states more easily, allowing us longer periods of heart rate variability, creativity and productivity with less effort. We can also find our way back into flow more quickly rather than feeling tempted to turn to coping behaviors we'd rather not employ.

Some call these say these regulating practices glimmers (as opposed to triggers). Glimmers can be planned, like spending time in beautiful nature, watching a sunset, dancing, drumming, listening to a song we enjoy, loving on our pet, and cuddling or hanging out with someone special. They can be unexpected kairos moments that result from being in the right place at the right time, including spotting a rainbow or shooting star, discovering a nest of baby birds, receiving beautiful flowers or discovering a wonderful restaurant, getting a meaningful message from someone we've been wanting to hear from, or any synchronicity that holds unique meaning for us.

These practices are fundamental to further engage and intentionally modulate our sensory gating.

Practice: Humming: See Thank you page

Reparenting

Relationships with parents can be very tricky for many people. And this is not just limited to those with parents that were abusive, neglectful, or dysregulated; even the most well-intentioned parents sometimes find their particular parenting style is a complete mismatch for one or more of their children. It's so common to experience primary woundings during our early years that feeling unwounded is the anomaly as opposed to the other way around. Rather than getting derailed by our "mother wound" and "father wound," we can engage in a practice called reparenting.

Sometimes one of the most healing practices we can offer ourselves is to show up as loving adults to protect the disempowered child we once were. The process is simple, and requires grace, care, and compassion. We breathe, sink into a relaxed, meditative state, and ask ourselves a question like: What care can I offer little me? Or we can also find a childhood picture of ourselves at any age and ask that child what support they'd like.

Oftentimes, people will see an actual image of themselves as a child at a particular age. The child's answers are often less involved than we may expect, for example: "Just play with me," "Hold my hand," "Listen to me tell a story," or "Tell me you love me." We can offer younger versions of ourselves exactly what they need by embodying the role of the loving adult we are now.

Another reparenting practice can be to write a letter to our child selves at particular ages or times of childhood, and share advice, insight, and even wisdom around how those periods influenced our future selves.

Slowly, this process can grow to become a daily practice of checking in with different parts of ourselves that are less at the forefront, asking what those parts need right now, and taking small actions in the present.

Practice: Reparenting meditation: See Thank you page

CULTIVATING A RELATIONSHIP WITH OTHERS

As we explore our relationship with ourselves, we can shift our relationships with those around us. True connection with others starts from reciprocity. How do we show up in our relationships, and how do others show up in return?

Some practices that enrich our relationships include clear communication and greater honesty with the people around us (think: kind but firm), engaging in hard conversations, and setting, sharing, and maintaining reasonable boundaries. We can learn when and how to be vulnerable and share feelings, and how to refine listening skills for others to share in similar ways.

After a ceremony, we may suddenly become aware that our lives are not populated by fierce tigers, which may mean we need to act differently than before. In some cases, we may realize that we've been highly guarded or overly anxious in ways that no longer feel necessary. In other cases, a relationship may need to drastically change or even end. Sometimes, what's needed is not immediately obvious at first.

After being in a ceremony or working with a psychedelic, we may notice we're not triggered the same way as before because we can inhabit the role of the audience – even for just a moment – rather than just a character responding automatically according to a karmic script. We may notice the other person's underlying pain or story in a way we didn't before. We may experience our own reaction differently, with new insight into the influence of an unrelated situation from our past or present.

Such moments can offer new spaciousness in our relationships as we respond in a more considered way.

Setting Boundaries

One of the most loving primary actions we can take toward ourselves and others is to determine, set, and communicate boundaries. Exploring boundaries is indicated when interactions with people or groups feel draining, triggering, or agitating.

It's easy to get angry at other people when we feel triggered. Whenever we blow up, the first thing to do is to ask ourselves why we're really upset. Sometimes, we haven't yet recognized that we need to set a certain boundary; sometimes, we haven't clearly expressed that boundary to people; and sometimes, we've clearly set a boundary that isn't being respected.

I grew up with my single mother, who struggled to regulate her severe anxiety. She frequently woke up in the middle of the night and wrote ten-page-long rants about how angry she was with me or how I was failing as a daughter. Beginning when I was a preteen, she slid her missives under my bedroom door so I would see them as soon as I woke up. When I left for college, she mailed them to me or filled my voicemail with message after recriminatory message. Naturally, I'd become upset, while her agitation had already dissipated. My distress was then framed as unreasonable and hostile.

For a long time, this dynamic was normal to me. I learned to tolerate what I later recognized as abusive behavior, which felt unpredictable and dysregulating. For a long time, I felt helpless. It never occurred to me that I had any agency in my experience of my mother's dysregulated behavior until I got married at twenty-three. The first time I listened to one of her messages with my new spouse standing right next to me, aghast, I realized: This behavior is not okay. This must stop.

I called my mother and calmly explained if she wanted to speak to me for any reason, she would have to call me. I told her I wouldn't listen to any voicemail messages longer than 15 seconds; they would simply be deleted. Any mail she sent would go directly into the garbage, unopened. She was angry, but I upheld my boundaries, and her behavior and communication eventually improved.

When we experience a sense of helplessness in an adult relationship, it's worth paying attention to what is driving that feeling. Typically, our desperation or distress puts a spotlight on an aspect of the relationship that requires our attention and courageous action.

Coregulating

Shared joyful experiences nourish relationships, even (especially) through difficult times of relationship growth. Think of these activities as joint deposits in our relational bank accounts. Meaningful connection does not require vast expenditures or exotic experiences, but simply presence and practice. The practices can range from sitting on the couch together sharing funny memes or watching a rerun of a beloved TV show to planning a picnic, stargazing, going to a concert, or returning to the spot of a first or early date. When appropriate, physical contact can also serve as a powerful form of connection and need not be sexual, even with a romantic partner. Hugging, spooning, holding hands, or leaning against each other allows for greater entrainment and shared heart rate variability.

Ask and really listen to what the other person enjoys. Finding new, common activities that each person enjoys can take time and requires a willingness to experiment. Remember that discovering something both people love (or hate!) can be a form of bonding. In general, expectations create pitfalls; no one is required to feel a certain way about an experience. Communication is key. Keep in mind that some shared experiences will be disappointing, others delightful. All can be meaningful.

As always, presence and practice are fundamental to building intimacy. Prioritizing time together will ideally include minimal distractions, especially from other people. When distractions consistently feel more appealing than being with the person with whom we've committed to spend time, it's worth reflecting on why our attention is being drawn elsewhere and what that might indicate about ourselves or our relationship.

CULTIVATING A RELATIONSHIP WITH THE LAND ON WHICH WE STAND

A relationship with the land can mean many things. Just as being in good relationship with people requires learning their nuances and needs, the land has her own needs, demands, and desires.

This practice starts with showing up. I recommend finding a sit spot for you to be with the land as a regular, daily practice. Oftentimes, the sit spot chooses us. When a location catches our attention because it's interesting, beautiful, or we feel an indescribable longing or pull, we may be receiving an invitation to begin a relationship with that place. What we notice is noticing us.

Bring an offering – whether it's compost, seeds, building a mandala, or singing a song - that shows that we are approaching with humility, reverence, and appreciation.

Then, we ask permission, listen for the response, and open our awareness. Spending time allows our sensory gating to open, and we begin to perceive the language of the place. When we spend time regularly, we start to be guided in a particular direction.

Then the conversation begins. That's the starting point.

Engaging in this conversation is what I teach in my Decertification program. One of my students had a beautiful passionflower plant that had beautiful flowers but never bore fruit. As one of our practices, she approached the plant and said: Dear Passionflower Plant, Thank you for being so beautiful. Would you be willing to make fruit for me this year? Lo and behold, weeks later, she discovered with joy her first passionfruit.

These practices can become a form of sacred play. We don't

know what will happen or how the conversation will go. We discover what is being asked of us and respond in the moment.

For all we get from Gaia, what we can offer in return is daily honoring: reverence, gratitude, appreciation, wonder, and awe. These can be expressed through many practices and in many forms. Traditionally, it has been through prayer, smoke offerings, corn, tobacco, or other sacred plants. An offering can begin with our awareness and attention through daily practices that slow us down, like meditation or mantra. We can offer words of thanks, songs, art, or nature mandalas. We can plant native pollinator-attracting flowers, tend our gardens in animal-friendly ways, or offer compost and seeds. We can rewild areas of our yard and allow for new ecosystems to develop.

Practice: Plant Brushing

Plant brushing is a beautiful sweeping practice starting from the head and ending with the feet that clears, cleans, lightens, and helps with release. The aromatic herbs – like mint, rosemary, basil, rue, lavender, oregano, mugwort, or evergreens like pine or fir – are most effective. Ideally, we grow these herbs ourselves in a garden or window pot, or source them from someone who does. By tending to the herbs, we cultivate an intimate relationship with them that helps us work together with them as a team.

Anytime we're working with plants, we can ask the plants which ones would like to be a part of the healing. This practice entails stopping, letting ourselves be drawn to one or another plant, and asking permission for their participation in our practice before harvesting. Once we have chosen one another, offer something – seeds, corn, a small crystal, special water, a feather or a coin.

Exercise: Plant Brushing: See Thank you page

CULTIVATING A RELATIONSHIP WITH OUR ANCESTORS

Dagara elder Malidoma Somé used to say we're not tough enough on our ancestors. Sometimes, he said, they forget it's a war zone down here. We may need to grab them, get in their faces, and not just request but demand their help.

When I teach the importance of connecting with ancestors in my Decertification program, many initially express reluctance for any number of reasons. Most often, people relate a sense of disapproval or shame concerning the actions of past generations, or feel that it's wrong to "disturb" them.

Dagara society is one of many that regards those who came before us as not being dead and gone, but playing as active a part in the present moment as we do. In this paradigm, ancestors want to help us, but require that we ask for it. To Somé, one of modern society's greatest deficits is that we have too many unemployed ancestors.

Whether we recognize it or not, we are in constant communication with our ancestors. They speak to us through every mineral, drop of water, and atom that comprised their bodies and now comprise ours. They speak to us through our DNA, epigenetics, mitochondria, microbiomes, and our very bones. They speak to us through our nervous systems and the way we react to the triggers that signal potential threats, and the glimmers that signal safety, joy, and pleasure. Ancestors speak to us through our tears, smiles and laughter.

Sometimes, we can hear their words and voices in our dreams. Often, they communicate through signs, symbols, and synchronicities. We can hear them in songs they loved, smell them in perfumes or smoke that drifts by, and see them in the light patterns shimmering through trees and animals we glimpse in the wild. We feel their guidance in our deepest longings.

Though we think of ancestors solely as blood relations, most cultures consider that definition far too narrow. In Dagara society, for example, ancestors comprised the entire village and beyond, including animals, plants, and even land within and around the community. Somé referred to this framework as "the relaxed web of ancestry." We may not know all of our ancestors, but they know us.

Even when we feel confused or lost, it's important to know we are never alone. We have support. When needed, we can always ask the ancestors to make themselves known to us.

Our ancestors bridge the indigenous and the modern. They help educate us as to what is needed at least seven generations before and ahead of us. They remind us that other worlds are available to us, and that our world isn't made better by keeping to ourselves. Keeping our hearts open enough to accept these many worlds helps us to embrace our constant state of metamorphosis. They want us to remember that magic and sacredness are woven into the terrain that connects us.

We can honor our ancestors for bringing us into the world. We can invite our ancestors to join us, and ask them to offer their assistance in the most truthful, helpful, and gentle way possible. We can allow them to become a part of our spiritual team. In return, we can ask ourselves daily if we are living our lives as an expression of gratitude to the ancestors.

We will one day become ancestors. What part can we play in re-enchanting the world as our offering to the present, past, and future? What will we co-create? What draws our attention and makes us feel most alive? How can we, as individuals, groups, and a society, make the celebration of life our work and play?

To begin our conversation with the ancestors, we can create a sacred spot where we quietly sit each day. This conversation may begin with saying: "Thank you for this day" or "Here's what I'll be doing today; please accompany me." We can share our problems as well as stories.

Building these relationships creates a symbiosis in ways practical and ethereal, inside and outside of ordinary time and space.

Practice: Build an ancestor altar: See Thank you page

CULTIVATING A RELATIONSHIP WITH IMAGINATION

When I have led ceremonies and people receive important messages or images, sometimes they ask me, "But what if it was just my imagination?"

"What if?" I reply.

We've been led to believe that what appears in our imagination is pretend and that inspirations that originate from within are thus not to be believed. As a result, creative pursuits are not considered consequential unless we employ them to make money or gain acclaim. Creativity is deemed "fun" but not a priority for most adults.

In Tarot, the first card in the deck is the Fool. In contrast to what we might think, the Fool is a deeply spiritual archetype. Fully present in the moment, he's liberated from the past and future in total trust and surrender. He is a sacred archetype that reflects patterns within all of us so we can better understand ourselves and each other.

Even the number associated with this first card turns upside down what we consider as having "value." It's not one, but zero. The circle reminds us that everything valuable comes from the void, the Great Unknown, and that our paths have no beginning or end.

The Fool is childlike and simultaneously a spiritual master. He embodies the beginner's mind discussed in Chapter 9. He asks questions fearlessly, no matter how basic, and assumes nothing. He speaks truth, even (especially) to power. Plus, he delivers potent commentary through lightness, humor, and laughter. Remember, the Jester could say things to the King that would have led to anyone else being executed.

Like the Fool archetype, our imaginations serve as vehicles that help us access the fertile void and the Divine. Our imaginations open windows and nonlinear doors that reveal vistas beyond what we could have ever summoned with our rational minds. Imagination allows us to alchemize our challenges and pains into lessons, inspiration, and new awareness rather than wreak havoc on us from the inside. Creativity turns us into cauldrons; whatever is within us can transfigure and emerge in magical ways.

In art, we can interrogate and express what we can't or won't otherwise. Like Master Plants, the creative force can be subversive, radical, liberating, and usher in new ways of being. The implausible becomes possible, and the possible becomes tangible. Our creativity makes manifest that which is not yet in the material realm but wants to be.

There's an easy way to connect with our imagination if it's something we don't do regularly. Hint: It's not asking ourselves whether we'll know what we're doing or be good at it, but exactly the opposite. We can sit – with pencil, paint, paper, flowers, piano, a drum, our voices – whatever calls us. Any canvas works: floors, walls, or the earth under our feet.

And then we make bad art. (Or dance. Or mandalas. Or poetry. Or stories.)

"Making bad art" means: No expectations. No judgment. No fear of what will come through. Not worrying about being disruptive or disobedient, or being good or bad or wrong. Making bad art isn't for approval, money, success, or displaying something post-able. This practice sets us up to receive and express without preconceived ideas and cultivate our connection to the divine spark within us.

Part of the joy of planting a garden is anticipating what might grow, recognizing that we may not get exactly what we wish for, and taking pleasure in what presents itself.

Experiment with impermanence and notice the joy we can feel within the cycles beyond our control. Make temporary art. Build mandalas or sand labyrinths. Plant flower gardens. Make up a song to perform for the trees. When we think we don't know how all the better to try it.

Exercise: Keeping a Dream Journal: See Thank you page

What to do when we don't know what to do

· · ·

Ask How
  • Connect with spirit
  • Make an offering
  • Ask for permission
  • Listen for guidance
  • Surrender

Heart
  • Attune
  • Breathe
  • Emote
  • Entrain

Head
  • Learn
  • Discern
  • Plan

Hands
  • Embody
  • Move
  • Tend
  • Create
  • Perform
  • Practice

Heal
  • Expand our capacity
  • Find flow

- Play
- Embrace change
- Cultivate and deepen relationships

Spiritual awakenings sound so much more glorious than they feel. While some are gentle and loving, others are akin to spending months in a high-speed blender. When we get right down to it, these periods tend to be more humbling than anything, so much so that we don't even recognize what happened as spiritual or an awakening until long after the fact. Yet the term often connotes a sense of spiritual elitism, disregarding hard-earned humility in favor of a shiny veneer of self-proclaimed enlightenment. Consider that the etymology of human and humility derives from the root *humus*, meaning of the Earth. When we are humbled, we become more human, grounded, and of this Earth.

As such, I've renamed these periods "provocations" because they provoke us out of long-held personal narratives and often age-old cultural constructs.

No matter how old or evolved we feel, provocations can knock us fully on our asses, sometimes seemingly right back to where we first started. Though these moments can feel like we've made no progress, the journey turns out to be a spiral. Even when we return to what seems like square one, we're never the same person each time. We're constantly deepening, refining ourselves, gaining more tools, and operating with more strength, self-compassion, vulnerability, connection, and whenever possible, grace.

For better or worse, no true shortcut or "hack" exists for this process, including Master Plants. We must travel through what I call the Ps: provocation, purposeful disobedience, presence, and practice.

We discussed provocation and purposeful disobedience in great depth in Chapter 9. These parts of the cycle get the most recognition because they are often dramatic and chaotic. The most meaningful, durable changes, however, emerge as a result of our presence and practices.

Presence begins with prioritizing moments of nonordinary awareness, which deepen each time we consciously choose rest, play, and acts of devotion. Presence attunes us to our inner compass, inviting us to engage with the invisible and recognize the enchantedness of the world within and around us. Presence is felt most prominently when we step out of the doldrums of chronological time and into kairos time – through flow states, contemplative experience, and deep time in nature – that create the "perfect" moment. Most importantly, presence offers opportunities to unlearn our domesticated thinking and become students of the greater-than-human world.

Practice describes how we show up and what we do every single day. Practice on an individual level can be committing to a bedtime, exercise routine, or spiritual practice, and on a communal level can be growing food, rewilding land, and responding to the emergent needs of our human and nonhuman communities. And of course, the individual and communal overlap.

Whether we're verbally expressing our needs to a partner (even when we feel more vulnerable than we ever have), comporting ourselves gracefully when we unexpectedly run into an ex, declining to devolve into road rage, or picking up groceries for someone in need, we're practicing. Practice is life.

Intentional practices build our spiritual muscle memories. They enable us to stay steady and find our way through the tumult of our lives.

Every day is filled with opportunities that invite us to operate with intention and agency in our thoughts, feelings, beliefs, and actions. The more we tend to ourselves and others from a place of meaning, purpose, imagination, and service, the more alive and empowered we become. As a result, our lives become part of an unfolding masterpiece that we co-create day by day. This masterpiece is a record of our ongoing conversation with the visible and invisible and becomes our contribution to the collective.

Within practice, we find another P: Pleasure. Pleasure is integral to life, as necessary as food, water, sunshine, and relationships. Hedonic pleasures describe those we can access through joyful, sensual, and ecstatic experiences, gratitude and appreciation, wonder and awe, or a simple sense of satisfaction. We experience eudaimonic (*eu* meaning good, *daemon* meaning for the soul) pleasure from living lives of meaning, purpose and service, and contributing to the greater whole. One describes satisfying experiences; the other, a satisfying life. A balance of both is important. And together, these open the door to peace, play, passion, possibility and plenty.

Pleasure is a nonlinear pursuit because opportunities are woven throughout the tapestry of life and thus can be discovered anywhere, in anything, at any time. Children are fluent in this skill; as adults, we can be too.

As the Zen saying goes: Before enlightenment, chop wood, carry water. After enlightenment, chop wood, carry water. This is not to say one or even one hundred psychedelic experiences mean we'll reach enlightenment. It's a reminder that any glimpses of enlightenment matter most in the ways we live our lives. Who can't relate to what Ram Dass said? "If you think you're enlightened, go spend a week with your family."

Amen.

12

THIS IS SOMETHING NEW

B y this point, you may be feeling profound enthusiasm around Master Plants. You've seen studies showing profound benefits. You've heard the captivating history and lore, feel the lure of the authentic and ancient and indigenous, and perhaps are drawn by the compelling promise of spiritual transformation.

Reality check time.

Despite all of the potential positives, simply ingesting Master Plants offers absolutely zero guarantee of benefit.

Much as we want it to be true – and even in light of the studies showing tremendous promise – Master Plants will not necessarily gratuitously reverse all of our depression, anxiety, PTSD, eating disorders, and trauma all on their own. They won't spontaneously cure everyone's chronic pain syndromes or Alzheimer's or cancer, either.

How often have I heard people say: "All the billionaires and world leaders should be required to take psychedelics." I guarantee many of them have. Master Plants are not the magic pill that will solve all of our ills.

Master Plants won't automatically make us more enlightened. They won't naturally make us better people. They won't fix society.

That's on us.

Now, the "us" I'm referring to is not just any of us alone as individuals. Of course, we have personal responsibility – through our attitude, commitment, and discipline around the way we choose to heal and actively comport ourselves. All of that is absolutely primary to our personal and collective healing.

But when I say it's on us, I mean "us" as in Me and We.

Achieving the promise of the Master Plant Experience depends on recalibrating and redeveloping our sense of connection and relationships.

By relationships, I'm referring to those between us and the Master Plants, yes. And also between us and our mitochondria, microbiome, cells, DNA, and epigenetics. Us and our nervous systems, our guts, our hearts. Us and our shadow parts – the parts we hide or feel ashamed of. Us and our family of origin and our ancestors. Us and our chosen family. Us and the land. Us and the elements and beings of the natural world. Us and our culture. Us and society. Us and the Invisible. Us and the Universe.

As cliché as it may sound, it takes a village, literally and figuratively, to stay grounded and embodied, to engage with Master Plants properly, and to allow healing and evolution, individually and collectively.

The reductionist, modern paradigm sees all of these – from cells, organs, plants, and animals to the earth – as concrete things, nothing more. And these things are connected only secondarily and mostly randomly, incidental "accidents" of time and space. According to that paradigm, an experience with Master Plants depends on the mechanism of an isolated "active" compound in the Master Plants stimulating our brains and bodies in a particular way and nothing more.

On the other hand, what if we could know that the Master Plant was lovingly grown, trimmed and tended, sung to when harvested? If we even had contact with the actual living plant before engaging with the medicine, or tended them with our own hands? If we knew their mythology and their personality? In that case, our experience with them might be quite different – with a very different outcome. If we make an offering, meditate, or pray every day for days, weeks, or months in advance as preparation, if we ask permission from the plant and receive it before we engage, our experience likely will be different.

While I'm not saying it's impossible to drink ayahuasca that we get over the internet on our own and still experience profound healing, I am saying that a disembodied, disconnected, and risky approach puts us at a disadvantage from the start. Why place ourselves behind the eight ball if we don't have to?

If we are blessed with a Master Plant experience that is ecstatic, one that allows us to touch the divine and recognize that we're all part of a magical web of connection, can we deeply inquire into the need to repeatedly and immediately dive right back into more experiences with Master Plants, again and again and again? Might this be another way to be a consumer in spiritual disguise, operating from a disembodied colonizer mentality not grounded in mission, purpose, or kinship?

All of this is to say we are engaging with ancient technologies with longstanding traditions, but we live in modernity. There is a sense that we are newly "discovering" these psychedelic plants through the lens of research: "Look! Psilocybin can reverse OCD!" "Ayahuasca can reverse depression!" "Iboga can reverse addiction!" "These drugs can save us from ourselves and the ills of modern society!" However, no one has discovered anything that wasn't already well known, albeit through a very different perspective and way of expressing that knowledge.

As an anthropocentric society, people find it unnerving to think of plants as having consciousness, let alone agency. For those of us who recognize the personhood – and, more than that, the spirit – of plants, however, it is clear that an array of Master Plants have decided to emerge from the communities they've nearly exclusively served and guided for millennia. They are currently knocking on our door. Given the epidemic of diseases of civilization that they may address, we in the Global North are heady with their potential benefit to people who are suffering, a population that seems to be growing larger by the day.

We don't yet know the cost to us – if any.

If the past is any indication, interacting with powerful plants in the same way we always have will come at a cost, likely a considerable one. Given that our greatest suffering has come from an extractive economy that commoditizes life, it's deeply concerning to see how quickly Master Plants are being commoditized and overharvested. In anticipation of changes in their legal status, entire warehouses are being outfitted to grow and sell industrial, scalable quantities of Maria Sabina's beloved Children, the psilocybe mushrooms, who were once considered so sacred that only children were considered pure enough to harvest them. Indigenous wisdom is again being stolen with little to nothing offered in return. Indigenous communities are being disrupted and corrupted by spiritual seekers and those in search of personal healing as well as those who want to support (as well as capitalize on) them. Powerful components of the plants are being isolated, manipulated, replicated, and trademarked. People smell benefit, need, and profit, and the excitement of these three converging has hit a fevered pitch.

All of it brings to mind the words of Albert Einstein: "We can't solve problems by using the same kind of thinking we used when we created them."

If we ask the question of why we're isolated, depressed, sick, and feeling a lack of spiritual purpose – the answers can be found in the kinds of colonizing, extractive behaviors listed previously.

This approach is like putting a fresh, pretty coat of white paint over a wall riddled with mold. It may temporarily look nicer from the outside, but it doesn't fundamentally change anything. In a way, the situation is made worse by masking the problem, disguising the wolf in sheep's clothing.

All of this is further complicated by the fact that a good number of people – some of them the very same people just described –

have the very best of intentions. They want to support indigenous communities in a good way. They are honoring indigenous wisdom and deeply authentic ceremonies surrounding these medicines. They believe there is incredible healing that should be accessed. They want indigenous people to receive fair remuneration, however that may look. Yet most of us have no idea what that would look like or how it would play out.

On the one hand, the current approach – even with lofty intentions – continues to be extractive, perpetuating a long-standing pattern of commoditizing everything possible from indigenous communities. Meanwhile, because peyote, ayahuasca, San Pedro, iboga, and so many others are being overharvested, indigenous people are being priced out of what is available, and healers and ceremonies are less available to their own local communities because they're being commandeered by retreat centers locally and abroad. The outcome of all of our well-meaning interest and enthusiasm is that indigenous people are struggling to access their own healing technologies, ceremonies, land, and ways of being that are the underpinnings of their very culture.

As doctors, scientists, and the government are exploring questions of the physiological safety of the compounds, few are asking what will happen when we extract Master Plants from their community connections – the land they're from; the plants, animals, insects and microbes they interact with; the people who have reverently engaged them as kin, who have lived according to their wisdom, and made offerings, transmitted their ícaros, and performed ceremony according to strict protocols over hundreds or even thousands of years.

Can we really experience that very same medicine from Master Plants when all of the systems surrounding them – so inherent to their healing powers – are removed? We want to benefit, but we're ignoring the fundamentals of the very indigenous science that allowed us to ever know these medicines to begin with.

Endless new psychedelic molecules are being created by industry labs as we speak, which on the one hand, is exciting. We can standardize concentration and control substance variation; ayahuasca – all the benefits but without the vomiting and hallucinations – get the good with no bad! Yes, please!

And yet we've been down this road before. Of course, there's a long-standing culture of pharmaceuticals made from ancient medicines without cultivating a relationship with the plant, without reverence and humility, without permission from the plant and the people who are holders of the wisdom of that particular plant. There's an idea that we've "discovered" things that certain indigenous cultures – and plants – have known and done since the beginning. From everything I'm seeing, this go-round may be no exception.

We can't yet know what will happen with those synthetics, but think back to the telltale story of the coca plant. Coca – the Master Plant – is not addictive or destructive. Cocaine – the pharmaceutical, the extracted chemical – is. Yet at the time, cocaine was seen as a miracle drug. And here we are, potentially doing the same thing all over again.

Master Plants are potent and offer incredible capacity for transformation. But do we want to take on their power without being grounded in right relationship – and if we do, where will we end up? Do we have the hubris to roll the dice and discover whether we get medicine or malice? Just as was seen with the sacred tobacco plant, the coca plant, and the opium poppy – each of which can offer powerful healing – extracting compounds for profit took us down a path of addiction, destruction, and death that continues to affect many millions at this very moment.

Could this problem be inherent to working with Master Plants or, at least, working with Master Plants without respect, reverence, and reciprocity?

Traditional ceremonies also fall into this category. When outsiders attend ceremonies in communities that have always been restricted to local members of that community, the community and the integrity of the ceremony itself are also disrupted. In the more extreme cases, wealthy foreigners throw thousands or even tens of thousands of dollars at local "shamans" to be trained or for the shamans to travel abroad to hold "authentic" ceremonies elsewhere. The question is, can we honor and appreciate that authenticity without colonizing it? For how much longer will authentic ceremony remain authentic? Or has the time for the authentic and ancient already passed?

Indeed, one of the most fundamental principles taught by indigenous Elders is that everything must be examined and interpreted only as they are found embedded in their stories, songs, dance, mythology and lineage. Gaining this knowledge requires that we form a respectful and positive relationship with ourselves and everything around us.

Traditional wisdom begins with respect and reverence for the spiritual essence that infuses and defines all forms. All forms of life must be respected as conscious, intrinsically valuable, and interdependent. We are all related. It is wrong to exploit other beings or take more than our share. The deep interest we felt as children in animals, plants, water, and earth can be trusted, encouraged, and continued. All creatures can be our teachers and while humans may readily affect other beings, we need not see ourselves as superior.

How will we honor the complex systems that allow Master Plants to continue to be effective healers and teachers – to offer their medicine and not their malice?

We can start by making offerings to plants, asking their permission before harvesting, and never taking more than we absolutely need at that moment; respecting animals by honoring their spirits, making offerings that support the well-being of the community of animals, and using every part of an animal's body; respectfully asking for guidance from the people who are wisdom holders of the ancient knowledge of the Master Plants; and asking Master Plants themselves what they want with humility and reverence.

We can start by shifting away from an anthropocentric, hierarchical view of the world where humans place ourselves before or above other life-forms.

Everything is alive, everything is people, everything has a voice, and all perspectives matter and must be heard.

There's no reason to think that stuffing psychedelics into the pharmaceutical-industrial complex of late-stage capitalism will deliver a better, different outcome than where this paradigm already has taken us. We know how this colonized way of being makes us feel – the soul loss, the perpetual sense of existential orphanhood, the commoditization of everything and everyone, the energy of domination and obedience. It's made us sad, lonely, and physically and mentally sick.

We are already familiar with this trajectory, and it isn't pretty.

Still, as much as we may long for part of the old ways, we can't exactly go backward either. Once upon a time, we were all indigenous – some of us more recently than others – but those who are no longer part of that world can't easily reclaim those ways. That's not an identity we can pick up and put back on once we've left it. Most of us are simply not part of a village where we have initiated elders who have been transmitting thousands of years of rich, multilayered knowledge through rituals and stories and place and community.

Change is afoot. At the same time, for most people, change can feel terrifying. Yet it's worthwhile to note that communities that have endured for millennia have done so not by remaining rigid but by knowing when to be flexible and what is fundamental and nonnegotiable. Survival depends on knowing both because the world is always in the process of changing. The world changes, so we change in response, and then the world changes again in response to our change. That responsiveness is the definition of being alive – of surviving and even thriving. It's a magnificent, ongoing, infinite conversation.

New ways are germinating, ready to emerge as always, and we can become midwives to this next way of being by showing up, staying present, and becoming curious rather than controlling. We can remain in apprenticeship with nature, imagination, and our own dreams. We can approach elders and indigenous wisdom holders with humility, respect, and appreciation and ask to learn their stories of survival and celebration.

The process of discovery begins with storytelling. What stories from the past and present do we want – need – to keep alive? Those are the stories to tell. As we tell them, new stories will naturally begin to emerge.

Then we can weave them into the next moment, and the next, and the next.

Together, we begin to combine old stories with the new that want to emerge as we co-create the next world that's calling to be born.

13

CONCLUSION

The modern world demands that we strive each as individuals to create it, shape it, and make and achieve our mark. In the process, our society makes it easy for us to become fixed – in our identities, in our narratives, in our labels, in our traumas. Think of the introductory question most people ask of each other: "What do you do?" We expect answers that are neat, a few words, and easy to digest. But in reality, we are all multidimensional, multi-hyphenate, out-of-the-box people. More and more, the boxes we live in, consciously or unconsciously, make us feel trapped, limited, sad, and even sick.

Master Plants challenge everything about us that is fixed or feels certain. They begin this process in the immediate moment, not simply when we ingest them. Simply in the discussion of them, in the writing about them, in the longing they elicit – we begin our relationship with these transformational beings that take us out of our ordinary lives and stories and reconnect us with the ancient, the infinite, the mystical and the invisible. The process is not always – or even often – easy.

After I finished the first draft of this book, I told my friend I felt I had been turned inside out – much more so than when I had written my prior book, *The Dirt Cure*. Writing a book about Master Plants had been so much more than I bargained for. I said I never would have agreed to write it had I known what the book would demand of me and I felt as though I had been squeezed out like a sponge.

She replied: "Well, that makes sense. You've been writing about plants that are not two-dimensional or even three-dimensional, but exist in dimensions we don't even yet understand. And your experience of writing sounds like every psychedelic experience I've ever had: like I'd bitten off more than I could chew, I never would have agreed to do it had I realized what would be asked of me, I had been turned inside out, and every bit of me had been squeezed out. All of this totally tracks."

Of course, I realized. This is exactly what I've known to be true with every Master Plant I've ever worked with. We take one step toward them, and they take one hundred toward us. We go backward and forward in a dance that is both carefully choreographed and also unpredictable. Any and every interaction – including simply giving them our attention – becomes transformative and starts us on a journey.

Psychedelics demand that all of these parts of ourselves we've previously considered fixed, certain, important and necessary become mutable and mysterious. Sometimes they condemn parts of us to death. They are anything but predictable, and they expect us to live into the most essential, courageous parts of ourselves. Every noun we'd use to label ourselves transforms into a verb – they show us that we are a collection of moving parts, each in relationship with others, always in a state of becoming.

At the same time, they show us that we are not in control of very much at all. The greatest lessons we learn during these experiences is that we sometimes discover the most not by trying to control our world, but in our surrender to it. We learn that we need more time to be still, to not do, but to be with and allow the movement all around us. In doing that, we see that we don't have to control the world, not just because we can't, but because we don't need to.

When we recognize we're part of something greater, that's alive and intelligent, it can reduce the anxiety around trying to strive alone as an individual – trying to insulate ourselves from the world – rather than being part of a massive orchestra that is partly harmonious, often dissonant, sometimes cacophonous, but always indescribably magnificent.

Making regular time for stillness, rest, calm, daydreams, connection, nature, creativity and beauty in everyday life – even just for moments each day, ideally for many, many moments – allow us to tap into this magic and enchantment that surrounds and supports us always. When we don't make that time, we are forced to rest and be in stillness in other ways – and it often feels far less pleasant to rest when we're lying sick or stressed beyond function than to make the choice to stop, be still, and tap into the mystery on our own.

One of the hardest parts of this process is bringing the hard-won discoveries we've made in a journey – or any underworld experience – into a reality around us that doesn't feel ready or receptive. Don't despair. We are all part of a collective process of reshaping, rebuilding, co-creating, and dreaming a new dream. As we release our resistance and surrender to what must fall apart, we simply begin by carrying ourselves in an authentic way. And as we rebuild, we bring more balance by applying non-ordinary ways of being to the ordinary, allowing the nonlinear to color the linear, valuing intuition to add greater dimension to the rational, bringing more spirit to the cerebral.

These sacred, nonlinear parts of us are necessary. Much as we've tried to put all our eggs in the science basket, the reality is that we can never know all the facts about anything. We are not disinterested observers but quite the opposite: invested participants. Part of life is always a mystery that lies beyond our five senses or rational brains.

We can't even rely on our eyes. When we watch a bird in flight, we don't see the flight itself. Our minds are taking a series of images, one after another, and pasting them together. These images are not the flight of the bird. To tune into the essence of that bird's flight, we can only feel into it through nonlinear means – through the sensing and knowing of our hearts.

Cultivating this awareness can take us beyond our preconceived linear and rational ways of knowing to light up these connections. The warmth of a hug. The sound of wind moving through trees. The magic of a close encounter with a hummingbird or an eagle. Recognizing that sense of joy – the yes! the wow! that is uniquely ours – comes only through carving out moments to step outside of ordinary time. In those moments, our intuition speaks to and guides us where we need to go.

In this process, we begin to recognize that even when we feel isolated and alone, we're connected, held, guided, and part of a wild, brilliant world that is absolutely, unmistakably alive. We may experience loneliness, but we don't have to. None of us are here on a solitary endeavor, no matter how much it may feel like we are.

We build the community within us and around us – looking for other beacon holders, building alliances, calling in our soul family, creating spiritual and practical communities that are committed to the principles of reverence and respect, gratitude and appreciation, reciprocity and kinship with all beings and peoples: the plant people, the stone people, the two-legged, the four-legged, the creepers and crawlers and winged and finned and furred and microscopic ones, Sun, Moon, Stars, and all the invisible beings unfettered by time and space.

And this is the magic of Master Plants, that they find us – every part of us, our resistance and deepest survival skills but also our gifts – and demand the utmost of us. So I can say that writing this book was a genuine psychedelic experience.

The call to mystery and re-enchantment isn't always easy – it takes courage and resilience and comes at the cost of our old selves – but the rewards for shedding our old, stale parts, mining ourselves deeply, and embracing our truest selves are profound. As we recognize aliveness in every aspect of the world around us, we become more connected to our own aliveness, and more committed to embracing life more fully and operating with more joy, reverence, and meaning.

Ultimately, Master Plants act as messengers, portals, windows, and doors to re-enchantment. They help us see and remember the other worlds that are accessible to us in any number of ways. Master Plants are indeed magical, and they transform us; however, their greatest gift is that they show us how to make new connection and see beyond what we've previously seen so that we can heal our relationships – with ourselves, those around us, the land, and the invisible – right here in our regular lives.

Master Plants can liberate us, but only if we want to be liberated.

As we recognize the wisdom of more ancient technologies and even mythologies, we are now being called to create a mythology for these new times – and not just with written words – but with spoken stories, music, art, dance, joy, play, dreams, imagination, ritual, rest, silence, listening in a new way, and sacred actions.

We're being asked to relate differently to one another – refugee to existential refugee, orphan to existential orphan, kin to kin. We're being asked to welcome each other and extend our arms to one another. We've endured so much alone. Now, we can hold each other. We can ask to hear each other's stories. We can listen to each other. We can become storytellers. We can listen to our kin, the plants and the living world. We can follow our inner compass to find our place in the web of life again and again.

The plants have already called you, and you have already begun to answer the call. A ceremony began when you first picked up this book, and as this book comes to a close, so too does this ceremony.

What now? Can we come out of this cauldron willing to humbly cooperate with nature's guiding genius?

If your answer is "I don't know," you're on the right track. Congratulations! Your unlearning has begun, and you have officially become a beginner.

Now mystery can find you.

ACKNOWLEDGMENTS

First, I want to thank the land I stand on and all of the beings who are here, that have been supporting, teaching, sustaining and inspiring me daily for my entire life. Thank you also to my beloved Master Plants who have guided and taught me as I tended them, in ways both difficult and delightful.

Thank you to the people who made this book possible.

Thank you to the team at Difference Press, especially Angela Lauria for her genius at translating ideas living in other realms into actual books in this one, and my editor Natasa Smirnov for her inspiring feedback, kind support and patience.

I will always be grateful to my teachers and mentors, past and present: Malidoma Somé, Robert Hand, Oly Schalow, Dr. Tieraona Low Dog, Rocio Alarcon and Dr. Robert Naviaux for starting me on my journey. My dear Ecuador squad who has stood beside me through thick and thin, especially Jaclyn Eisman, Tammi Sweet, and Janet Blevins. Thank you to the brilliant, big-hearted scientists and experts who have shared their inspiring wisdom in The Master Plant Experience events.

To my wonderful Decertification students: Thank for trusting me, and for being engaged, excited, brave, honest, curious, delightfully beautiful humans always open to the Mystery. I love you all.

To the other wonderful humans who kept me sane through this process: Constance Klein, Gail Schorsch, Ariela Migdal, Rob Sarno, Valerie Van Oettl, the earlybird coffee shop staff, Stargazer Li, Victoria Williams, Erika Robinson, and Denis Poitras. There are others. It truly takes a village.

Thank you to my parents. My mother, who modeled enthusiasm for beauty and the magic of nature ever since I can remember. My father, whose support I still directly receive nearly 40 years after he moved into the next world. My grandmother and grandfather, who saved my life many times throughout my childhood. My dear family, spread across the world, that loves me from afar. My ancestors, who guide and welcome me home to who I truly am and where I come from, no matter how long it takes me to remember.

Thank you to my loves. To my beautiful children aka muses aka teachers, who are on this journey of becoming with me - Margalit, Elan, and Erez. To my beloved dog and protector, Leo. And to Jesse Mendez, who has been my rock, my cheerleader, my massage therapist, a shoulder to cry on, a best friend, and beloved throughout this process. Thank you for believing in me.

ABOUT THE AUTHOR

Dr. Maya inhabits more than one identity. She is an adult and pediatric neurologist who has spoken around the world, and also listens and talks to plants every day. She is an ancient astrologer who is grounded in mitochondria, the microbiome and mycelium. She is an herbalist, urban farmer, forager, and ceremonialist. She is the author of *The Dirt Cure*. Dr. Maya is an expert in many things and also always endeavors to remain a beginner.

In short, she is an emergent system, and wants to show how we can revel in our own individual and collective emergence.

Dr. Maya created Quantum Drops, also known as Ceremony in a Bottle, a vibrational Master Plant product that is legal, safe and deeply transformative. She is the founder of the Terrain Institute, where she offers a Decertification, an unlearning journey for those who are interested in exploring mystery, and a Certification, for those who want to become psychedelic professionals.

She is passionate about finding and showing us the way out of loneliness and into accessing and embodying our aliveness. All of her work is intended as an invitation into a sense of kinship, re-enchantment, trust, open sensory gating, and inhabiting the role of invested participant rather than disinterested observer. She wants to lead the way for us all to celebrate the miracle of being here every single day.

THANK YOU

Beautiful Human!

Thank you for reading my book and being a part of this ceremony.

As my gift to you, please scan the code or follow the link below to access some of the meditations, practices, and other activities I've described in this book. You'll also find a list of references, current research, and wonderful resources, at no cost to you.

This is just the beginning.

Love,

Dr. Maya

DrMaya.com/Resources

OTHER BOOKS BY DIFFERENCE PRESS

The Profitable Startup: Launch On-Time, Delight Customers and Investors, and Generate Profit Fast by Elissa Bordner

Outside in Recovery: Dancing My Way Back to My Self after Breast Cancer by Jenny C. Cohen

Why the F#@ Am I Still Not Organized?: Stop Struggling with Clutter Once and for All* by Star Hansen

Stop Getting Triggered in Mediation: The Art of Managing Triggers as a Mediator and Increasing Your Impact by Tamir Hasan

Help Your Child Fight Cancer: A Nurse's Guide to Getting Through Every Parent's Worst Nightmare by Amy G. Kohler

Morning Cup of Jo: Proof That Love and Life Never Die in a Sacred Conversation between a Medical Doctor and Her Son in Spirit by Shaunna Menard, MD

The Quiet Quitting Nurse: 8 Steps to Help You Decide Whether or Not to Leave Your Job by Maricea Muhammad, RN, MSN, MHA, UZIY

Lead by Design: Applying Human Design Principles to Leadership Strategies by Kristin Panek

7-Figure Goddess: Making the Leap from Six to Seven Figures in Two Years (Or Less) by Elizabeth Purvis

Alcohol Made Me Do It: Why People Act Out of Character When They Drink and How to Stop by Amy Turk

Her First Place: The Black Woman's Guide to Building Generational Wealth as a First-Time Home Buyer by J. René Walker

Made in the USA
Las Vegas, NV
27 December 2024

15469272R00162